PEOPLE FIRST

Reflections on Leadership

EDWARD A. MALLOY, C.S.C.
President Emeritus, *The* University *of* Notre Dame

Ⓢ SOULSTIR BOOKS

Published by SOULSTIR Books, a division of SOULSTIR LLC
12412 Bittersweet Commons Blvd W #365, Granger, Indiana 46530
soulstirbooks.com

SOULSTIR Books and SOULSTIR are trademarks
or registered trademarks of SOULSTIR LLC.

Special thanks to Carri Frye
Editing by Cara Krenn
Book design by Maryn Arreguín

Hardcover ISBN: 979-8-9850370-3-6
Paperback ISBN: 979-8-9850370-4-3

Printed and bound in the United States of America.
First Edition 9 8 7 6 5 4 3 2 1

I dedicate this book to Fr. Mark Poorman, C.S.C.,
a good friend, colleague, and fellow community member
who has been an outstanding leader in his own right at the
University of Notre Dame and the University of Portland.

CONTENTS

FOREWORD

In the pages of *People First: Reflections on Leadership*, members and friends of the Notre Dame family will find a first-hand account of senior-level servant leadership, written by someone who was recognized early in life for his potential, worked hard to develop his abilities, and ultimately picked up the mantle of leadership from a living legend and carried it forward in his own unique style to great success.

I first came to know Fr. Edward "Monk" Malloy during my sophomore year as an undergraduate student at Notre Dame when I found myself enrolled in a small theology seminar that he taught. I would like to say that he instantly saw my potential for university leadership, but actually, the reverse was true; I saw his. You would have been blind not to see it. His love for his subject, for his students, and for his university were clearly evident, and would eventually see him named as President of the University.

I was proud to see my Theology professor so honored, and I followed his work closely—not only because I was a loyal alumnus, but also because our younger son, Brent, earned two degrees from Notre Dame during Fr. Malloy's tenure. I was then privileged to have the opportunity to work with him when he became a member of the Board of Trustees at Vanderbilt University, from which he had earned his Ph.D., and where I was serving as provost.

Finally, when I returned to Notre Dame as provost, where I served from 2005 through 2020, I experienced the leadership of Fr. Malloy simply by seeing and benefiting from the advances he led at Notre Dame after assuming the presidency from Fr. Theodore Hesburgh. Under Fr. Malloy's leadership, Notre Dame became more widely recognized as a leading research university, excelling across a wide diversity of disciplines and attracting some of the most talented students and faculty in the nation and beyond. But as Fr. Malloy makes clear in this book, he never lost sight of the importance of undergraduate teaching and the faith-based values that "enhanced our identity and mission as a Catholic university."

Over the years, I have come to know Fr. Malloy as a person deeply committed to his faith and priesthood, and also as someone who cares passionately about students and their intellectual and moral development. Fr. Malloy's tenure as president was marked by his dedication to the central thesis of Notre Dame's mission—to help curious, talented, impressionable 18-year-olds become mature 22-year-olds, instilled with the values, moral compass, and leadership skills to become forces for good in the world. In Fr. Malloy's words, he worked to ensure that Notre Dame was a place where "you students…can learn to think for yourself, to be exposed to new ideas and different points of view without abandoning the core values that you arrived with."

In *People First: Reflections on Leadership*, Fr. Malloy reflects on the myriad leadership situations and challenges he faced in his years as a student, athlete, professor, and as President of the

University. Using an engaging question-and-answer format, he offers bite-sized stories of his experiences and the opportunities they presented to teach the principles, skills, and moral dimensions of leadership.

Fr. Malloy also discusses the value of mentoring, how he benefited from the guidance of Fr. Hesburgh, and how he used the lessons he learned from Fr. Hesburgh to help others. Throughout the book, Fr. Malloy emphasizes the importance of ethics and the tenets of Catholic social teaching as critical components of leadership.

In the book's later chapters, Fr. Malloy highlights leaders he holds in high regard and dissects the qualities that made them successful. He includes several pioneering women, many of them Holy Cross sisters, who contributed significantly to his success as University President and more broadly to the success of the Notre Dame community.

In this largely autobiographical book, Fr. Malloy is candid about his own leadership experiences, both successes and challenges. Because of this personal approach, *People First: Reflections on Leadership* is about more than leadership; it is also about the often unseen, difficult, selfless, and disciplined acts that form the basis of a good and rewarding life.

For those of us fortunate enough to have known Fr. Malloy and seen his leadership in action, this book will be an uplifting and engaging highlight reel of the man whose qualities we remember and revere. For those who are younger and know Fr. Malloy's leadership only through its effects, it is a chance to crack open a book, find a cozy chair, and learn some lessons of life and leadership from a great teacher and joyful priest.

—Tom Burish, Former Provost

INTRODUCTION

I have been teaching college students most of my adult life. In my early years, I taught introductory classes to both undergraduate and masters students, as well as specialized courses in moral theology at both levels and doctoral seminars. I also gave lectures on and off campus, including throughout the U.S. and in other parts of the world. The largest course I ever taught had 270 students and the smallest 6 students in a Ph.D. seminar. I always tried to include discussion formats, either directly with me or with University staff in small group settings.

When I became a full-time administrator, first as Vice President and Associate Provost and later as President of the University, and now as President Emeritus, except for two years off for sabbaticals, I continued teaching. Most recently, in my Presidential and post-Presidential years, I have taught almost 70 individual seminars to first year undergraduates.

When I began thinking about writing a short book on "leadership," instinctively I imagined interacting with a class of undergraduate students in a seminar format where the conversation could be free-flowing and no type of question would be out of bounds.

As a result, this book will take the form of an imaginary seminar in which students get to ask me questions that range from the theoretical and aspirational to the everyday and practical. By design, all my answers will be relatively brief but hopefully on point. My intention is to draw some conclusions in most cases that would encourage students to reflect upon their own individual potential as leaders and the steps that they might take to prepare for such responsibilities.

The book is divided into eight sections that gather questions and topics that have some natural affinity. My answers spring from my extensive reading in the literature on leadership as well as my utilization of memoirs, biographies, and autobiographies in classes that I have taught through the years. I have deliberately chosen to avoid footnotes, bibliographies, and other scholarly apparatus since this would drastically change the tenor and the potential audience for the book.

In my life, I have met and come to know leaders in government, business, higher education, the military, athletics, entertainment, religion, medicine, law, law enforcement, not-for-profit organizations, and other sectors of contemporary life. In addition, I have served on 32 separate boards for various lengths of time. From all these experiences, I have developed perspectives on leadership that, I hope, may be of interest and helpfulness to young people in particular but also to older generations who have their own thoughts on this significant and often complicated topic.

Finally, I am a Catholic priest and a moral theologian so I have incorporated some of my learning from these roles into my answers, particularly in sections three and four. I consider these thoughts one of the strengths of the book.

In the course of my reflections, I will provide concrete

examples as much as possible and I will refer to real people whose principled leadership I very much admire. In this day and age, when contending parties seem averse to any search for compromise or any admission of failure, I hope to promote a notion of leadership that seeks mutual understanding, a common sense of purpose, and respect for one another.

I have titled this book *People First: Reflections on Leadership* because I believe that it is our common humanity and our search for truth, beauty, and goodness that undergird all successful efforts to achieve consensus and move forward on the pursuit of worthwhile goals and bridge-building outcomes.

SECTION ONE

What Makes a Good Leader?

"In my eyes,
leadership is
ultimately about
~~people~~, ~~people~~,
~~people~~."

QUESTION 1

What is a leader?

In the dictionary, a leader is defined as "a person who leads," a "guide or conductor," a "person who has commanding authority or influence," or "the principal officer" of a military force, political party, or legislative body. I do not disagree with these definitions but I think much more needs to be said.

For me, a leader is a participant in some network of social relationships and dynamics. Within this context, a leader is an initiative taker, a reinforcer of a common sense of purpose and function, an articulator of directions and goals, a solicitor of resources, an evaluator of performance, a representative of the group and/or activity in the public forum, and a chooser of other responsible agents in echelons of cooperation.

A leader is, first, a human person with a range of God-given talents and potential. In some situations, the fit for a given individual to function as a leader is clearly manifest, usually based on levels of experience and preparation. I do not believe that anyone is "born" to be a leader, but some are quick learners and confidence-inspirers at a relatively young age. Then, it is a question of opportunity coupled with various forms of mentorship.

In religious terms, some are called to be leaders as a vocation from God. Think of the Scriptural portrayals of Abraham, Isaac, and Jacob, of Moses, David, and Solomon, and of the twelve Apostles (plus Paul). In the post-biblical period, we have Augustine of Hippo, Benedict, Francis of Assisi, Dominic, Ignatius of Loyola, and many founders of religious communities of women. In the broader Christian community, the same could be said of Martin Luther, John Calvin, and John Wesley. Not all religious vocations involve organizational responsibilities as such. The concept of "vocation" can have secular resonance as well.

One of the reasons that I have been teaching seminars in recent years on biography/autobiography is that I am inherently interested in how people's lives and sense of purpose evolve over time. Each of those genres has the potential for insight into the motivation, life experiences, and challenges of recognized leaders. What can we learn about George Washington, Alexander Hamilton, Abraham Lincoln, Queen Elizabeth, Nelson Mandela, Che Guevara, Margaret Thatcher, Condoleezza Rice, or Napoleon Bonaparte that can inform the preparation of potential political leaders in the university context? The same is true in other areas of human endeavor.

In my eyes, leadership is ultimately about people, people, people. It involves recruiting, hiring, or otherwise attracting to a common work those who are committed, well-prepared, and properly motivated. Leadership at whatever level, whether in higher education, business life, government, the Church, the military, not-for-profit organizations, or whatever begins with this recognition that people are at the heart of the activity and people are the ones that the leader has primary responsibility for. People are more important than strategic plans, budgets, fundraising, the issuing of reports, and community relations, even though they are all related. My more comprehensive definition of "leader" will inform the remaining sections of this book.

QUESTION 2

Are leaders born or made?
Can leadership be taught?

At birth, each of us inherits a set of genetic characteristics, physiological attributes, and mental capacities that distinguish us from others. Even identical twins, while similar in many fundamental ways, are distinguishable based on the concrete experiences that they have. This is most obvious when identical twins are separated at birth and then reunited in adulthood. They are then seen as alike in many ways but are still distinguishable.

The nature/nurture dilemma will never be finally resolved. As we go through the states of life from infancy to adulthood, we develop a range of defining characteristics. Some are shy, others are gregarious. Some are gifted athletically and others in artistic representation, musical performance, or the culinary arts. Some have a type-A personality and are full of energy and enthusiasm for life. Others are more hesitant to stand out from the crowd or are fearful of fitting in.

Sometimes one's parents or other family members or teachers, coaches, or mentors play a pivotal role in encouraging involvement in peer activities or volunteering to be an initiator or planner and organizer. On other occasions, it happens more spontaneously, on the spur of the moment, or in the absence of anyone else to get the job done.

For me, I was a good athlete, tall for my age, and successful academically. This mix provided the grounds for a certain level of self-confidence. In grade school, I was a team captain, a leader on the safety patrol, and someone assigned to important liturgical occasions as an altar server. In high school, I was student body president and a captain of the basketball team. At Notre Dame, I served as a dorm vice president and president and was a member of the Blue Honor Society, which was made up of leaders from across the campus. In the seminary and after ordination, I was either appointed or elected to a succession of responsibilities. Finally, I was elected a Vice President and Associate Provost and President of the University.

Based on my personal experience, I could argue that it was a mix of native gifts and fostered opportunities that led me to become a leader. I was fortunate in having gained the respect of my peers, in receiving constant affirmation from significant others, and in knowing a degree of accomplishment in the various leadership roles that I was allowed to play.

For you my students, the question lingers on—can leadership be taught in a class or in internship programs or by a tutor or simply by being in the company of impressive leaders? My first answer (as a lifelong teacher) is that elements of leadership can be learned in a structured academic setting. But, there is no necessary connection between passing formal tests on leadership and actually functioning as a leader. There is no substitute for experience.

And how does one gain experience? I recommend that, drawing from your self-knowledge and self-awareness, you seek out opportunities for service that are close to home, such as in a dorm setting, a campus club, or in an extracurricular activity like the school marching band, the student newspaper, student government, or an intramural sport. If you happen to be a scholarship athlete, your coaches over time will be seeking out those players who have the potential to serve as captains or a positive presence in the locker room.

The important thing is that you have to start somewhere. Normally, leaders emerge from among those who have put in hard work in a given activity and displayed enthusiasm, gained social support, and displayed the capacity for planning, implementation, and fruitfulness. Once recognized by others as a potential leader, it is likely that other opportunities will present themselves. All things being equal, I recommend starting small and close to home and letting your record speak for itself. The great thing about being young is that you have your whole life ahead of you (including different levels of leadership).

QUESTION 3

Must a leader be liked?

Likeability depends on a whole range of variables. Abraham Lincoln was revered in the North and detested in the South during the American Civil War. The same could be said in reverse of Robert E. Lee. Joan of Arc was a national hero among the French and was eventually declared a saint, but was considered a spawn of the devil by the British, especially because she was an unprecedented female military leader. Mahatma Gandhi became a spiritual and political leader during the struggle for independence for India, but the British considered him a strange, misguided, unpredictable revolutionary presence.

In recent Catholic Church history, certain groups looked to Pope John XXIII as the father of the Second Vatican Council with his call for reform and, after his death and the publication of his spiritual memoir, celebrated his spirit of openness. Later, Pope John Paul II won favor among those who thought the Council had gone too far and too quickly. More recently, Pope Francis has been very appealing to some Catholics and others outside the Church for his call for simplicity of life and the priority that should be given to the poor, immigrants, women, and non-Western Catholics. Others have castigated him for abandoning the Church structures that they are most comfortable with.

In my life as a leader, I never sought to win any popularity contest. I felt that good decision-making and participatory processes would carry the day. Only seldom did I lie awake at night worrying about how particular decisions would be interpreted by our constituencies. I knew instinctively that some information could not be shared for good reasons related to privacy or other's reputations.

One example was the University's decision not to join the Big Ten Conference, which I announced at a press conference. There was speculation both before and after, much of which was not factual. Another example was the decision to have Nathan Hatch replace Tim O'Meara as Provost. Nathan was not a Catholic but a Christian of deep faith (his father was a Presbyterian minister). Some saw this as a weakening of Notre Dame's commitment to our Catholic character and identity. From my experience working with Nathan previously, I felt he was the best choice from the available pool. And, in my subsequent judgment, this turned out to be true.

You students know the pressure in grade school and high school to be liked, to have the right group of friends, to dress stylishly, and to be invited to popular parties and social events. College life is generally better but such peer judgment is always precarious. That is why it is important to do the right thing, to seek to be guided by the right set of values, to be a leader for the contribution you can make. If these principles guide you, then ephemeral popularity will seem progressively less important.

QUESTION 4

Must leaders be optimistic?

Yes, leaders must be optimistic. A true pessimist may be talented in critique and recognition of the flaws of human nature and the sometimes-overwhelming nature of public events, like wars, natural disasters, and the capacity of individuals in leadership positions to cause widespread death and destruction. But true leadership requires inspiring visions of the future and the ability to motivate others in the organization to work for the common good.

I have always said that legal counselors, accountants, and risk management have vital roles to play in the decision-making process, but they should not have the final say. Their role is to provide a note of realism with a concern about budgets, legal requirements, and risk factors, all of which are important in their own right. But, data banks, court decisions, and precedents and projected future challenges are not sufficient to capture the big picture.

In my presidential role at Notre Dame, there were a couple of decisions that reflected this point about optimism. One was the proposal to expand the football stadium from 59,000 to

80,000 seats. I knew that at face value a certain group of faculty would see this as a misguided priority. So, I put together a committee made up of the athletic director and a group of respected faculty. When this group saw the benefits for academics from the additional revenue to be gained, they recommended that we proceed. Then, I knew that waiting and consulting had been crucial to the process.

A second example was the DeBartolo Performing Arts Center. I had said in my inauguration address that a great university needed a great performing arts center. The first iteration of this possibility provided a tentative plan for such a structure, but we could not find sufficient funding for the project. Other proposals gained greater support. For years, this was the case. However, I swore that before I stepped down as President, we would have our performing arts center. It became the last major project completed in my 18 years as President.

You students should be excited about the future and the contributions you can make to cure diseases, create solutions to complex social ills, reform the Catholic Church, run for president (or governor, or mayor), form happy marriages and loving families, and be responsive to neighbors in need. If you are not ready to take on these challenges, who will be? To those to whom much has been given, much is to be expected. Only those of an optimistic spirit can imagine a better world.

QUESTION 5

Does a leader need to be a good public speaker?

Some people have the gift. They can be serious or humorous, tell stories effectively, engage their audience well, and keep their reflections within manageable limits. Some public speakers seem to have an innate capacity for their fundamental role in leadership. But most must develop their skill by hard work and a lot of practice.

I learned many lessons along the way. I am no good at telling jokes. But I can be reasonably good at telling stories about people, events, and circumstances that are amusing in themselves or capture a certain sense of irony.

I have been comfortable speaking in public settings going back to grade school and high school. In high school, I was elected Student Body President and this provided many opportunities for me to speak to my peers and others. Some people die a thousand deaths every time they are called to address an audience beyond the members of their immediate family. Yet, even they can learn to calm their nerves and focus on the task at hand.

I normally speak without a text or notes or even an outline. That is not to suggest that I ad lib my talks and do not prepare. On the contrary, I work through my material in my head beforehand and give myself various options, depending on the audience. When I talk about Notre Dame or teaching or student life or athletics or my personal experiences, I have a fund of material that I can draw from. In more academic settings or in my classes, I may put up an outline on the blackboard or distribute one to students. That way, we can all keep on track. I think every public speaker must find a format and style that works for them.

As a Catholic priest, one form of public speaking is preaching, which I very much enjoy. It is always a privilege to speak about Jesus Christ and fundamental Christian beliefs and practices. The Bible is full of interesting and pertinent material. It is our challenge to make it available to contemporary congregations in ways that touch their basic human needs, desires, and aspirations. My Holy Cross colleagues at Notre Dame are, on the whole, quite talented preachers. I enjoy listening to them. Collectively, I believe we set a high standard, and now with Masses on the internet, we have an even wider audience.

Public speaking should never be boring or self-serving or excessively long. The attention span of contemporary audiences is much shorter than it was a few generations ago. Sincerity and respect for one's listeners are important virtues. Martin Luther King, Jr. was not only a great preacher and teacher but he also adjusted his material to his audience. Abraham Lincoln's "Gettysburg Address" was amazingly brief but it followed a peroration that went on for longer than an hour.

Before I was elected President of Notre Dame, Dave Tyson, Bill Beauchamp, and I spent two days with an expert on television as a medium of communication. She taught us how to turn negative questions into positive audiences, how important posture and eye contact are, and how to participate in group conversations on television. This was wonderful advice that I came to fully appreciate later on.

Public speaking is about having a message and delivering it effectively. Every leader needs to aspire to that goal within his or her natural gifts and developed capacities.

My best advice to those of you contemplating how your

leadership skills might be developed in your college years is to exercise and refine your oratorical abilities as often as you can, particularly before different audiences. Some campuses have a Toastmasters Club, which can be an effective format for getting peer feedback and testing out different styles of presentation. Even the simple act of reading Biblical texts at worship services can provide a backlog of public exposure. Many college students have participated in debate as a high school activity and, even though this club has rather rigid rules about content and time, it can build up significantly the confidence level of those who participate.

Public speaking usually involves one's whole body, so attention to appearance, gesturing, tone, volume, and unconscious verbal fill-ins like "er, uh, you know, and like," are all important. I have watched myself on videotape many times and it has always been helpful. You might try the same.

QUESTION 6

How does one find their leadership style?
How does yours differ from your
predecessor or successor?

An authentic leadership style should reflect one's unique personal characteristics, prior experiences, and cultural expectations. When search committees look for candidates to fulfill certain leadership roles, they want people of strong character, solid integrity, sound judgment, good social skills, refined work habits, inspiring visions, emotional maturity, and manifest intelligence. What they get, if the search process goes well, is certifiable evidence that the person under consideration has the capacity for all these qualities even if the available evidence is mixed. This can be the result of the age of the candidate, their previous level of responsibility, or the opportunities they have been given. For example, in a university setting, not everyone has been directly involved in fundraising or the number of people who reported directly to them may have been limited.

I mention search processes because in that context there is usually more attention to "leadership style" than otherwise would be the case. An academic setting may put more emphasis on process, collaboration, and transparency than the military, for-profit corporations, or elected government offices.

Some of the elements of my personal leadership style include:

→ Surrounding myself with colleagues whose strengths and weakness are complementary to my own (for example, I am a word person more than a numbers person). However, if experts in certain areas cannot explain it to me, they will not enlighten the conversation;

→ Running meetings efficiently by being well-prepared, starting on time, and ending on time;

→ Not scheduling too tightly since things will always come up that need to be attended to quickly;

→ Visiting the sick, celebrating or attending funerals, and congratulating people for successes;

→ Allowing time in the calendar for reading, reflection, and relaxation;

→ Trying to assure widespread participation in important discussions, including explicitly inviting all individuals for their opinions;

→ Respecting the prerogatives of other leaders within the organization. When away or otherwise preoccupied, let them handle things;

→ Bringing together the leadership team each year to look back on the past year and look forward to the coming year; inviting spouses to attend. (I did this each year at Land O'Lakes, Wisconsin); and

→ Preparing the next generation of leaders, especially among the Holy Cross community, by giving them a lot of personal access.

Father Ted Hesburgh, my predecessor, was a polyglot with broad interests and the capacity to master new material quickly. He was rather traditional in terms of his personal piety but a big supporter of Vatican II. He traveled extensively and in his later years he gave over much of the daily operation of the University to the Provost. He was a quite effective and popular public speaker. He relished being involved outside of the University on behalf of presidents and popes. He did not teach as President although he gave many lectures.

Father John Jenkins, my successor, is a philosopher by nature and by academic discipline, a bit shy but an effective communicator. He seems not to relish public speaking and travel the way that Ted and I did but he has worked hard at it. People see him as a holy man and a good priest. He is always open to invitations to interact with student groups but he does not have a regular schedule of such events. He is more focused on the campus than Ted and I were. He is excellent with the trustees.

Ted, John, and I all consider the priesthood our fundamental professional identity and our years as President flow from our membership in the Congregation of Holy Cross. I think all three of us come across as sincere, hard-working, open to new ideas, and proud of our achievements but with full recognition that it has always been a team effort. Of the three, John is the most adept at the utilization of internet technology, I am the most experienced in athletics, both as a participant and as a fan, and Ted is the most honored outside the University.

In the end, each of our leadership styles seems to have been effective for the needs of the University during the years we served as President. For you students, it is a good reminder that there is no one type of personality or no particular degree path that can guarantee that a given leader will be just right for the responsibility. In Christian terms, the Holy Spirit can surprise us all.

QUESTION 7

*What is the most important risk you took
and why? Should leaders be risk takers?*

Risk-taking is about weighing benefits and liabilities both in the short and long term. The most important risk I took was agreeing to become the successor to the iconic, 35-year President of Notre Dame. The first stage was accepting the responsibility of Vice President and Associate Provost (the #2 academic officer) as part of a pool of three applicants (the residency being restricted to a Holy Cross priest of the Indiana Province). Four years and five months later, after a formal selection process, I was chosen. All three of the candidates (which included Bill Beauchamp and Dave Tyson) were given a lot of leeway (to attend officer, trustee, and advisory council meetings and to familiarize ourselves with a cross-section of the University). After I was chosen, I asked Bill Beauchamp to become my Executive Vice President and Dave Tyson to remain on as Vice President of Student Affairs.

While it was implicit in my willingness to become an officer that I would accept the appointment of President, if offered it, I could have discovered that I was not up to the task or did not enjoy administration and said, "No."

Many observers at the time had predicted that Ted Hesburgh's successor would have a hard time, being constantly compared unfavorably with Ted. In fact, I was never afraid of this challenge. As a former athlete, I relished competitive situations. Ted encouraged me to be myself and chart my own path and that is what I tried to do.

As I expected, I enjoyed being President. I considered it to be an honor and a privilege and I felt that, as a Holy Cross priest, I was part of a collective mission that Holy Cross had been exercising since 1842. Of course, not every moment was sheer bliss. I made my share of mistakes and there were controversies and debates. For example, after I prepared a ten-year plan at the conclusion of a long planning process, some members of the faculty felt that I emphasized too much "the presence of committed Catholic faculty." Fortunately, we were able to work out a clearer articulation.

To answer the original question more directly, I believe that leaders must be risk-takers since the status quo will only suffice for a while in a world subject to constant change and in a higher education system where research and constant dialogue can lead to sharp breaks from the past.

Think, for example, about the computer revolution or the changing role of women or the greater appreciation of threats to the national environment or the wonders of modern medicine. In all of these cases, faculty and students at a modern college or university must adapt, rethink, mull over, and rearticulate the central perspectives of every discipline.

Hopefully, you students are more comfortable in this new worldview than even your teachers are. But, your risks revolve around what to study and major in, how to properly answer a vocational call, and how to decide what balance you will be looking for between your professional and personal lives. Few students had a clear vision of what they wanted to do with their lives even back in high school. But, most of the rest change majors, accept internships to try out possibilities, and are sometimes limited by the opportunities available.

Be ready to take risks, but do not be overwhelmed by the process of personal decision-making. You can change your mind.

QUESTION 8

How does a good leader view and respond to adversity and accept criticism?

Let me respond to the criticism question first. In some ways, leaders need to have thick skin and short memories. In the public forum, every decision, judgment, policy, priority, and public presentation can be subject to a variety of responses. Gossip, rumor-mongering, and insider information can all make a leader's life and work more uncomfortable. Observers can attribute all kinds of motives and intentions to particular issues and decisions. Is he/she a power seeker, a revenge-getter, an ignoramus, or an underqualified representative of the work of the institution?

Some higher education leaders have assumed their roles during budget crises, enrollment challenges, old turf wars, underfunded financial aid, and inadequate fundraising offices. Right from the start, if people must be laid off, operating budgets cut, or programs and academic departments terminated, a group of unhappy people has been created. Even if individuals understand the need for drastic action, they are inclined to think it should not apply to them.

I was fortunate in that I became president when Notre Dame had a lot of positive momentum and impressive resources. Nevertheless, there were still neuralgic issues. For example, our older dorms and structures did not have adequate fire safety equipment and systems, but corrections could only be implemented over time. The urgency of becoming more coeducational and more diverse was not given the same priority by all units of the University. Despite new efforts in improving relationships with the broader South Bend/Mishawaka community, some parts of the citizenry felt unwelcome on campus.

Perhaps no aspect of Notre Dame could generate more negative responses than failures in the Notre Dame football program. We won the national championship in my first year as President (we expected to do so frequently in the following years, and we came close a few times). After several bad seasons, we made coaching changes several times. On each occasion, part of the fan base was concerned that there was some available coach elsewhere who was guaranteed to turn the program around. When we went elsewhere, we found that these coaches were usually not available or there were mitigating factors in their background or there was no institutional fit. The negative publicity before a coaching change meant that we lost a year of recruiting and, after the first year, there was a deficit of talent.

Athletics are a big part of the Notre Dame tradition, especially the football program. We have also won national championships in women's basketball, women's soccer, fencing, and men's lacrosse. We hold ourselves to high standards for admission, academic performance, and student athlete behavior. We consider the coaching staff as part of the teaching mission of the institution. When we fail to live by our high expectations, we try to address the problem directly and forcefully. As a former student athlete myself, I am proud of the role that athletics has played and believe that we can remain a model for other programs.

Problems in higher education have their own significance, but they are not at the same level as a wartime president, or a CEO whose business has been outstripped by competitors and may have to declare bankruptcy and close, or mayors of large cities overwhelmed by crime and citizen unrest.

For students, the fundamental lesson is that life is often complicated and not everyone will appreciate your efforts in service of the common good. Some criticism is valid and well grounded. In those cases, one needs to learn from experience and make whatever changes in one's leadership functions that seem necessary and then leave the past behind.

I used to meet each year with the newly elected student government leaders. I encouraged them to lay out their goals for the year and then engage in their own evaluation of their success or failure at the year's end because the next candidates for the same offices would, in their campaigns, act as if the previous holders of the offices were not impressive.

In the end, all leaders are subject to criticism but also acclaim. Often, it is in retrospect that great leaders are recognized. Let us hope that we are among those so honored.

SECTION TWO

Leadership and the Global Stage

"It is important that you, as members of the younger generation, develop confidence in your ability <u>to stand up for what you believe in</u> and not remain complacent on the sidelines."

QUESTION 1

Is it dangerous to be a leader in today's world?

We all know that some great leaders like Abraham Lincoln, Mahatma Gandhi, and Martin Luther King, Jr. have been assassinated by those opposed to their views or their roles in their respective societies. A much longer list could be compiled of heads of state, corporate executives, media influencers, and public figures who were murdered for one reason or another, even though many had security agents who were expected to protect them from harm. Today, to visit the American Congress, a governor or mayor's office, or corporate headquarters requires going through a magnetometer or a similar device and stating your business to a guard.

In a higher education context, there have been occasional but quite serious outbreaks of violence like those occurring at Virginia Tech and Northern Illinois.

Unfortunately, the United States, with more guns than people, is experiencing widespread multiple death shootings, more than any other developed country. We have come to appreciate that no one is immune. I am sure that all of you students in grade school and high school were required to engage in protective drills as well.

What worries me more than the odds of directed physical violence targeting leaders at all levels of society is the pervasiveness of character assassinations on the internet. When someone runs for political office or is being considered for a major position in a corporation or other major activity, smear campaigns can begin based on thin or no evidence. Rumormongering, false accusations, and spitefulness can make the prospect of serving in a new capacity rather daunting. In some cases, events from decades ago can emerge as though they revealed something still problematic about the person. The existence of blogs, videotapes, and personal diaries can make for a tawdry dynamic.

On the other hand, true leaders need to keep focused on a positive message, on their vision for the future, and on their positive achievements in previous roles. You must have confidence that truth will carry the day. One's friends and allies can provide a critical role in reemphasizing one's virtues and fit for the new leadership role.

One good reason for students to exercise leadership roles in college is that the enjoyment of a job well done can outweigh whatever negative experiences that one has had. Jealousy and resentment can always exist but they should never disincentivize somebody who feels the call to be a leader and looks forward to the good that can be achieved. When it comes to physical danger, the odds are extremely low that one will be at risk.

QUESTION 2

There are a fair number of concerns in society today about the revival of authoritarian government, many sprung from democratic tradition. Do you share this concern?

Yes, I share that concern. Democracy is a fragile form of government that depends on the consent of the governed. If the people are ill-informed or distracted by other matters or deluded by false information or desperate for an improvement in their everyday lives, then demagogues may arise who promise to restore the glorious days of the past or reinforce national identity or eliminate the perceived threat of those who are different in race, class, language, or religion or promise to achieve a new level of prosperity.

Hitler's rise to power is a classic example. His supervisors in WWI evaluated him as lacking in leadership potential. He was a failed artist. He was small in stature and had no particular sources of wealth or influence. But, he got involved in local politics and was savvy in achieving some lower levels of power.

From then on, Hitler's malevolent genius came to the front. He became a master orator with an emphasis on the greatness of the Aryan race and grievances from the end of WWI. He created a common enemy—the Jews. He surrounded himself with criminals, incompetents, and sycophants. He created a new military force, the SS, totally loyal to him. He staged mass rallies with banners, the singing of patriotic songs, people in uniform, including youth, and the effective use of flames and lighting at night. He lied about his intentions to foreign leaders. He invested heavily in the military and he suppressed the power of the courts. When all was in place, he sought to take Europe by storm and establish a new conception of German greatness.

In our lifetime, we have seen similar efforts in Russia, Argentina, China, Vietnam, Cuba, Rhodesia, Italy, and Japan, among others. And, with the advent of the information revolution, there exists a new method for deceiving the masses and seizing power.

In the American context, we have a strong tradition of checks and balances among the three branches of government. But, there are no guarantees that this system will continue to function effectively. It seems that we have arrived at severe differences of opinion between the two main political parties. There are many one-issue voters. Even in the same family or church community, it has become more difficult to have a rational, fact-based conversation about politics and related matters.

Despite all of this, I remain optimistic about the future of our country and other democratic societies. As one pundit claimed, democracy may not be the ideal form of government but it is the best, most just, and most effective one humans have devised.

I hope that you students will recognize how to read the signs of the times, how to learn from the past and recommit yourselves to playing a proper role in the body of politics. First, be sure to get registered and vote. Seek to be informed about the great issues of the day—discrimination, respect for life at all of its stages, immigration, the provision of the basic necessities of life, workplace opportunities, peacemaking, the environment, and many others. The more that your generation gets invested in thoughtfully discussing the issues, the more that you mobilize to bring out the vote. The more that some of you run for political office (or serve in government positions), the better the chance that democracy will be preserved and certain authoritarian tendencies suppressed. It is important that you, as members of the younger generation, develop confidence in your ability to stand up for what you believe in and not remain complacent on the sidelines.

QUESTION 3

In an exposed social media-driven, share-everything world, how should a leader protect their privacy and security?

To some of my peers, I seem like a Neanderthal since I am usually a late adapter of the latest forms of communication. However, I remain acutely interested in how the internet and all forms of social media have over time transformed the nature and risks of social interaction.

On the positive side, it is possible to meet and keep in touch across natural boundaries like oceans, continents, and nation-states. During COVID-19, families, university classes, and governing boards could exchange news, reinforce bonds, teach material, and make important decisions.

On the negative side, one's personal life and intimate relationships could be the subject of rumormongering and bullying behavior. In an instant, young people's reputations could be maligned and one's inner vulnerability reinforced. Furthermore, the nature and availability of truth and honest communication could be called into question.

At the institutional level, malware and ransomware can be costly and a reminder that there are people out there (in the cloud so to speak) who are ready to do you harm and who have no moral scruples.

The best advice is to be prudent and discreet in the use of internet vehicles and services. Better to build a positive reputation over time than to regret premature personal revelations.

One of my friends who was the CEO of a major New York

City-based company discovered that members of his large management group were sending late-night emails to him (long after he had left work and was otherwise involved) that protected them if things went wrong by a presumptive approval of their decision by the CEO. After a court case when all these emails were made available to aggrieved parties, he made the decision to get off email entirely. In fact, there was no way in which he, as the head of a multinational company, could keep on top of all the information that was supposedly flowing to him for his approval.

Obviously, email is just one form of internet communication. But, more and more, leaders in all fields are becoming increasingly aware of the risks of this kind of interaction. Face-to-face is one thing. Telephone conversations or Zoom are another. Much of contemporary board work (especially after COVID-19) is being done remotely and this is not only relatively impersonal but also a source of potential misuse.

In my own leadership roles, I am usually thought of as not really up-to-date. Yet, I have never really felt it held me back, partly because I had colleagues who were very good at all aspects of internet technology and were also aware of their limitations and risks and partly because I chose to utilize it when I needed it.

Privacy is described as the quality of being apart from company or observation or freedom from unauthorized intrusion. Just about every leader I know would say to their subordinates, "Do not surprise me." They want access to all the appropriate information that might affect their decision-making process and they want to know it in advance if possible. That puts a corresponding responsibility on the leader to decide who needs to know what and when. Usually, there is a group of trusted advisors for major decisions (often hierarchically established but not always). But there will be clear situations where secrecy is paramount and public revelation is deferred until the circumstances are right.

Privacy is a relative thing. In this country, observation cameras are present throughout downtown neighborhoods, on storefronts, on government buildings, and in dangerous parts of town. This is also true inside buildings. In London and Manhattan, you can be followed sequentially from one place to another, an effective tool against thieves and terrorists.

But, I am thinking more of privacy in the workplace, especially for those with leadership responsibilities. It is important to step out of the public eye, at least occasionally, for a sense of peace and quiet, for the opportunity to mull over important decisions. The ubiquity of cell phones and computer connectivity has eroded this possibility for many.

Privacy is also connected to confidentiality. Some reflections and decisions need to remain private, especially those that directly affect the reputations and well-being of others. You need to be able to decide who to share your most difficult challenges with. It could be a spouse, a key advisor, or a personal friend. The very act of revelation may put everything into a clearer perspective.

For me, having a private office is a critical component of privacy. Some people simply do not deserve access. On other occasions, you need to be focused on central issues rather than peripheral matters. In general, I have never been a big fan of open office areas which may seem efficient but have several negative impacts as well.

As a priest, privacy is essential in sacramental contexts like Penance (or confession) and in pastoral counseling. It is important that conversations not be overheard. This provides a kind of assurance that penitents and counselees can speak from the heart and their trust will not be violated.

Privacy can never be total, since leaders need to be evaluated and their contributions honestly reviewed. But, relative privacy can contribute to a healthier work environment and a more confident mode of decision-making.

When I was President, I would sometimes get calls from *Observer* reporters (our student newspaper) who sought my response to some important issue in their eyes. I found from my experience that this was not a good time to react since I sometimes knew nothing about the issue they brought up. The same was true with the *South Bend Tribune* or any of the local television or radio stations. It was better to respond in an organized way at the proper level of authority and with the assistance of our media team.

In addition to University-wide topics, some inquirers were concerned about my personal life, my schedule, my routines, my sources of relaxation, or my friendship group. While some of this attention was harmless, I always wanted to control what I revealed lest it become part of the social rumor mill. I felt that my public persona was one thing but my personal life was another. Fortunately, I never felt that I was of great interest to investigative reporters or law enforcement. The mistakes and errors of my life never amounted to much compared to certain politicians or media celebrities.

Students tend to be less concerned about such matters. So, my advice to you is never to give up your deserved right to privacy in the leadership roles you assume and trust the locals when it comes to good counsel about staying safe in other environments. Your generation has become so accustomed to internet communication that you, seemingly, cannot function without it.

Yet, there are real dangers in oversharing and in not retaining a degree of privacy. Just presume that whatever is in the cloud could become public knowledge someday, much to your potential embarrassment.

QUESTION 4

What has your experience taught you about the dangers of being a leader?

Security involves freedom from danger and/or freedom from fear or anxiety. During my leadership role at Notre Dame, I had one major threatening encounter at my office in the Main Building when a mentally ill man of about 50 years sought to meet with me. My assistant at the time recognized the danger and called the Notre Dame Police, who arrested him. He had a knife and a gun on his person and the makings of a bomb in his car. He claimed that he was a pacifist and resented that we had "God, Country, Notre Dame" on the side of The Sacred Heart Basilica. After that incident, we placed a quite physically impressive security guard in our office area and put panic buttons under desks of the various assistants of University officers. (In retrospect, I know that I was lucky relative to the horrors of Virginia Tech, Northern Illinois, and several other higher education institutions).

I later learned that other presidents had encountered threats and subsequently ratcheted up their security protections.

On some of the international trips, I had the assistance of the

Coca-Cola Corporation. Don Keough, the Chair of the Board of Trustees at the time, was the #2 Officer at Coke. The company had a protocol in which they divided up the countries of the world into categories of relative risk. Most of the trips where I sought their assistance revolved around providing a local driver or facilitating a meeting or two. Only later did I discover that, on trips to countries thought to be of higher risk, they assigned a second car with armed personnel to accompany my car at a discreet distance. I presume that most for-profit companies have similar practices.

On a trip to Honduras to visit with Notre Dame alumni and others, I found out that our host had several security personnel with automatic weapons who accompanied him and his family at all times. (In fact, earlier they had had a shootout and all the attackers had been killed). In Guatemala, I had a similar experience. At a gathering of Notre Dame alumni at someone's home, there was a whole contingent of guards for the various families present. In the Philippines, we had dinner at the end of a cul-de-sac and everyone had to go through a security post on the way in.

None of those experiences really bothered me but they were a reminder that life can be quite dangerous for business and government leaders in many parts of the world. The American Ambassador in Honduras was a Notre Dame graduate and when I joined him on a visit to an agrarian site in the countryside, we were accompanied by a contingent of military in jeeps both leading the way and following up from the rear.

Notre Dame is, overall, a very safe campus and we have an excellent police/security operation. On home football weekends as well as graduation and other special events, we add police personnel to supplement the members of our own force. I have personally spent time on campus with Presidents Jimmy Carter, Ronald Reagan, George H. W. Bush, Bill Clinton, and George W. Bush, not to speak of a whole host of foreign leaders. They have always had their Secret Service protective squads with them or an equivalent group. I guess you could say, I was never safer or at greater risk.

As a priest, occasionally, you meet individuals with crazy notions about religion. Most are relatively harmless, but you never know ahead of time. On one occasion, I found a young man in front of the altar after Communion with a crucifix who was spread-eagled over what turned out to be a Kentucky Fried Chicken dinner in a plastic container. He was making strange noises. After I made it into the sacristy, I found out that he was a drug user who needed help. Later that night, Notre Dame Police took him to a psychology ward for evaluation.

Leaders need safety to do their jobs effectively. But, as I found out, there are no guarantees on a low-crime campus or when traveling on behalf of the University.

QUESTION 5

What steps, specifically, would you recommend leaders implement to promote diversity and inclusion?

My answer to this question would be different now than when I was serving as President. In the earlier period, we had large gaps in representation of the diversity of American culture. Early on,

I appointed Roland Smith (a Black man with roots in South Bend and, eventually, an advanced degree from Harvard) as my Executive Assistant. Roland later went on to a major administrative post at Rice University. Later, I added Chandra Johnson, a Black woman, to my staff (a former student of mine who came to Notre Dame in her 30s). Chandra became a kind of guru with minority students and with women staff members. Both Roland and Chandra had great people skills and were an extension of the Office of President with various constituencies on and off the campus.

I also sought to diversify the administration at the vice president and dean level. This included African Americans, Hispanics, and women. In addition, we developed protocols for seeking out faculty across the academic disciplines who were both diverse and supportive of our Catholic mission and identity.

When it came to undergraduate students, we gave a high priority to recruiting for diversity both in census-category terms and also relative to socio-economic backgrounds. This entailed substantially increasing our financial aid resources, which made it a priority in our fundraising campaigns. Derivatively, we did the same in the law, business, and graduate schools.

A related issue was building up support structures for students of diverse backgrounds (including international students). This usually entailed personnel and facilities. The Student Affairs Operations worked hard on cultivating a welcoming environment in dorm life for all students.

One of the things we did, which surprised some people, was to create within the Notre Dame Alumni Association separate groups for Black, Hispanic, and Asian-Pacific alumni which were synchronized in their activities with the broader association. These moves substantially increased the participation rate of minority alumni.

Today, the context of higher education has changed drastically. Every search process I have been involved in (at Notre Dame and elsewhere) has highlighted the importance of diversity and inclusion. Meanwhile, the courts continue to take on lawsuits that challenge the use of preferences in admissions for underrepresented groups. The two major political parties disagree about how all this should be adjudicated going forward.

I personally operate with certain presumptions

→ We are all equal before God, our creator and redeemer;

→ Our national and world history needs to be taken into account;

→ The scourge of slavery and institutionalized racism cannot be ignored;

→ Patterns of discrimination and neighborhood segregation have severely influenced the socio-economic opportunities for parts of the population;

→ Public schools at the primary and secondary levels are vastly unequal in various parts of the country, especially in large cities;

→ The cost of higher education is a disincentive for many minority families;

→ The amelioration of all of this requires a collective effort by the allocation of government resources and the cooperation of all institutions of higher education;

→ In my lifetime, much progress has been made and this needs to be gratefully acknowledged;

→ The demographics of America continue to change rather significantly and, unless we solve the immigration crisis, the number of college-age students will continue to decline. As a result, schools will close and the types of higher education institutions available will be reduced; and

→ We need a national strategy that all of us can play a part in.

In the seminars I teach, the composition is usually much more diverse than the student population in general. I have taught students from every continent except Antarctica and from a rich array of American cultural backgrounds. I believe that this has enhanced learning opportunities for everyone. I am always gratified by the sharing that goes on and the friendships that are formed.

Finally, I hope that more of our underrepresented students will consider going on to achieve advanced degrees so that our future faculties will more closely represent the makeup of the broader society.

QUESTION 6

What sources of information do you find most trustworthy? How should leaders filter/choose information sources?

I am "old guard" when it comes to my commitment to keep up on local, national, and world events. Every day I read the following newspapers: *South Bend Tribune*, *Chicago Tribune*, *Chicago Sun Times*, *USA Today*, *The Washington Post*, *The Wall Street Journal*, and *The New York Times*. I use the print editions but others might choose the online editions. I know the sections I am most interested in and, often, similar material appears in multiple sources. I know the general orientation of each of these papers and can factor that into my perusal. I also subscribe to *Time* and *The Week*. On the religious side, I receive *America*, *Commonweal*, *Theological Studies*, and *National Catholic Reporter*.

I have a special interest in history and consider myself a Civil War buff and a Lincoln-phile. I have read widely about the American presidency. I have learned much from novels and autobiographies set in every continent, including Australia/New Zealand and Antarctica.

Over the course of my professional career as a moral theologian, I have developed some expertise in Catholic social teaching, biomedical ethics, war and peace, police ethics and law enforcement, terrorism and anti-terrorism, sexual ethics, race and ethnicity, and family issues. In a sense, I have been trained to take my theoretical background and apply it to some of the most important ethical issues of the day.

I am a big believer in keeping an open mind and learning

take decisive steps to respond to it. Juries have awarded huge settlements to victims in order to address the wrong (but this has also severely affected the ability of religious groups to perform their appropriate pastoral functions). And now law firms who specialize in these cases are pursuing similar legal strategies against other youth-serving organizations like Boy and Girl Scouts, Big Brothers/Big Sisters, and Boys and Girls Clubs.

When it comes to political leadership, our deeply divided country has become accustomed to counternarratives, the propagation of false information, and the widespread use of social media to appeal to almost primordial fears by different parts of the population. In recent years, Bill Clinton was impeached and Donald Trump impeached twice. In Illinois, several governors have gone to the penitentiary for crimes committed during their term of service. Some politicians have always been corrupt but the trend seems to be worsening.

The real question is how credibility can be regained. In my judgment, it revolves around a combination of factors: a commitment toward lives of personal integrity; a system of checks and balances where no one is above the law; professional groupings that promote the highest standards of leadership in various walks of life; and the public description of role models and inspiring stories that highlight examples of successful and honorable leadership.

For college students, the most important thing is to avoid cynicism and pervasive distrust. As students, your peers are observing your choices. They make judgments by the choices you make, who you hang out with, and how you treat people of different ages and from different backgrounds. It will be the same in future years when your leadership skills are manifest in more complicated social dynamics. Seek for a level of consistency when you are young and it will serve you well later in life. While some leaders may fail and violate the expectations placed upon them, there are plenty of counterexamples who can lead you to recognizing both the privileges and responsibilities of leadership.

QUESTION 8

How can students foster credibility in their own lives by their choices?

Perhaps the hardest influence to counteract is peer pressure at every stage of one's education and social interactions. Everyone wants to be liked and to be socially acceptable. However, reputations are guided best by concrete decisions. Who engages in gossip or rumor spreading? How reliable is one's friendship when faced with opposition? Who takes the initiative in reaching out to newcomers or to those who seem marginalized?

Regular, reliable acts of welcome can establish a positive reputation. A willingness to take responsibility for mistakes and failures can convey a genuine humility and a desire to start anew. A good sense of humor can help one avoid excessive self-preoccupation.

Credibility is won by a life of genuine openness and a consistent desire to live by high personal values. Once such a reputation is established it can be the solid grounding for successive levels of leadership and a spirit of confidence that can inspire trust.

QUESTION 9

As you have seen decades of Notre Dame alumni assume leadership positions, what sets them apart? What is your biggest hope for alumni leaders of the future?

For many years, the Notre Dame College of Engineering honored three of its graduates who had gone on to positions of leadership in industry, research, government, or elsewhere. I used to join them for lunch. I was curious about how they evaluated their Notre Dame education many years later. Almost all were convinced that our core curriculum had helped provide a broad background that served them well later in their careers. They felt that their technical training had been fine, but what distinguished them from their peers who had gone to other acclaimed institutions of higher education was that they could fashion a coherent essay, engage in a public debate, give an inspirational talk, and run a smooth meeting. Their background in philosophy, theology, literature, history, the social sciences, and the fine and performing arts had helped them avoid institutional sclerosis.

My hope is that our graduates will bring to their future lives in the professions, in business, in government services, in the military, and in the Church, a strong sense of the values they would like to guide their lives and the commitment to abide by them day in and day out. This means that personal integrity is a *sine qua non*.

I also think that the earlier decisions about where to live and work, whom to marry, what group of friends bring out the best in us, and how to raise a family are all relevant. There are some career paths not worth pursuing. I mean by this not only criminal activity or utter self-indulgence but also situations where peer pressure is intense and/or there is little to no opportunity for a personal life or contribution to the broader society. It may be that in the early stages of a career, in order to establish a positive reputation and be promoted, one has to work long hours and travel frequently, but if you notice that people 20 or 30 years later are doing the same, it should be an opportunity for self-examination.

Among the Notre Dame graduates I have greatly admired, there is usually a mix of deep family involvement, willingness to get involved in various professional and not-for-profit organizations, and regular financial contributions to prized causes and institutions. For example, Art Decio ran a successful business in Elkhart in the recreational vehicle and pre-built housing business, served on the Notre Dame Board of Trustees, was involved at the national level with The Salvation Army, and supported so many good causes that he was called "Saint Art." He also had a great wife, Patricia, and helped raise five children.

In my travels, I have found Notre Dame graduates serving in Congress or as governors and mayors. Others ran homeless shelters or rose to the top ranks in the military or in higher education. Some of the doctors I have met established traditions of volunteer service in poverty settings abroad. A number were in the forefront of civil or human rights organizations. We have had bishops and archbishops, and people in leadership of religious communities. Many are active today in athletics at the college and professional level and in the media. There is hardly any worthwhile walk of life where you cannot find a Notre Dame graduate making a difference.

All of this is to say that our present generation of students has a lot to look forward to. The world needs bright, well-educated, and generous young people who want to make a difference and who want to build on the legacy of those who have gone before them.

SECTION THREE

The Virtuous Leader

"The intention should be to say, when one of us is honored, _we all are._"

QUESTION 1

What does it mean to be a humble or servant leader?

Humility involves honest self-appraisal, often facilitated by appropriate feedback from others. In an age when personal, objective testing is taken for granted, early in our lives we can learn our IQs, our SAT or ACT scores, and later our scores on tests for professional and/or graduate studies. Not only can we find out about our own performance but we can also figure out where it fits in competitively with others who took the same test. Psychologists can also develop a profile of our inner world, socialization skills, and potential as a leader. These results in total may be comforting or challenging or depressing, but they are one way to assess our unique assets and capacities as a person.

In competitive circumstances, we may have our musical, artistic, literary, mathematical, or rhythmic talents appraised. Usually, only a limited number of people make the team or are chosen for the band, choral group, or cast of the school play. There are a specified number of cheerleaders, class presidents, student newspaper editors, or officers of student government. Failure to be selected for one of these roles may induce a lack of self-confidence or motivate us to move on to other areas of interest.

The **first lesson** about being a humble leader is that few people are equally gifted in every area of human activity, so you have to choose on the basis of feedback from multiple sources and your own enduring passion or lack of it.

A **second lesson** is that we should never forget our roots. Each of us has a unique personal history. Even identical twins, who have comparable genetic endowments, have different personalities and senses of themselves.

Having written a three-volume memoir in which I basically relive my life from birth to the end of my presidency at Notre Dame, I am very aware of the role my parents, two sisters, extended family, teachers, coaches at all levels, local parish priests, and the Holy Cross community had in my personal development. Through their presence, I have known and experienced love, belonging, inspiration, and support in times of both success and challenge.

The problem with some leaders is that they act like they were masters of their own destiny right from the start, that their talent was self-derived, and that their opportunities along the way were duly deserved with no dependence on others.

While each of our paths is different, we are all part of social and personal networks that either bring out the best in us or hinder our potential for leadership roles. That is why inauguration ceremonies and retirement events are full of potential for a formal moment of thankfulness and acknowledgment of our family members and the legions of others who supported us along the way.

The **third lesson** about being a servant leader is to recognize that you can never say thank you or congratulations too often.

The role of a leader can be a lonely one, if you let it be. In the end, only one person is responsible for the most basic decisions. The temptation, in order to avoid accusation of favoritism, is to deliberately isolate oneself from normal social interactions.

Contrariwise, leaders need to cultivate a spirit of thankfulness and appreciation for a job well done. A healthy organization establishes formal procedures to recognize significant moments in the lives of one's colleagues, no matter their station. The intention should be to say, when one of us is honored, we all are. It is often the times of personal hardship, like sickness in the family, or a natural disaster, or the death of loved ones that allow, through words and deeds of support (including from the leader directly), a closer bond to be created.

In my own life, I have tried to be alert for opportunities to provide positive feedback. I send congratulatory messages to faculty, students, and administrators who achieve something out of the ordinary. I send words of condolence to anyone who has lost a loved one. As a priest, I offer Masses for people in distressed circumstances. All of this I have learned from leaders whom I have admired.

For you students, I encourage you to be self-aware and open to solid feedback, to always remember where you came from, and who has supported you along the way, and, finally, to be thankful in explicit ways as a reminder that the good things you have achieved were dependent on a whole network of others.

QUESTION 2

How can we best cultivate the gifts of the Holy Spirit in our lives?

In Christian tradition, there are seven gifts of the Holy Spirit— wisdom, knowledge, understanding, counsel, piety, fortitude, and fear of the Lord. They are gifts in the sense that they help to perfect certain human capacities. Each of them can be seen as related to effective Christian leadership. I will concentrate on the first four since they have the widest application, even outside the Christian community of belief.

WISDOM

In some senses, wisdom can be seen as the work of a lifetime. It requires native ability, disciplined study, accumulated experience, and the capacity for discernment. It allows us to recognize the connection among various pieces of evidence, to rest uneasy until we have probed the inner meaning of things. The wise person is both humble (there is much more to learn) and confident (real discoveries have been achieved). Wisdom is not a solitary virtue since it is the work of poets, seekers, scientists, philosophers, and theologians. It involves shared knowledge and reliable implementation.

The wise leader fosters cooperative endeavor, comfortable sharing, and a humane agenda. He or she is not overwhelmed by data or process but seeks consensus and common ground. Projected timelines can be neither too short (like business quarterly reports too often are) nor too long (when no real criteria of success are operative). In large collective endeavors, the wise leader recognizes and fosters the gifts of other leaders within the operation so that each might contribute within their realm of effectiveness.

KNOWLEDGE

Knowledge is the gift of awareness or familiarity of some fact or relationship or reality that is gained by human experience or through the exercise of science, art, or some technique. The knowledgeable person, in contemporary society, is presently educated in school or through internship, a tutoring relationship, or a lifetime of perceptive observation.

Individuals blessed with great memories may even, on rare occasions, function with total recall. I knew a theology professor, a New Testament scholar, who claimed to have written sophisticated books full of relevant details entirely out of what he had previously read without having to go back and check his sources. Others may have a quick recall of extensive data or a mastery of mathematical figures and financial information.

Knowledge can be used for good or ill. In and of itself, it does not determine what priorities should be, or how to pursue a given goal, or who to include in a common endeavor. That is why a knowledgeable leader needs to engage in consultation with trusted others and seek a variety of points of view about how to establish goals based on the best knowledge available. Too much knowledge, in the sense of unlimited data banks or endless patterns of appraisal, can lead to inertia, a waning of enthusiasm, or a fear of misdirection.

Transformative leaders are never afraid of diverse contributions to a conversation about goals, processes, or desirable participants since some are blessed with a greater capacity for absorption of relevant information. But, in the end, it is the effective leader who will oversee the implementation of the best knowledge available in the service of the common good.

UNDERSTANDING

Understanding is about comprehension of the general relations among particulars. It involves the application of concepts and categories to make experiences intelligible. When people visit other cultures, especially when they do not speak the native language, they can feel lost. Most social interactions become problematic. The same can happen when they immerse themselves in a subculture that presumes a certain language game or jargon like experimental science, information technology, war strategy, or artistic critique. Jews, Christians, and Muslims do, in fact, share notions that God is one and that a book like the Bible or the Koran is central. But, their theologies, forms of worship, and leadership structures vary widely and may interfere with understanding.

Understanding can also refer to emotional connection in human relationships. We enjoy the company of some people more than others. We may give priority to family members, neighbors, schoolmates, and fellow adherents of a religious tradition more than other humans whom we know less intimately.

Leadership involves both notions of understanding—both the ability to recognize connections in our experience and find vocabulary to conceptualize and make sense of them and the ability to forge human relationships within our sphere of influence and across artificial boundaries. Search committees want to choose from among candidates who are both smart and savvy.

COUNSEL

While wisdom, understanding, and knowledge are virtues that describe attributes of an individual, counsel is prototypically about a certain kind of interaction between two or more individuals. Counsel is about the rendering of advice, presumably in a spirit of generosity and mutual regard. Parents may counsel their own children about ordinary things like nutrition, civility, healthy habits, or the need to pull one's weight around the house. More importantly, they may discuss the need to study for school, peer pressure, moral values, religious participation, and the demands of love and forgiveness. Doctors, lawyers, law enforcement personnel, teachers, clergy, and individuals who have experienced a lot of life will be called upon to offer counsel and advice in their professional capacities or as trusted others. In addition, there are counselors with specialized training that qualifies them to take on a role with individuals who suffer emotional disturbance, who have been traumatized, or whose life circumstances have been unsupportive or chronically painful.

In all these senses, counsel can be exercised by a wide variety of individuals from the highly trained to the willing amateurs. But, relative to leadership in complex institutions like businesses, schools, government organizations, the military, and religious communities, counsel is a role intended to draw upon the wealth of one's own experience, and that of others, to establish goals, mobilize resources, overcome divisions, reward successful activity, and energize the common enterprise with vision, enthusiasm, and a sense of achievement.

In theological terms, the gifts of the Holy Spirit are gratuitous, freely given by God. They are not qualities that one can claim credit for. The sacrament of Confirmation is seen as a particular moment of grace-giving for Christians to live in the world as agents of virtue, example, and leadership. You students should recognize the pivotal role of the three sacraments of initiation—Baptism, Confirmation, and the reception of the Holy Eucharist. It is the faith community that sends forth every new generation to bring the Good News of the Gospel to the world.

QUESTION 3

How can leaders encourage spirituality?

My experience at Notre Dame as a priest President is very much connected to promoting spirituality on campus. Since I was elected President, I have lived in Sorin Hall as priest-in-residence. This means that I celebrate Mass there on Sundays and on Tuesday and Thursday evenings at 10:00 p.m. Now, I am the only priest in the hall, so I celebrate more Sunday liturgies than I did before when often the Rector was also a Holy Cross priest. All of this has meant that the residents of the dorm (and others) have the opportunity to worship there on a regular basis. We are also right next to Sacred Heart Basilica, so they have other convenient places to worship. There has also been a tradition in the hall of paying visits in groups to the Grotto of Our Lady of Lourdes, which is nearby.

In addition, all other dorms have a regular Mass schedule. Some also have Holy Hours or other spiritual gatherings. Notre Dame is rather unusual among Catholic colleges and universities in having so many priests available plus a quite active Campus Ministry. On home football weekends, we have large congregations for Masses before or after the game depending on the starting time.

Each year the RCIA program accompanies members of our broader community, (most of them students), who are interested in the possibility of either being baptized or becoming full members of the Catholic community at the Easter Vigil service. Their sponsors through the whole process are usually peers.

The multiple liturgical choirs at Notre Dame recruit

participants who sing at the major Masses in the Basilica and on special occasions like First-Year Orientation, Junior Parents Weekend, and Commencement. Periodically, these groups tour the U.S. or abroad sharing their musical gifts with alumni and others.

Today, with the ready availability of internet communication, many of the Masses at the Basilica, or on special occasions, are carried online. During the worst of COVID-19, many Notre Dame graduates or friends began watching these Masses on a regular basis. I received several emails from those who watched the Monday Mass at 11:30 a.m. that I celebrate on a regular basis.

As a leader, I also gave talks on campus on religious, spiritual, or theological topics. This included reflections on Notre Dame's status as a Catholic university and our special sense of identity and mission. A number of other Catholic institutions reached out to us for advice about best practices.

Some of the most enjoyable experiences that I had as President were weddings and baptisms which usually involved young people I knew (and normally a host of their friends). Such events were the equivalent of reunions for friendship groups. I also had the privilege of celebrating funeral Masses of Notre Dame-related people both on and off campus.

Furthermore, the offerings of the Theology Department (with our two required courses at the undergraduate level) and the various Institutes and Centers provided a more theoretical rationale for the life of faith and Christian practice.

Spirituality cannot be forced, but it can be heartily promoted. I know that I was positively influenced at various times in my life by the inspiring example of peers and leaders who took their faith seriously. They worshipped regularly, participated in parish (or campus) life, and were generous in the service they rendered. This provided me with a model to emulate. That is why I encourage the students that I teach to take full advantage of the array of opportunities available at Notre Dame.

QUESTION 4

What is the effect of prayer on leadership?

Prayer is a necessary Christian practice (as well as in other religious traditions). In Catholicism, the central context of prayer is the celebration of the sacrament of the Holy Eucharist in which we consecrate the bread and wine and they become transferred into the very body and blood of Jesus. The other sacraments and other forms of common prayer are derivative of the Eucharist.

In my experience as a priest President, the public prayer that I have participated in (and often led) has been an essential part of my leadership. At Notre Dame, in First-Year Orientation, during Junior Parents Weekend, and on Commencement Weekend, the celebration of the Eucharist symbolizes and enacts our sense of community and our turning to God to seek blessings on all members of our campus family. At the beginning of the school year, this, in some sense, is in prospect, an affirmation of what we hope will happen. At Commencement, it is a sending forth by the parents and the University of their sons and daughters to become active members of other communities, guided by the values of Notre Dame and supported by the friends they have made.

In addition to these pivotal moments of transition, we celebrate the Eucharist daily in Sacred Heart Basilica and Sacred Heart Parish (down below) and in all the student halls and several academic buildings on a regular basis. In my years as President, I tried to lead the liturgies at least once in as many of the chapels as I could. We also had Masses when the trustees and advisory councils gathered on campus (to properly reflect our nature as a Catholic university).

As President, I also did my share of baptisms, marriages, and funerals (as did other priest members of the officers' group). The funerals of students were very emotional both for the family members and for their campus friendship group. (The funeral for the women's swim team accident victims was especially memorable). On the more positive side, I celebrated anniversary Masses for couples and on fundraising weekends and often held Mass in the Log Chapel.

At Notre Dame, we always try to cultivate other traditions of prayer like visits to the Grotto, participation in dorm or Campus Ministry-sponsored retreats, Bible study groups, and other forms of student-led religious reflection. And, we are quite fortunate in having so many choirs and musicians who provide music at the Basilica, are available for weddings and funerals, and participate in special Eucharists.

While much of what I have said revolves around my status as a priest President, our lay administrators and lay rectors also have an essential role to play in promoting the practices of prayer, from Eucharistic Adoration to praying the rosary to modeling prayer as an integral part of one's life.

As a Holy Cross religious, I also have participated in our common prayer life, which has been a great source of personal support for my particular ministries at Notre Dame. On occasion, I have been invited to lead retreats off-campus for various groups including diocesan clergy and other groups of Holy Cross religious as well as lay groups. I surely was invited to play these roles because of my leadership position but it was never part of my formal job descriptions.

Despite my nickname, I have no attraction to the monastic life. I see myself as an active religious for whom the apostolate is central to my identity as a priest. So, my own prayer life undergirds and flows from my ministry to others. If I err on occasion, it is because of the demand of the apostolate, but my identity as a Holy Cross religious always calls me back to the essential practice of prayer. I would encourage all of you as students to develop a rhythm of prayer that fits your own spirituality and other time commitments. For example, a daily quick visit to the Grotto is easily adaptable.

QUESTION 5

How can this daily essential prayer practice guide and inform students who will become leaders?

In addition to the Grotto visits, there are countless ways in which student leaders can develop a rich and meaningful prayer life. As a student, I regularly attended daily Mass either at the Sacred Heart or in my hall chapel. This is still a readily available tradition at Notre Dame. Each evening at 6:45 pm the rosary is recited at the Grotto. There are student groups who gather for Bible study or faith sharing. The sacrament of Penance is available at the Sacred Heart and elsewhere on most days. Chapel visits can suit anyone's schedule. In addition, some students seek out a spiritual director to assist their development as a person of prayer.

The important thing is to start simply. A regular practice of a comfortable form of prayer is more valuable in the long run than some elaborate schedule that becomes impossible to keep up. A leader who prays is better prepared for the challenges of office than in the absence of this spiritual practice.

QUESTION 6

What are the responsibilities of Catholic leaders that sets them apart?

In some ways, as President of Notre Dame, I had a major leadership role in the American Catholic Church. I put a strong emphasis on the mission and identity of Notre Dame as a Catholic university. I frequently referred to our founding by the Congregation of Holy Cross, the continued presence and activity of a significant number of Holy Cross religious, the various services we rendered through our faculty, graduates, and students to the local, national, and international Church, the role our institutes and centers in undertaking research projects in Church-related issues, and our presence as a major pilgrimage site through the Grotto of Our Lady of Lourdes and Sacred Heart Basilica. In addition, we have a major commitment to Campus Ministry and regular worship opportunities in all our dorms and many academic building chapels. Many think of Notre Dame as the preeminent Catholic university in the nation, and perhaps in the world.

Because we are an institution of higher education in the American context, we try to negotiate the delicate balance between being faithful to our Catholic intellectual heritage and our commitment to full-blown academic freedom. This means that, at times, various segments of the Church may think of us as too liberal or too conservative. Occasionally, we attract the attention of national media, the American bishops, or the Vatican. Usually, these concerns revolve around ecclesiastical issues, moral teachings, or political advocacy. In most cases, there is a period of debate and then some sort of resolution. My role as President was to make sure that the prerogatives of each of the contributors to the conversation were preserved.

By my participation on various boards (like other universities, higher education associations, not-for-profit organizations serving youth, addiction treatment, and service learning), I tend to bring my training as a moral theologian and my role as a priest President into broader circles of influence. For example, I serve on the Board of Governors of the Boys and Girls Clubs movement as its official ethicist.

As a writer and frequent speech-giver, I have had many opportunities to address relevant topics in both civil and Church-related worlds. Addiction is a complicated topic depending on the substance or practice, the age of the afflicted, and the prevailing wisdom about various modes of intervention, structured reforms, and treatment. The opioid crisis is an example where criminal law, law enforcement, treatment options, and financial support are all relevant. An addictive person is a sick person, but their behavior can also put other people at risk. Alcohol abuse remains a major problem on almost all our college campuses and is the source of many of the most severe disciplinary problems.

Among the challenges that I think Catholic Church leaders of today have to take on are the following:

→ Proclaim the Gospel of Jesus Christ with energy, faithfulness, and enthusiasm;

→ Establish and reinforce the community of faith (this means bringing together the sometimes divided Church communities that are split on often superficial grounds);

→ Rely on the Holy Spirit for the power of renewal;

→ Strive to be both humble and forthright; and

→ Yearn for the eternal banquet when all will be brought to completion, which will be a fitting reminder that, in this world, we have to leave all things in God's hands.

I hope that you who are Catholic learn your heritage well, bring your own talents to bear on contemporary Church discussions, and develop a well-informed voice to promote the necessary ongoing reform of the Church itself. For students from other faith traditions, the same general principles apply. It is the necessary and critical entity to convey the Gospel to the world.

QUESTION 7

How can religious faith be an asset in optimal leadership?

What we believe about God, about God's relationship to human-ity, and about the human grounds for hope and commitment are all relevant to how we see ourselves as leaders. As a Catholic Christian and a priest, I have spent my life in pursuit of the truth as passed down in the Judeo-Christian tradition and interpreted by centuries of philosophers, theologians, and Church leaders. All of this has given me a head start in determining my own personal values and goals in life. I have tested out the wisdom of it all as I have lived out my life, encountered human sinfulness, recognized the gift of forgiveness, and had my values reinforced by the active presence of a community of believers.

Eventually, everyone will go through the stage of life in which self-knowledge will be possible and one level of decision-making will lead to another. When I joined the Congregation of Holy Cross, made my final vows, and was ordained to the priesthood, I chose one path of Christian commitment. In order to pre-pare for that step, I spent years in study and spiritual formation. Later, I pursued a doctorate in Christian Ethics at Vanderbilt University, where I was also involved in parish ministry on the weekends. Those provided a solid formation for the leadership roles that I would finally undertake.

Through my involvement in many not-for-profit boards, I have met many leaders from other faith traditions who impressed me with their deep sense of faith and their service orientation. A number were actively involved in their own places of worship.

One result of my formal theological preparation was the Christian anthropology that I derived from it. Human persons are created by God and called to holiness. However, our capacity for sin and our potential to misuse human freedom means that there is an important place for law and its enforcement. It is naïve to believe that goodness will always prevail. On the other hand, we are also capable of love, justice, and mutual forgiveness. In other words, we are neither devils nor saints but humans on the journey of life where our choices make a difference and where social structures, value systems, and accountability structures are all important.

As leaders within this frame of reference, we need to serve the common good, appeal to the best in those entrusted to our care, and recognize our own need for feedback and periodic evaluation.

For a Christian believer, the mystery of Jesus' life, death, and resurrection is a constant reminder that suffering and pain and disappointment are part of the human condition, but our final victory as faithful followers of the Lord has been assured. In light of Easter, we can be people of hope and aspiration and meaningful engagement in the vital issues of our day.

As a Catholic Christian person of faith, I continue to be inspired by the example of the holy men and women who have gone before me, some of whom had significant leadership roles both within and outside the Church. I think of Peter and Paul, Ambrose and Augustine, Francis, Dominic and Ignatius, Theresa, Clare, Catherine of Siena, Elizabeth, and many more.

One of the most important things that students can do during their college years is to pursue their own life of faith, participate actively in a worshipping community, and take classes that enhance their knowledge of the traditions. On that basis, they can then test out the applications of that faith within the parameters of their own families, neighborhoods, and societies and later as adult leaders.

QUESTION 8 (A)

How can leaders best embrace the cardinal virtues? How are these foundational for leadership?

While these categories of moral analysis are rooted in the Catholic ethical tradition, they all have relevance for those who seek to be leaders of integrity and purposefulness. The **four cardinal virtues** are basic orientations or habits of the self as a free agent in the world.

For example, **prudence** is a virtue of practical reason. It involves sagacity or shrewdness in the management of affairs including personnel and resources. In fact, prudence is not a disinclination to action or an excessive fear of making a mistake. It is not about hesitancy, indecision, or reluctance. Instead, prudent leaders possess a broad vision and a proper concern for detail. They recognize that planning is necessary, that all voices must be listened to, and that action should not be done hesitantly or precipitously. However, in the end, action must be taken, workers properly empowered, a vision of success entertained, and a full evaluation undertaken after the fact.

The prudent leader hires well, inspires by word and action, cultivates proper cooperation, and rewards hard work and exceptional performance. The prudent leader is guided by the highest ideals and a sense of confidence that there will be consistency between preparation taken and hoped-for results.

A second cardinal virtue is **temperance**, which seeks moderation in action, thought, and feeling. It implies that it is appropriate to set limits relative to appetites or desires. Despite the public connection of temperance with the historical movement to abstain from alcohol, temperance is applicable to a whole range of human behaviors. For example, how we dress, where we live, what kind of things we indulge in, and the concern for appearance and possessions as indicators of one's social status are all relevant in this regard. Of course, it is possible to be rich and humble and quite generous (the tradition of philanthropy depends on this willingness).

The temperate leader operates from within according to recognized values and established practices of operation. Leaders who depend on one-upmanship, glitz, and glamor will ultimately find that the roots of their authority are shallow. It is the deeper sense of colleagueship, shared goals, and collective responsibility that can really support the most important endeavors.

Fortitude is the third cardinal virtue, which leads to strength of purpose in good action. It enables a person to persist, to carry on, and to encounter pain or adversity with courage. It is more than stubbornness because it is manifest in the pursuit of worthy goals and agreed-upon ends. Even in the face of public denunciation, imprisonment, or threats of death, the leader who is gifted with fortitude will not withdraw from the fray or betray his or her companions or fundamental values. Some leaders will find themselves in the face of unexpected opposition, untrustworthy colleagues, or circumstances beyond their immediate control. It is in such moments that their character is tested. Some will continue on despite ill health or familial challenges or the aging process. Sometimes, only in retrospect will their contributions be fully appreciated.

Fortitude is about interior strength, not physical endowment or inherited fortune. It requires a maturity of judgment and a range of prior experience. Like athletes or entertainers, the persistent leader will benefit from earlier tests and focused reflection. A politician or a military leader may know moments of real failure before rising to new opportunities. A business leader may undergo bankruptcy or a corporate buyout before finding the right fit.

In religious terms, fortitude is about renewal of purpose in the face of the recognition of human weakness and limitations. It is about a conversion that more effectively includes the whole person.

The fourth and final cardinal virtue is **justice**, which is the virtue that springs from the desire for fairness and equality in human life and activity. It is the principle of just dealing or right action. It includes conformity to truth, fact, or reason. The opposite of justice is injustice, bias, mistreatment, coercion, intimidation, and sometimes physical, psychological, or moral violence. In democracies, political leaders take oaths that commit them to upholding the constitution, bylaws, and regulations passed by legitimate authority.

Justice can describe:

→ the dynamic between two people or entities;

→ the relations and expectations that pertain to life, trade, and reciprocal responsibilities in society; and

→ the special demands that accrue to some in society who are deprived of the basic necessities of life or whose appeal is deeply rooted in our common humanity (There but for the grace of God go I).

All leaders in a just society are expected to care about the well-being of those entrusted to their care. In business, this entails fair hiring practices and opportunities for promotion, safe working conditions, proper remuneration, attention to group morale, and regular celebrations of achievement and personal markers in their employees' lives. In contemporary practice, this also includes an explicit recognition of obstacles to effective and satisfactory employment that may spring from gender, age, religion, ethnicity, race, or sexual orientation.

Some leaders are promoters of causes (abolitionism, women's right to vote, immigration, temperance, civil rights, abortion, the death penalty, pacifism, or religious freedom). Gandhi was the great advocate of Indian independence. Dorothy Day began Catholic Worker Movement. Mother Theresa worked with the poor and dying in Calcutta. Martin Luther King, Jr., was a stalwart in the efforts to achieve justice for African Americans. Nelson Mandela sought racial justice and peace in South Africa.

In American society, with its tradition of not-for-profit

organizations, many volunteer their services to work with young people, the homeless, the elderly, recent immigrants, and those afflicted by addiction or other human ills. Each of those efforts requires full-time staff with committed leaders as well as governing boards. In my life, I have served on boards connected to higher education, addiction to alcohol and other drugs, promotion of the health, education, and job skills of young people, the well-being of sick children, homelessness, and service learning opportunities for college students.

Leaders need to be just in their dealings with others. But they also need to be treated fairly by those with whom they work, periodic evaluators, and outside observers. No one is perfect. Leaders make mistakes. Compromise is sometimes necessary. That is why the Golden Rule, "Do unto others as you would have them do onto you" and the Silver Rule, "Do not do unto others as you would not have them do unto you" are always operative.

In a good society, the standard of justice is relevant for all, from those with explicit power, influence, and authority in relation to those easily forgotten. It is the committed, generous, and self-aware leader who will set the standard for all who participate in the different levels of the social, economic, and political order.

For you students, the cardinal virtues are learned and hopefully practiced on the path to adulthood. That is why each of these virtues requires a degree of maturity that can only be learned by practice. Most of us make a lot of mistakes along the way. But, with healthy self-reflection and the advice of trusted others, you too can become prudent, temperate, persistent, and just. Those are all attributes of great leaders.

QUESTION 8 (B)

How can leaders best embrace the corporal works of mercy?

In answering this question, I need to explore a particular biblically based understanding of the demands of justice. This list generally derives from Matthew 25:31–46, the Parable of Judgment at the end of time when God will separate the sheep from the goats, those who respond to the needs of others from those who do not. The seven works of mercy do not specify how to ascertain who qualifies for aid or how to properly deliver such assistance.

FEED THE HUNGRY

This can entail sharing a meal with a stranger, a group of refugees, those deprived of the basic necessities of life, the unemployed, or victims of natural disasters. While individuals or small groups may take on this responsibility, more organized and structured efforts will require leadership at the local, regional, national, or international level. I think of St. Vincent de Paul Society, Goodwill, the Salvation Army, Bread for the World, Catholic Relief Services International, or various local food banks and feeding programs sponsored by different religious or humanitarian groups. In my experience, local Boys and Girls Clubs often distribute lunch and dinner to young people who otherwise would go without.

GIVE DRINK TO THE THIRSTY

This effort is often directly connected to feeding the hungry, but it can take a special urgency in regions suffering from prolonged drought and civil conflict where wells, water pipes, and purification systems have been negatively impacted or destroyed. Military forces can sometimes be deployed to assist in this effort. Water is a basic necessity for human survival.

CLOTHE THE NAKED

In this regard, so much depends on the time of year and meteorological conditions how imperative clothing can be. Children, the young, and the elderly can be especially susceptible to harsh weather conditions. In cold climates, proper clothing can prevent hypothermia and the risk of death. Footwear, shorts and pants, hats and gloves, and other components of covering the human body can also influence peoples' sense of self-worth and belonging. Leaders need to be alert to the difficult levels of the social significance of clothing, e.g., teenage peer pressures.

SHELTER THE HOMELESS

In the United States, the number of homeless went up precipitously after reformers sought to deinstitutionalize parts of the population that lacked the capacity to house themselves, including the mentally ill and the addicted. The unintended consequence was the proliferation of homeless encampments, especially in warmer urban environments. In this day, this has become a chronic problem across the country. Outside the United States, the number of people forced from their homelands by civil wars, natural disasters, and population pressures is unprecedented. The United Nations and other international agencies are doing their best, but the situation is urgent. This is especially true for those seeking access to Europe from Africa and Asia and to the United States from Mexico, Central America, Asia, and the Middle East. We need leaders who pursue both short-range and long-range responses.

VISIT THE IMPRISONED

The United States has the largest imprisoned population in the world. They are disproportionately Black, Hispanic, and lower-income whites. Much of this has been driven by the illegal drug trade and organized gangs. Prisons are usually highly segregated by race and ethnicity by self-selection and the survival instinct.

Efforts are underway to reduce the prison population and find other ways to hold felons accountable for their misbehavior. These reform steps require good leadership both in the law enforcement and penal fields.

VISIT THE SICK

A good part of the U.S. annual budget goes into health care and this is rising because of the aging of the population and the increased cost of high tech treatment and pharmaceutical medication.

In this area, there is a great need for leadership in scientific research, including on college and university campuses, in the allotment of federal and state dollars and in medical care in hospitals, clinics, and other patient-oriented facilities.

Patient-centered care, family presence, cordial and welcoming treatment environments, and a recognition of the

social, emotional, and religious needs of those being cared for
are all critical areas of need for future attention.

BURY THE DEAD

While in the Catholic context, there is now provision for
cremations as a part of the celebration of the life and death
of human persons; this is not intended to undermine the
importance of the funeral liturgy and burial rite. Each
individual is unique and has a distinctive history. This needs to
be honored and celebrated. Funeral directors, pastoral staffs,
and loving family members all have a role to play.

In certain circumstances like wartime, natural disruptions,
plagues, and viruses like COVID-19, there are limits on
how the dead can be safely laid to rest without endangering
others, but in normal times, community and religious leaders
need to preserve the sense of dignity and value for those
who have died. As people who believe in the Resurrection of
the Lord, we need to assure that the hope for eternal life is
manifest in the way the dead are buried.

For students, the corporal works of mercy can be practiced
during one's undergraduate days through various service organizations where leadership roles are readily available and usually
turn over on a regular basis. On campus, one can participate in
hall clothing drives or food pantries or fundraising. In town, one
can volunteer at the South Bend Center for the Homeless, the
Robinson Community Learning Center, Dismas House, or the
local Boys and Girls Club. There are also tutoring opportunities.
After graduation, the Notre Dame Alumni Network puts great
emphasis on club service projects. We all hope that this is a hallmark of a Notre Dame education.

My early involvements in Latin America provided an exposure to the culture of poverty and gave me the opportunity to distribute food, engage in simple medical procedures, work in orphanages, help construct housing, and otherwise be involved in ameliorative activities. The availability of internships and subsidized summer programs can provide an introduction for decisions about major areas of study and lifetime career goals.

QUESTION 8 (C)

How can leaders best embrace the spiritual works of mercy?

Such a question presumes that the human person has both physical and spiritual dimension and that one of the responsibilities of leadership is to nurture both attributes and needs of the integrated self. Some might prefer the term psychological or emotional to "spiritual," but similar challenges for leadership are at stake.

My premise is that the spiritual works of mercy are applicable beyond the domains of bishops, pastors, and lay leaders or psychologists and psychiatrists. Mental health is a serious need today at various levels of education and also in business, corporations, the military, athletics, the performing arts, and elsewhere.

COMFORT THE SORROWING

In every workplace, neighborhood, and social network, at any given moment, there are individuals who are grieving the loss of a loved one (a parent, child, neighbor, or a good friend), or who have received unexpected news about their health or that of someone close to them, or who have lost their job or been demoted, or who have been suffering from emotional turmoil from whatever source.

Of course, these are opportunities for words and deeds of support and encouragement. Many companies and institutions have structured ways to respond holistically to such situations. Churches and other religious communities should be especially adept at reaching out to its sorrowing members or others brought to their attention. At Notre Dame, we pride ourselves on all the services available (and committed people to deliver them) when people may not know who to turn to.

COUNSEL THE DOUBTFUL

This can refer to people who lack self-confidence and need reassurance or those in the process of making difficult decisions (like career choices or what to study in school or whether and who to marry). This is when good listening skills are essential. In my undergraduate seminar, the final assignment is an autobiographical essay. Even though the students are in the first year of college, most of the papers I receive are quite revealing and full of descriptions about the fears and hopes they bring to college.

Academic settings and other places where professional counselors are available need leaders who will respond to a broad understanding of the needs of those entrusted to their care.

INSTRUCT THE IGNORANT

Because our various levels of public and private education are so diverse in quality and because parental and family involvements are, in some cases, unreliable, I have served on many not-for-profit boards who have sponsored studies to figure out how to improve public education at all levels and private education as well. Notre Dame's Alliance for Catholic Education (ACE) is a quite successful model for how to encourage our graduates to become teachers (and principals) and prepare them well for these important responsibilities.

But, this work of mercy also includes the sharing of wisdom by elders and others with a broad range of experiences. Various media have tried to create advice columns and T.V. shows purportedly to help the inexperienced, but too often these become only a form of cheap entertainment.

WARN THE SINNER

While "sinner" is an explicitly religious category, it could also refer to those who put their and other lives at danger or violate the common good or ally with others to seek profit from illegal or immoral activity. Parents, neighbors, schools, houses of worship, and the legal/judicial/penal system all have a role to play in this kind of confrontation. The best remedy is early intervention. Sin, or moral misdeeds, tends to be habitual behavior. As a result, silence or inaction is not a helpful strategy.

Some political candidates run on law-and-order platforms. However, often, their solutions involve draconian interventions and harsh treatment. That is why we have the largest prison population in the world.

FORGIVE ALL INJURIES

One of the most pervasive themes in the Christian Scriptures is the call to mercy and forgiveness. In a sense, this is one manifestation of the command to love (even our enemies). It is easier to carry grudges and seek to get even than to give those who may have harmed us another chance. To the realists in our midst, this work of mercy may seem utterly naive, yet I recall that in my lifetime formerly hostile nations were able to become allies and partners (Germany, Italy, Japan, Vietnam, and to a lesser extent, the Soviet Union). We have also seen Pope John Paul II publicly forgive the man who shot him, members of the Black church in Montgomery forgive the white man who murdered so many members, and others step forward in acts of forgiveness in individual cases to our amazement and inspiration.

BEAR WRONGS PATIENTLY

All of us make mistakes and need to apologize for our poor choices and occasional harmful actions. Some among us, like Job, seem to incur a disproportionate number of ills and pains, sometimes from those we love the most. Our instinct might be to lash out and seek redress from the courts or somehow gain the upper hand. In the face of this potential gut response, we need to structure at the personal, family, and social level means for patience and tolerance that can prevent any untoward behavior and keep open the possibility of wholehearted reconciliation at a later date.

PRAY FOR THE LIVING AND THE DEAD

Prayers of petition are much more common than prayers of

thanksgiving. Prayers for our own personal (perceived) needs are more common than those focused on others, those far removed from our social circles.

People of faith need to pray to the living God as one form of recognition of our ultimate dependence on God for our very life and for all we enjoy in the world. We can legitimately pray for anything that reflects a God-filled world and our role within it.

We also pray for the dead in order to recognize our bonds with them as members of the same families, workplaces, civic communities, religious communities, or worldwide concern. As Christian believers, we believe that we will be reunited one day with all those we have known and loved in this world and many others as well. Only God gets to choose who will be part of this community of lovers and saints. Yet, amidst our grief and pain, we indeed pray for the dead and celebrate their lives in their funeral liturgies and burials.

Leaders who believe in the value of prayer should seek to incorporate it, insofar as possible, into the everyday life of those for whom they are responsible. People never forget who visits them in the hospital or comes to the burials of their beloved dead.

In general, students on residential campuses have endless opportunities to practice the spiritual works of mercy in their relationships with their roommate, in the dynamics of hall life, in participation in various support groups, and with an openness to people of different backgrounds. Any initiative taking in these areas can be an excellent preparation for leadership focused on the fullness of the human person.

SECTION FOUR

Leadership Gone Awry:

Negative Attributes of a Leader

"Always see leadership as a _collective responsibility_. Whatever particular role you play will always be part of a much bigger enterprise."

QUESTION 1

What are attributes of harmful and destructive leadership?

There are many such attributes, but I will focus on three of them: dishonesty, coercion, and lack of self-knowledge.

With regard to **dishonesty**, leaders are rightly expected to be people of their word, to have a reliable sense of reality, to be, in the long run, trustworthy and dependable. In their public utterances and in their written communications, words count.

In certain spheres of endeavor, like politics, there may be some leeway for exaggeration or excessively idealistic promises. People on the campaign trail may have a set number of speeches that emphasize key points or attack the persuasiveness of their opponent's arguments. But, in the end, there need to be a few main points that lay out a feasible set of directions for the future.

When political candidates call into question the very nature of truth and propound falsehoods, self-serving constructed realities, and malign plots by their opponents, then those who respond to them need to have access to different and provable versions of reality. Otherwise, they become victims of the lie (or, more likely lies) that may make it impossible to repair the harm done.

The dishonesty of leaders can come in many forms. For example, they may falsify their credentials or invent pasts that never existed. At Notre Dame, we once hired a new football coach, but after a local reporter in his hometown checked his curriculum vitae, it was determined that he made a couple of false claims that eliminated his eligibility for the job.

A second form of such behavior revolves around suppressed information like troubling accusations about theft or overbilling or excessive spending in a previous position. The same is true regarding discriminatory treatment of colleagues or subordinates or sexual misconduct. This does not mean that forgiveness and/or reform are out of the question, but rather that deliberate silence may cloak underlying tendencies and troublesome patterns.

A third issue is the misuse of inside information for one's financial advantage or to harm unnecessarily someone else's reputation. Leaders, especially at the upper levels, often are familiar with a wide range of normally undisclosed information. This can become a weapon in the face of certain desires for revenge or to win out in particularly competitive environments.

Dishonesty, over time, can become a characteristic way of approaching the world. In a worst-case scenario, the person may forget (either deliberately or not) where truth lies. In that case, the reliability of social communication simply breaks down.

With regard to **coercion**, some governmental/political leaders come into and stay in power through various means of coercion. Think of Mao Tse Tung, Stalin, Hitler, Mussolini, and Pol Pot, who collectively were responsible for the deaths of tens of millions of people, not to speak of those imprisoned and tortured and stripped of all their possessions. It is amazing to me that sometimes one individual through demagoguery, false propaganda, the mobilization of police and military forces, and the creation of a common enemy can attain such an all-encompassing power over the life and well-being of others.

Even in less dramatic circumstances, we can find individuals who have all the asocial skills of bullies. They intimidate physically and psychologically. They engage in rumormongering to smear the reputations of potential rivals. They look for weakness in others and embarrass them in public. They lure others into minor misdeeds so that this evidence can be brought forth at critical moments.

Sometimes, the coercive capacity of leaders is seen most clearly when superior debating skills or access to extensive financial resources or long-time affiliations can be strategically drawn upon. All of this can create an atmosphere of fear or suspicion in the workplace or other contexts of leadership. In human history, we have had unworthy governors and mayors, amoral business executives, untrustworthy not-for-profit chiefs, and self-serving bishops, ministers, and rabbis.

On occasion, coercion can take a physical form: hard handshakes, unexpected pushes, unfriendly pokes. More commonly, it can include harsh words, screams, prolonged tirades, and dismissive vocabulary and phrases.

A coercive leader only survives by shrewd alliance-building and constant disruptive social dynamics. Group meetings are always unpleasant and sometimes deeply feared. One-on-one situations are unpredictable and include suspicion that job stability may be at stake.

They say that there is no honor among thieves. The same could be said about leaders who rely on pressure and disruptive behavior to stay in control. When the truth is eventually told, there is no one with whom they can find support. After their exit, it is a scorched earth and a dysfunctional common life that they leave behind.

Third, and last, is a **lack of self-knowledge**. I will leave it to psychologists and sociologists to weigh how powerful nature and nurture are in influencing and, in some cases, determining our personalities, our value systems, and our life ambitions. My own sense is that early emotional deprivation (an unhappy family life, the experience of bullying in our youth, unfulfilled desires for love and acceptance, peer rejection) often sets individuals on a negative path in life. If so, some such individuals cope by creating false notions of who they are and how they are perceived by others.

Harmful and destructive leaders create false narratives of their own personal history, surround themselves with others who are insecure and angry about their place in society, and move easily from one concocted self-created persona to another. Untroubled by the growing discrepancy between their inner and outer selves, they become accustomed to unexamined lives and unreflective social roles. In the end, they do not trust others because they do not really believe in themselves.

One method of avoiding patterns of harmful and destructive leadership is to have a friend (or group of friends) who can be available (at least periodically) for honest feedback. They can identify troubling patterns and harmful tendencies. For example, when one is straying from truthfulness, either out of fear or laziness, they can urge you to return to a life based on facts, honest appraisals, and genuine emotions. Or, when one is becoming bossy and characteristically stern in human dynamics, they can point out the harmful impact this has on others, especially those who are most vulnerable. Or, when you become the center of every story you tell or take credit for every achievement, they can remind you of the valuable contribution of others and the vital necessity to share credit for all one's moments of glory.

The main moral lesson that you students can learn from all of this is that honesty, mutual respect, and mature self-awareness are essential qualities of well-grounded and successful leaders.

Receiving periodic peer reviews and feedback can enhance this process of informed and self-conscious decision-making.

QUESTION 2

Why is demagoguery one of the most prevalent forms of harmful leadership?

A "demagogue" is a leader who makes use of popular prejudices and false claims and promises in order to gain power. Such behavior is rooted in negative emotions and not in rational analysis. Demagogues either create, or play on, historical precedent, in order to establish scapegoats who are said to be responsible for most, or all, of the ills of the present society.

For the emperors of Rome, like Nero, it was Christians who were blamed for his own failures of governance and eventually sacrificed in the Roman Forum or elsewhere. During the Crusades, the leaders on both the Christian and Muslim sides saw each other as enemies and encouraged their followers to engage in battles with no limits. During the Inquisition, it was witches or Jewish converts or members of various heretical groups that were castigated and punished severely, even to the point of death.

More recently, during the Nazi Holocaust, Hitler depicted the Jews as the contamination of the Aryan nation, along with homosexuals, gypsies, and others. For Stalin, it was those who had benefited from the rule of the Tsarists and, later, those who opposed the Communist world order. For Pol Pot in Cambodia, it was the educated class, those who wore glasses, and those who owned property who had to be incarcerated and/or killed. In Rwanda, it was the Hutu majority who pictured Tutsis as "cockroaches" worthy of destruction. These examples reveal how demagogues rely on the debasement of others and the creation of an "Us vs. Them" mentality to precipitate horrible deeds and utter dehumanization of others.

Two more examples of demagoguery in the American political contest are Huey Long and Senator Joseph McCarthy. Huey "Kingfish" Long rose to power in Louisiana in the 1920s and 1930s. He served as governor and United States Senator and enjoyed almost total control of his state by playing to the negative passions of his constituency. His goal was to become President of the United States but in 1935, he was assassinated. Joseph McCarthy served in the United States Senate and eventually became chairman of the Permanent Subcommittee on Investigations in 1953. He initiated, on false evidence, a witch hunt against supposed Communists in the federal government and elsewhere. Many lives and reputations were ruined in the process. It was later discovered that both Long and McCarthy had sordid private lives.

Demagogues engage in propaganda of a vicious sort. They employ visual caricature, inflated rhetoric, concocted examples of malfeasance and symbols of solidarity among themselves to open a vast chasm between the "ins" and the "outs." Today, with the proliferation of internet communication, facts can be fudged, false interpretations established, and suspicions aroused.

The audience for demagogic activity can include the poor, the unemployed, the restless and ruthless, and those with legitimate grievances. What the leader does is serve as a person who forecasts ill will and fosters the desire for hostility and organized vengeance. Often, it becomes an all-or-nothing perception, apocalyptic in its significance. You are either for us or against us.

For the demagogue, it is all about power, gaining it and maintaining it. In democratic settings, the process of public conversation and expression of opinion are attacked as predetermined or stacked against the true believers. This makes the use of violence more attractive because it sees the results as guaranteed. Thus, military coups or intimidating tactics are justified.

Demagogues are not genuine leaders since they lack character, truthfulness, and the capacity for forgiveness or any sense of responsibility for the common good. Their inflated sense of self-importance and their need for adulation prevent them from committing themselves to any semblance of positive enhancement of the broader society. Their role in history is the promotion of themselves and not those entrusted to their care and concern.

There are two brief lessons for you students. First, learn how to identify leaders whose goals revolve around their own power and advancement. Do not be duped by their false narratives and malicious ascriptions of malevolence to their opponents. Second, always strive as a leader to serve the common good. That is the best antidote to ambition run amuck.

QUESTION 3

How can Catholic teaching about the seven deadly sins help leaders to resist temptation?

The **seven deadly sins** are pride, anger, lust, envy, gluttony, avarice, and sloth. They all result from fundamental human drivers that have led us astray. Fortunately, there are corresponding virtues that can keep us on a moral path.

In its worst sense, **pride** is inordinate self-esteem or utter self-preoccupation. Pride is the opposite of humility or a proper sense of one's place in the world. Prideful people strut, seek attention, and try to put themselves in the center of every social situation. They relish adulation, public recognition, and the reception of publicity and honors.

Egotism is another name for pride. It is a form of psychological underdevelopment. It is the relative absence of empathy or other concern.

There are, of course, legitimate forms of pride—for a job well-done, for the fruits of one's labor, for a proper response to a complicated situation, or for properly meshing the talent of a group toward a common goal for one's family, culture, or nation.

In most books on leadership written today, groups are encouraged to pick leaders at all levels of responsibility who are process-oriented, who set a cooperative tone, and who bring out the best in their colleagues. This perspective presumes that leadership is not a solitary venture or a matter of sheer talent or force carrying the day.

By reputation, certain stellar performers in the arts and entertainment field are known for their self-absorbance and defining idiosyncrasies. They are hard to deal with and sometimes end up in self-destructive patterns of behavior. This leadership model is more second-hand, but it influences all who are involved in the same activity.

The old adage proclaims that "Pride comes before the fall." This could mean that prideful leaders inevitably build resentments and spark opposition. Those who must put up with their chronic cockiness will look for opportunities to balance the ledger, to achieve a more realistic appraisal, to oust those who rule now.

One of the problems with leadership in the political realm is the need on the campaign trail to brag about one's proposals and policies, whether in prospect or as achieved. It is hard to be both ambitious and modest. Yet, it is possible. In Church leadership, pride is an even more contradictory trait. It usually entails confusing the message that one proclaims with one's own gifts. Pride and power together are antithetical to the Gospel.

The second deadly sin is **anger**, which is an intense emotional state in response to some displeasure. It seems that some anger can be righteous when in response to realities or actions that are unfair, mean, or shameful. We think of Jesus driving the moneychangers from the temple or parents responding to harm against their children or religious or civic leaders in the face of offenses to the common good. Indignation can be justified if it is proportionate to offenses rendered.

On the other hand, individuals who are temperamentally inclined to lose self-control can be a danger both to themselves and to others. They rage and lash out and may even physically attack those who are subject to their hostility.

For some, anger can be a pose and form of intimidation, a method of controlling circumstances and remaining in command. There are leaders who exercise their authority in such a way that people cower in their presence. They selectively lash out and create an atmosphere that is pervasively unpleasant and threatening. This stance, when seen from the top, can become rampant across a whole organization.

One of the great gifts of a successful leader is a thick skin—the ability to not take criticism personally, to not let the events or challenges of one day or week carry over into the next. One needs to be open to legitimate critique and be prepared for improvement of one's behavior. But, when things go wrong, it is important to avoid the anger that leads to verbal displays or a get-even mentality.

All of this is especially important when working with children or adolescents in school settings or athletic and extracurricular involvements. I have always found athletic coaches and band directors or agents of discipline who yell and scream at those entrusted to their care to miss the point entirely about their proper role in the learning process and in emotional development.

Lust is the third deadly sin. It is intense or unbridled sexual desire. From the onset of puberty, human beings may experience this emotion. It is different from the forms of love that we call friendship and other serving commitments. Lust is more about self-satisfaction and power than it is about relationships and a deeper knowledge of the other.

Individuals in leadership roles can be faced with loneliness, work preoccupation, or the absence of appropriate opportunities for living a well-balanced life. In their circumstances, both inside and outside the work context, the temptation can exist for unexpected or unacceptable sexual dynamics. Trysts, flings, liaisons, and other such clandestine meetings, whether for leaders who are married or single, can compromise one's integrity and call into question one's legitimacy as a leader. To most observers, it is patterns of behavior more than an isolated instance that are most problematic.

There have been leaders in business, entertainment, and government, who have established a lifestyle that presumed they were masters of their own futures, that no one would ever find out or, if they did, no one would really care. Despite the ever-changing social mores and legal context, every year scandals abound and careers are shattered. For married leaders, the demands of the job may entail long periods of travel, especially internationally. This may cause a real emotional distancing, including with one's children. In some work settings, there may be a plethora of attractive individuals who may seem like possible substitutes for emotional support.

Lust has led to the fall of emperors and empresses, kings and queens, czars of industry, academic gurus, creative artists, and religious personages. In human history, this deadly sin seldom survives the light of publicity, the glare of criticism, or the coming to grips with the truth.

The fourth deadly sin is **envy**, which is an awareness of some advantage that another possesses and a desire to possess it oneself. It is a form of comparison in which one begrudges another's success. Children can have sibling rivalries in which they vie for the attention or love of one or both parents. In school, students can resent the academic, social, athletic, or other competitive successes of peers. In the area of social dynamics connected to dating and marriage, the pressures of winning the affection of the other can be especially severe.

In the workforce, the hiring process often emphasizes natural or earned credentials that can distinguish one candidate from another. Some businesses may adopt an up or out policy that regularly both rewards and punishes some part of the employee base. The winners are then prepared for the next level of continuous competition. Presumably, the very best will rise to the top. In the military, professional athletics, music, theater, and the other arts, similar processes may exist.

Envy can provoke jealousy, bitterness, and belittlement of others. Gossip, rumormongering, and verbal innuendos may be weapons of revenge for those who feel left out. Especially in a dog-eat-dog professional world, there may be no safe and secure position of leadership. Historically, royal courts or salons or subcultures of critique may constantly pick apart those who happen to exercise power at a given moment.

Even those who are well-established in a certain area of endeavor may feel inferior to others who function in comparable spheres. What level of power and influence is enough? What degree of public acclaim or recognition is sufficient?

Good leaders need both thick skins and self-generated standards of achievement. To be self-aware is to be comfortable as a leader with a certain set of opportunities to make one's mark, to bring out the best in others, and to prepare for one's own eventual retirement. For some, it is the allure of another level or context of leadership that fosters another round of comparison with others.

Gluttony is the fifth deadly sin. Gluttony is normally associated with excessive eating or drinking. I would expand it to include excessive dress, personal accouterments, residence décor, and accumulation of artistic representations and other forms of self-presentation. In other words, a glutton is someone who employs the things of this world for personal pleasure and impressive social status.

In the political order, heads of state and other representatives of government have historically lived in palaces, mansions, and military citadels where they could be protected from harm and hold court surrounded by various personal retainers. This lifestyle often included feasts and festivals where sumptuous food and alcoholic beverages were made available to those who had been invited as a source of privilege. They would also entertain representatives of other reigns and domains with a cornucopia of aliments and exotic brews. This included, on many occasions, musical entertainment, dancing, and professionals like storytellers and clowns. The intention in all of this was to impress and amaze with no limits.

The tradition of military parades had a similar purpose. The more troops, horses, and later armaments like tanks, rocket launchers, and overhead aircraft, the better. The presumption that strong leaders had no limits in what they could muster for public display meant that the word spread quickly about the indulgence of the leader and his or her presumptive power.

In the academy, the accumulation of endowments, the building of impressive campuses, the attraction of world-class faculty and competitive student bodies, and the preoccupation with rankings can serve a similar purpose.

On a personal level, some leaders have been ruined by bacchanalian lifestyles where their capacity for discipline and self-control has been lost. Either out of addiction or neglect, they have indulged in practices of appetite satisfaction that have distracted them from their primary responsibilities and eventually led to loss of reputation and, in some cases, shortening of lifespans.

In ecclesial circles, such behavior is even more antithetical. An ethic of service and a commitment to all of God's children, especially the poorest and most vulnerable, is simply incompatible with any image of cultivated excess, and a church title or high level of recognition can be an excuse for public pomp and circumstance and a tendency toward finery and luxury.

The sixth deadly sin is **avarice**, which is the excessive or insatiable desire for wealth or gain. It is a form of greed, which can lead to a preoccupation with one's relative level of possession of certain goods of the earth. The instrumental value of certain things, like money, land, and property, is less important than the control over one's life circumstances that these things seem to promise.

Avarice can be correlated with one's public reputation and various hierarchies of success and belonging. If you have $500 million, a billion is better. If you own two companies, why not four?

Avarice is disconnected from generosity, from a sense of responsibility for the well-being of others. Things, instead, are accumulated for their own sake, not for the way they may be utilized in service of the common good.

An avaricious leader may occasionally donate or participate in raising money for a worthy cause, but it is done for its public relations value and not for any higher purpose. One of the ironies of inherited family fortunes is that the beneficiaries, who were never directly responsible for the monies that had been earned, may feel no obligation to reach out beyond a self-perpetuating family circle.

The temptation to avarice can crop up in any area of leadership. One form is a monopoly, where companies seek to dominate an industry and render their competition incapable of response. Another form is public relations campaigns that provide a false narrative and allow an individual leader to dominate a field of operation like entertainment, publishing, international agencies, or athletic ownership. A third form focuses on glitz, glamor, and high-profile associates so that one is never out of the public eye.

In the worst cases, avaricious leaders do not face any public accountability. They fear no reputational or judicial restraint. This is true in tyrannies of any kind. In ethical terms, this suggests a real one-uppance either in this world or in the one after.

The last, and seventh, of the deadly sins is **sloth,** which is a disinclination to action or labor. For me, it can be a form of spiritual apathy. The slow-moving arboreal mammal that hangs from trees upside down seems a fitting representative of this disposition.

It would seem that most leaders are type-A personalities and more inclined to have busy lives and constant involvements in all aspects of work than not. It may be that sloth is more of a temptation later in a term of leadership when the excitement may have gone out of one's role and some of one's reservoirs of energy are used up. Then, one may rest on one's laurels, allow inertia to set in, and hide behind formalities and customary practices. There may be no room for initiative-taking and forward thinking. Action plans may resemble each other and receive comparably tepid responses.

Sloth may accompany the aging process or be impacted by health concerns or exterior factors like financial challenges, changing markets, and political instability. Turnovers in other top leadership positions may make one's daily and weekly routine more unpredictable.

Psychological factors, like depression and fear of the future, may also lead to indolence. Or, a kind of spiritual malaise may lead to moments of intense introspection. For an activist, this may convey to multiple constituencies that one is not the same person that was originally chosen for a leadership role. Rumors may start that one's marriage is in trouble or one is suffering from a severe illness.

Sloth is a kind of sluggishness, a torpor of spirit, a limited lethargic interaction with others. Hopefully, such a disposition of the self is temporary, a function of a brief setback rather than a defining personal characteristic.

In religious history, some of the saints have written about "the dark night of the soul" when everything looked bleak and inner-directed prayer seemed impossible. Something similar can happen to leaders. But these same spiritual gurus also acknowledge that the "dark night" can be succeeded by a new burst of enthusiasm and a deeper commitment to full engagement in the central activities of one's life. We can all hope that whatever setbacks we know will be temporary and serve to make us stronger and more resilient in exercising our leadership responsibilities.

The seven deadly sins are all vice-ridden temptations that are a misuse of human freedom. They are not inevitable. Human agents possess the capacity to orient their lives in a virtuous way. For you students, the important thing is that appropriate patterns of behavior need to be practiced by leaders at all stages of their personal life journeys. It is likely that all of us will fail to some extent in living a virtuous life. That is why forgiveness and the capacity for conversion in small patterns and major moments of decision-making are central elements in Christian life. To ask for and receive forgiveness (sacramentally or otherwise) can begin in one's early family dynamics, in school settings, and in one's leadership roles. Like all virtuous behavior, forgiveness (like love, patience, and understanding) can begin early in life and grow into characteristic qualities of the self.

QUESTION 4

How can students handle temptation to participate in the seven deadly sins?

There is what some would call a theological anthropology built into the concept of the seven deadly sins. As creatures of flesh and blood with a degree of freedom in decision-making and with an array of seeming goods vying for our attention, we are regularly facing choices about the values we want to live by and the means to achieve these goals. In addition, we are creatures of habit. Each choice we make, whether for good or ill, makes us more inclined to follow that same path in future decision-making.

We call the proper exercise of the higher values "virtue" and the improper exercise "vice." For example, in establishing our proper place in the universe and our degree of dependence on others, a virtuous person will recognize that God is the source of our native talents and other humans are potential colleagues in the good things we are able to achieve. A proud person will want to hog the limelight and take all the credit. A humble person will express thanks to his or her compatriots and supporters. Such humility is not false modesty but rather can become an antidote to prideful self-preoccupation.

The more that a student leader learns to share the credit, the better prepared such a person will be for exercising successive levels of responsibility.

QUESTION 5

What is the biggest trap for leaders?

I think the biggest trap for leaders is to **focus on themselves** rather than the organization, cause, or entity that they are leading. In a sense, this is about ego, satisfaction, pride, or a poorly developed social barometer. Only dictators or tyrants or innate bullies can survive for long in the absence of high goals and dictated support structures.

One way to think about this is to focus on trust and loyalty. If a leader conveys a constant spirit of suspicion about the motives of colleagues and regulatory boards, then that spirit will become pervasive in the organization. Such social environments become preoccupied by constant rumormongering about who has the leader's favor, "who is in, and who is out." A leader who plays the subordinate leaders against each other will, inevitably, pay the price in reduced morale and chronic bitterness.

One dimension of focusing on oneself as a leader is the perpetual use of "I" language in talking about the work and, especially, in attributing success to oneself rather than a team effort. It is interesting today in search processes for leaders at the top levels of management how the questions asked try to sniff out such attitudes. I have been involved in a lot of searches for presidents, provosts, vice presidents, and deans in institutions of higher education and comparable leaders in various not-for-profit organizations. None of these search groups is interested in someone who conveys a strong self-preoccupation. Instead, they seek out team builders and visionaries who seem capable of inspiring their would-be colleagues and those being served.

It may be in the for-profit world and politics that this is not the case. If that is so, it would be worthy of further scrutiny.

One of the complicating factors in all this is that a CEO in any organization will normally be its public face. This entails media time, speeches at public events, and quality time with governing boards and benefactors, all of which implicitly suggest that the top leader oversees, and is responsible for, everything that goes on. As President of Notre Dame, I always felt that I got credit for things I was not directly involved in (like major faculty grants, favorable admissions reports, or athletic victories) and correspondingly blamed for the bad things that took place (like inadequate snow removal, some speaker who made a controversial remark, or athletic losses). The great antidote to excessive preoccupation with oneself as a leader is a spirit of humility. In fact, no leader is indispensable.

I have met leaders at all levels of responsibility who seemed to be in it for reasons of ego gratification. Instinctively, I felt sorry for them since they seemed to have missed the point. Leadership is a privilege and not a possession. Whether one succeeds or fails in a given role, life goes on.

You students can learn from the models that you come to know in your various learning environments and from the historical and contemporary leaders that you study.

Strive to work for the common good and you will be on the right path as a leader.

QUESTION 6

What is one mistake that leaders make more frequently than others?

It is difficult to choose just one mistake, but I would sum up a multiplicity of potential problems under the rubric "going it alone." Leaders are not hermits or solitary folk. They are not nomads, robots, or self-actualizing individuals. Rather, leaders are normally chosen from within institutional and social contexts to play a particular role. What makes them attractive to search committees and institutional representatives is their innate ability to inspire others, foster cooperative endeavors, articulate short and long-term goals, evaluate and reward talent, represent the group to the broader population, handle the media, and operate with high values.

While all these attributes are challenging separately, the combined expectation for some combination of them can indeed be daunting. That is why leaders need disciplined preparation, good mentors, and a network of friends and trustworthy colleagues. For example, when I was elected President of Notre Dame, I had already served as a Vice President for four+ years. I had been encouraged to participate in all of the governance structures of the University, to meet as many faculty, administrators, students, and alumni as I could. I consulted regularly with Ted Hesburgh and Tim O'Meara as President and Provost and Don Keough as the Chair of the Board of Trustees. I deliberately went to higher education association meetings and met with sitting presidents. Their collective advice was invaluable. I also read books about leadership, especially in the context of higher education. And, equally valuable, I sought to preserve my roots in my religious community and in teaching, research, and residential life.

The "going it alone" option includes several different forms. First is the mindset that pictures oneself in total control of an organization from day one, as though one's predecessors were not worthy of time and attention or the past was a dead letter never to be referred to again. I have known presidents and other leaders who cleaned house or cast aspersions on those who had gone before or began to concentrate as much power under their control as possible. The notion of allies and colleagues (and friends) was seen as determined exclusively on pragmatic grounds.

A second form of such a mindset might be called "deliberate ignorance" or a desire to avoid information, opinions, or judgments that originate elsewhere in the organization. That means that deliberative bodies (like the Faculty Senate, Student Government, or Academic Council) are seen as obstacles to be overcome, pesky units to be silenced by indifference, or a dead letter file.

A third form is a function of how a leader uses their staff. One of the jobs of executive assistants and those who report directly to CEOs is to pass on unpleasant information or potentially troublesome realities. I know that I relied on my staff not only to represent me across the institution and to take on particular tasks but also to keep me up-to-date and give me advanced warning of troubles on the horizon. My secretary/assistants organized my schedule, saved me from strange callers and correspondents, and created a welcoming environment in the office. They got to know my family members and close friends and those who deserved ready access and a quick turn-around time. They also read my moods and reminded me about haircuts, laundry, medical check-ups, and other such things. My other assistants brought invaluable expertise in academics, student life, Church, and staff matters. In the absence of their help, I could never have served for 18 years as President.

My advice to you students is the more that you foster your relationships with others, the easier it will be to avoid thinking that it is "all about you."

QUESTION 7

In a polarized world with an "us vs. them" mentality, how can leaders promote compromise and moderation?

This may be the most difficult question to answer in today's environment in both civil society and the Catholic Church. For a variety of reasons, extreme groups have emerged that are suspicious of those who disagree with them and often attribute malevolent motives to them. If individuals or small groups derive most of their information from rather narrow sources like one newspaper or television network or website, then it is unlikely that they will be open to others' claims to the truth or a credible view of reality.

In political circles, the very nature of truth or patriotism or claims to citizenship is progressively less agreed upon. In Catholic Church circles, it is about orthodoxy or respect for tradition or proper sources of authority.

This is why the academy can play a crucial role in preparing the next generation for proper participation in the meaningful debates of the day. Higher education can be the ideal place to discuss the nature of truth, the limits of human understanding, the role of public discussion and debate, the different sources of insight and persuasiveness, and the capacity of the open-minded to reverse course, change their mind, and move to new levels of consensus.

As the President of a Catholic university, I was always a defender of established notions of academic freedom. This meant that we needed to be an open forum with the presumption of mutual respect among those who held differing opinions. In some cases, there would be individuals or groups who moved too readily from debate to advocacy. But, in the vast majority of cases, it was important for us as a distinctively Catholic university to model our commitment to freedom of thoughtful exchange among those who constituted our community of learners.

For example, we invited representatives of both the major political parties in the United States to our campus, including Presidents of the United States. We did this out of respect for their role of leadership in the country. But we never did this to implicitly or explicitly endorse a particular opinion, body of legislation, or financial consideration. We also invited individuals who were well known for some point of view to participate in panels or seminars where their position could be debated and critiqued by others.

For some, the awarding of honorary degrees was a particular point of contention. The decision to do so was usually well vetted, but there were organized groups who disliked some aspects of certain honorees' history or present role. We were then criticized as being unfaithful to our religious heritage. In any case, such is life in the modern university.

From my perspective, there are specific values and attitudes that are critical to achieving an appropriate mode of compromise and moderation. First, it is trying to find common ground. In most cases, we share more values and opinions than those that divide us. Second, it is spending time in each other's company when we can simply relax and be sociable. For example, Ted Hesburgh took the U.S. Civil Rights Commission to the University's place in Land O'Lakes, Wisconsin, where they had drinks and a meal and went fishing together. He claimed that was how they found common ground. Third, it is providing a context for discussion where the ground rules are known and respected. This is a good antidote to harangues and personal attacks. Finally, if action is required, everyone needs to respect the pre-given lines of authority. Many groups have consultative authority only, but that can be an important step in the overall process.

In most cases, I have seen compromise and moderation work for the common good. In complicated group interactions and reward systems, there do not have to be winners and losers. Ideally, we can all be respected for the unique contribution we make. With the proper give-and-take, everyone can at least feel that their voice was respected.

All of this is quite applicable at the student level as well. Just as athletic teams shake hands after a spirited contest, so should other student groups. It is a potent gesture that can create the right level of expectation.

QUESTION 8

What steps would you recommend to minimize divisiveness and promote unity?

In my lifetime, I have participated in a number of movements for social justice and cultural change. This includes human and civil rights and concomitant legal protection. As a result, I have participated in many discussions and debates in which different points of view were articulated. Sometimes disagreements led to public protests and even civil disorder.

My father and I, for example, played a quite small role in the provision of hospitality during the famous March on Washington when Martin Luther King, Jr., delivered his "I Have a Dream" speech at the Lincoln Memorial. We welcomed people near the Washington Monument grounds as they arrived on buses for the event. Later, we were quite close for the speech itself. As I remember it, I knew that we were part of something quite significant. Only later did we realize that we were witnesses to our equivalent of the Gettysburg Address. It ended up as one of the most peaceful gatherings in the history of the capital city. Later, after King was assassinated, I was caught in a new car on 14th street N.W. in D.C. that died out amid rioters who busted out the windows before I could get the car started again and escape. Finally, I was invited by Coretta Scott King to be one of the speakers on King's birthday at Ebenezer Baptist Church in Atlanta (along with Governor Bill Clinton, among others).

On several trips to Northern Ireland, I experienced first-hand the hostility between the so-called Catholic and Protestant groups and the misguided role that British troops ended up playing in the conflict. We met with neighborhood leaders, advocates for both sides, and government officials. We offered to facilitate business investment in the North. I toured Derry with John Hume (who won the Nobel Peace Prize) and discovered why his role was so critical in the eventual peace talks. John Hume was a leading Catholic figure in Northern Ireland. Born in Derry, he was the leader of the Social Democratic Labour Party. In 1993, he and the Sinn Fein leader, Gerry Adams, began a series of talks intended to bring about peace.

I have overseen the evolution of Notre Dame from an almost all-male institution to a more fully coeducational one. This has involved academic, social, attitudinal, and structural transformations. Together we have had to challenge our presuppositions and develop a new sense of collective identity.

When asked about the most effective way forward, I would emphasize physical time in each other's company, an opportunity for both speaking and listening in public settings, and an openness to companionship and eventually friendship. Books, films, and various artistic expressions can all be helpful. But concrete experiences and orderly reflection are even more important.

As an undergraduate, when I went on summer service projects to Mexico and Peru, I learned about the culture of poverty, what life was like in a stratified society, and the role that education and the Catholic Church could play in bringing people together and helping to articulate various goals of social improvement and mutual understanding.

I believe that friendship is the most effective antidote to division, anger, hostility, and the false ascription of motives to one's seeming opponents. Friendship requires time together, conversations, the sharing of life stories, and a growing recognition of the full humanness of the other.

For college students, friendship can begin with roommates or dormmates. Participation in classes and in extracurricular activities is also important. Working on a common project of social amelioration can expose the other's highest values. In my judgment, friendship breaks down barriers of whatever kind and our network of friends is the greatest safety net for any of us. College is a great time to take the initiative in broadening our friendship base and in spending quality time with a broad cross-section of peers, faculty, and staff. Study abroad programs can be an integral part of this process of recognition of the diversity of cultures, religions, and ways of life that vary from our own. Standing in the middle of Beijing or Moscow or Nairobi can be eye-opening experiences.

QUESTION 9

How does a leader inspire loyalty? How does an obsession with loyalty spoil leadership?

One of my favorite books about leadership is *Team of Rivals: The Political Genius of Abraham Lincoln* by Doris Kearns Goodwin. Abraham Lincoln deliberately chose members of his Cabinet who would represent different points of view and different political persuasions. He felt that the great chasm in the nation between the North and the South could only be repaired by examples of cooperation and mutual respect among those invited to leadership positions in the Northern government. This did not preclude a successful conclusion of the military effort but, rather, an example of what the future might look like.

Barack Obama referred to that book as he put together his Cabinet and leadership team. How one can inspire loyalty is a complicated question. First, it entails some **shared values**. For example, in my situation, all the central administration had to be convinced about the mission of Notre Dame was for it to be a great Catholic university, whether they were Catholic or not. How they might contribute to that distinctive identity could be a matter for further conversation. But they could not be indifferent or adverse to that fundamental value. I am sure that the same could be said about other institutions with a particular sense of themselves and their role in the broader culture.

Second, those who work together in leadership roles in whatever structure of governance and interaction must **appreciate the character and integrity** of those with whom they work. Even amid intense disagreements about an issue, there needs to be some leeway for moving on without rancor or hostility. I realize that this is asking a lot of people who are highly competitive or make quick judgments about their feelings about another person. One of the things I learned from my athletic background is that I could be friends with competitors before and after the contest. There was always another day or another match when the outcome might be reversed.

A third way to inspire loyalty is to **be consistent** in one's approach to a variety of issues and concrete judgments. You cannot be wishy-washy or seemingly arbitrary or fearful of public criticism. That does not mean that a leader cannot change his or her mind based on prolonged discussion. An open mind is an asset to be prized. However, this willingness to respect arguments is not the same as an incapacity to decide in the end.

A fourth and final component of building loyalty is to be willing to **pay the price** to choose what is right and to do it for the right reasons. In Robert Bolt's play, *A Man for All Seasons*, Thomas More is faced with his dependency on King Henry VIII, on the one hand, and his conscience, on the other. Even the appeals of his wife and children cannot turn him away from paying the ultimate price for a value-based determination of the right thing to do.

I agree that an obsession with loyalty can deprive ultimate leaders from hearing other voices or engaging with more than sycophants and "yes" men. One of the characteristics of tyrants is that they cannot tolerate disagreement. That is why they so often try to buy off and/or terrorize their assistants.

In the end, true loyalty is generated by a cooperative spirit, mutual regard, and even friendship. If those are missing, it is a kind of forced participation that runs shallow and easily disappears at the first crisis.

You students should practice loyalty and expect it in return. If your experience in your early years is positive, it will be easier to pursue it in the future. Being a true friend or colleague involves investment in the relationship, reliable moments of mutual presence, and the fostering of a sense of confidence. You need to feel that the other will be there for you when disappointment or failure takes place or when sickness or the loss of a loved one creates emotional stress. All of this can begin at an early age, even with roommates, hallmates, or participants in common activities.

SECTION FIVE

Leadership and Inspiration

"In the end, it is character and a record of service that counts. Let those types of people be your _role models_."

QUESTION 1

What leaders inspire you and why?

One of the reasons why the Catholic Church canonizes individuals as saints is so that we as individuals or as part of similar social groups can be inspired by their example. Obviously, the preeminent Christian holy person is Jesus Christ whom we honor as our Lord and Savior. His public ministry was characterized by the profundity of his teaching and preaching, the tender concern of his miracle working, the breadth of his welcome into community across human boundaries, his acts of forgiveness and healing, and the example of his suffering and death on the cross as a prelude to his resurrection from the dead. As a Catholic priest, he is my ultimate model of faith, hope, and love and his gospel is the source of the ministry I am called to exercise.

A second great model is Mary the mother of Jesus who was responsible (along with Joseph) for preparing Jesus in human terms for his later role. In that sense, she was a leader behind the scenes.

Among the apostles, I find myself drawn to Paul, who spent his life, after his conversion, on a mission throughout the Mediterranean region. He was relentless in establishing nascent churches and resolving difficulties among those so gathered. As a world traveler myself, I hope my experience of diverse cultures and peoples can continue to inspire my leadership role.

When it comes to my role as a theologian, I have learned much from Augustine of Hippo, Thomas Aquinas, and a whole host of contemporary theologians. As the leader of a Catholic university, it has been important for me to have a solid background in a range of theological subspecialties from Scripture and methodology to moral theology, pastoral theology, and liturgy.

As an administrator, I have always been inspired by Thomas More, a British martyr, who sought to serve King Henry VIII faithfully, but when faced with the choice of obeying the King or the dictates of his conscience, he chose the latter and suffered martyrdom.

As a Holy Cross religious, I have tried to follow the words of our founder, Blessed Basil Moreau, who proclaimed that true Christian education was about the cultivation of the mind, body, and spirit of those entrusted to our care. He also wanted his priests, brothers, and sisters to be open to serving throughout the world.

Most immediately, I have been influenced by the example of Fr. Ted Hesburgh, my predecessor, who withstood the rigors of the presidential office for 35 years and was constantly open to the necessary changes that new circumstances required. He kept alert to challenges and opportunities in both society and the Church and tried to assure that Notre Dame would remain a force for good.

In a broader sense, I have my own list of heroes and heroines including: Abraham Lincoln, Nelson Mandela, Mother Theresa of Calcutta, Pope John XXIII, Pope Francis, Dorothy Day, Sister Madeleva, Peter Tannock, Martin Luther King, Jr., Cesar Chavez, Karl Rahner, John Courtney Murray, Raymond Brown, and a whole host of others.

I encourage you students to search for examples from history and from your own concrete experience who can model the good life, the generous life, and the life of leadership and service. Maybe, someday, you will be a model for the next generation yourself.

QUESTION 2

What leader(s) would you most like to meet?

I hope this question is not limited to the present day. First on my list is Jesus Christ. As a Christian believer, a Catholic priest, a theologian, and a former college administrator, I have all kinds of questions. We do not know what Jesus looked like so simply meeting him would answer some of my interests. What kind of personality and temperament did he possess? As an itinerant preacher, he was constantly on the road, so where did he stay, who provided his food, who were his best friends? (We have suggestions regarding John the Beloved Disciple and Martha, Mary, and Lazarus). When he arrived in a new place, did he light up the room, did he have gravitas, did he simply observe the dynamics among the people around him? As a preacher, did he have a strong voice or did people have to lean in to hear him? When confronted by his enemies, the scribes and Pharisees, how did he control his anger, or when experiencing the utter humanity of his disciples, how did he keep his cool?

Some of these concerns might seem trivial, but since the four Gospels were written from the point of view that focused on his public ministry, his death, and his resurrection, they did not have to take up many questions connected to his humanity (true God and true human) which would have been a distraction.

I would have loved to listen to Jesus preach and teach. As a teacher myself, I am struck by the recognition that some of Jesus' parables (the Good Samaritan, the Prodigal Son, the Separation of the Sheep from the Goats) are among the best remembered bits of wisdom ever uttered. When his enemies tried to trap him, he always had a counter move (his time had not yet come).

To see one of his miracles would be a great gift indeed. I think, in particular, of his combining physical healing with spiritual forgiveness. While John's Gospel is parsimonious on the miracle accounts, the last of the seven signs, the raising of his good friend Lazarus from the dead was a great foreshadowing of his own resurrection.

And, most of all, I would love to encounter Jesus risen from the dead like the disciples on the road to Emmaus or doubting Thomas or Mary Magdalene. What a great privilege that would be. Like Paul the Apostle to the Gentiles, I too could say, I have seen the Lord and it makes all the difference.

In the absence of the chance to meet Jesus in person, I continue to draw upon the Biblical evidence, the theology developed in Christian history, the liturgical tradition, and prayer. Many who met Jesus in the flesh did not become believers. I have been gifted with faith so I have a responsibility to share the good news. As a university person, the challenge is how to effectively share that experience with the next generation.

QUESTION 3

What leaders have been most impressive to meet?

I have met two Nobel Peace Prize winners—John Hume and Bishop Tutu. In 1998, Hume and David Trimble received the Nobel Peace Prize in the same ceremony. I hosted John Hume earlier on campus and also interacted with him at various Irish American events in the States, including at the White House. On a trip to Northern Ireland, Hume gave me a guided tour through Derry, including where the violence had taken place. John Hume paid a big price medically for his involvements. He was a courageous person who was never intimidated.

Bishop Desmond Tutu was a leader in the Anglican Church in Cape Town, South Africa. Along with Nelson Mandela, he was involved in the struggle against apartheid. He was especially effective in making the case for a peaceful resolution of the conflict to international audiences in Europe and North America. One time, when he was visiting the States, he came to Notre Dame. I spent time with him and later introduced him for a talk in the Continuing Education building. The mostly undergraduate audience was overflowing, so we also had his talk on T.V. in adjacent rooms. Bishop Tutu's presentation was both inspirational and humorous. He was less confrontational and more aspirational.

In the course of my duties as President, I have met and spent time with 23 heads of state as well as Kofi Annan when he was head of the United Nations. What I enjoyed about interacting with the various American presidents was the informal time either here on campus, in the White House, at some public event, or elsewhere. For example, I was with Ronald Reagan, Gerald Ford, Jimmy Carter, George H. W. Bush, Bill Clinton, and George W. Bush in such contexts. I also visited with Donald Trump in Trump Tower long before he was elected president (not an edifying experience). I once hosted five former presidents of Costa Rica over lunch where we discussed their peace heritage.

I have enjoyed being with Popes John Paul II and Francis. The latter welcomed the Notre Dame Board of Trustees to be with him for a formal event with picture-taking at the Vatican.

On multiple occasions, I have spent time with Mary Robinson, the President of Ireland, and five different Irish Prime Ministers.

Of course, there have been many less well-known individuals who have impressed me deeply, from writers, artists, business leaders, and educators to heads of not-for-profit organizations. One of the greatest compliments I can offer is that I have known several "living saints" whose profound love for others and manifest generosity has inspired me deeply. This includes members of my personal and extended family and other Holy Cross religious.

In the wake of 9/11/01, I can honestly say that I met many impressive police officers, fire fighters, and EMTs who put their lives on the line—some of whom paid the ultimate price. People like them continue to serve in our local communities, at the federal level, and in the military. The same is true of religious community members who serve in the missions, often under stark and dangerous conditions.

For students, there is nothing wrong with celebrating public icons. But, in the end, it is character and a record of service that counts. Let those types of people be your role models.

QUESTION 4

What female leaders during your time at Notre Dame do you most admire?

Father Basil Moreau, the founder of the Congregation of Holy Cross, attempted to establish a religious community in which priests, brothers, and sisters would work closely together as part of the same apostolate. While the Vatican ruled that the Holy Cross sisters would have a separate administrative structure, Father Edward Sorin was eager to have Holy Cross sisters active at Notre Dame in its earliest years where they played a variety of roles. He was also instrumental in the establishment of St. Mary's College, our sister institution. So, the first women that should be highlighted are the Holy Cross sisters. I served for nine years on the Board of Trustees at St. Mary's and I was delighted to be able to repay, in a sense, the stalwart and generous contributions of Holy Cross women in our early, often precarious origins.

Moving up to my own years as President, I came to admire in a particular way the role of many other women. First was Sister John Miriam Jones, S.C., who served as Associate Provost and was charged by Fr. Ted Hesburgh with administering every aspect of the transition to coeducation from 1972 on. In many ways, this was a daunting task. Except for a few graduate courses, Notre Dame had been, student-wise, an all-male institution for all its history. There were some traditionalists who totally opposed the decision. And, there were many more who wondered what the impact would be on the overall culture. (As Father Ted later said, it improved every aspect of the culture).

While the first years included some embarrassing incidents, as the number of undergraduate women increased and the support services improved, most of the early opponents changed their minds, especially if they had daughters or granddaughters who were eager to attend Notre Dame. Sister John Miriam was a strong and popular presence who emphasized the positive and kept problems to a minimum. Looking back, it is hard to imagine the University being constrained by the previous strictures on enrollment.

A second person of note is Isabel Charles, who served as the first female Dean of the College of Arts and Letters and later joined Sister John Miriam as an Associate Provost. Isabel was an enthusiastic supporter of the arts, language studies, and international programs. She personified a public intellectual who was a perfect fit for Notre Dame. She took the initiative in our efforts to have more women serve in leadership roles in the colleges, in student affairs, in athletics, and in other major areas of University life.

In the Student Affairs area, a critical component of Notre Dame life was Sister Jean Lenz, O.S.F., the Rector of Farley Hall and later an Assistant Vice President of Student Affairs who played a decisive early role. She was a great people person who encouraged residents not only to study hard but also to get involved in every area of student life from student government and *The Observer* to inter-hall sports, the Marching Band, and the Center for Social Concerns. Eventually, she wrote a book about her experiences, *Loyal Sons & Daughters: A Notre Dame Memoir*, which has become a Notre Dame classic.

Looking back, I see a whole host of women who had a transformative impact on the University. Chandra Johnson, who came to Notre Dame in her 30s and was a student of mine, later served in the President's Office and became a guru and friend to minority students, women students, and staff members. She was also active in Campus Ministry.

Patty O'Hara was a graduate of Notre Dame Law School who, after a period of practicing corporate law, returned as a faculty member in the Law School in 1981. In 1990, she was elected by the Board of Trustees as Vice President for Student Affairs, the first woman to serve as an officer of the University. Then, in 1999, she was appointed Dean of the Law School and served in that capacity for 10 years. Patty was an agent of transformation in two critical areas of the University while volunteering for service in a number of higher education and not-for-profit organizations.

Carol Ann Mooney was a Law School faculty member and administrator who served for years as a Vice President and Associate Provost and later became President of St. Mary's College. Carol Ann tightened the bonds between the two institutions.

Dolly Duffy succeeded the indomitable Chuck Lennon as head of the Alumni Association and expanded its mission, the diversity of participation in leadership roles, and the number of clubs. She also supported the spiritual dimension of Association Services as well as the travel opportunities.

Carol Kaesebier was a first female Vice President and General Counsel. Her portfolio grew with the increasing complexity of the modern university and the litigious nature of some of its interactions. Carol brought a calm and measured voice to many public and private challenges.

Two other pivotal women leaders at Notre Dame are discussed later. Fortunately, today, there are so many women worthy of recognition that it is impossible to mention them all.

My hope is that our present women students, both under-graduate and graduate, will move into leadership positions in every walk of life and that they can be inspired by the example of some of the women I have mentioned and many others whom they have come to know.

QUESTION 5

What is the most important part of your legacy?

Periodically, historians of the American presidency provide lists of the best and worst presidents. It is safest for them to give priority to those men long dead and well-established in the popular consciousness (and they have all been men, unlike many other countries). In most lists, Abraham Lincoln, George Washington, and Franklin Delano Roosevelt are the top three. How to evaluate the most recent presidents is much more precarious and subject to debates about contemporary issues and the level of available evidence.

I had the opportunity to interview two presidents of Latin American countries after they were elected and before they took over their new responsibilities and then, later, after they had completed their terms of service. The first was Patricio Aylwin of Chile, who served from 1990 to 1994. He was the first democratically elected president after the long dictatorship of Augusto Pinochet. Aylwin's top priority was to bring peace and reconciliation to Chile after the pervasive violence and human rights violations of the Pinochet years. After stepping down as president, he reminisced about what he had achieved and what he was unable to effect. Indeed, he became a world-renowned expert on holding officials accountable, including the military and the police, while avoiding wholesale imprisonment or capital punishment.

The second was Fernando Enrique Cardoso, who served as president of Brazil from 1995 to 2003. Cardoso, who spent time at the Kellogg Institute at Notre Dame, along with his wife, took over after periods of authoritarian rule with a heavy presence of military and he set out, as he described it, to reinforce democratic traditions and open political discourse. His two terms were relatively placid. In 1995, after a free election, Luiz Inacio Lula da Silva (from a different political party) took over as president. This successful transfer of power from one political party to another was rare in Brazilian history and Notre Dame honored both men with a Coca-Cola sponsored award at a ceremony in Brazil that I attended. Once again Cardoso shared with me his own evaluation of the high and low points of his eight years as President.

The comments about historical figures are simply to suggest that there will always be short-, medium-, and long-term evaluations of the quality of leadership provided by any individual.

Even though not all priorities were achieved equally well, I am proud of the progress we made through the commitment and hard work of so many. I leave it to others to give further appraisals.

My sense of my own legacy is based on events and experiences that have already taken place. When it comes to you students with much of your life still ahead of you, I want to quote part of the advice that Father Ted Hesburgh gave me at the time of the transition at Notre Dame from one president to another.

He said, "Just be yourself. Do not try to be me." I think this is wise counsel for anyone.

While you are in school, you have to make countless decisions about what your major will be, who you will room with, what extracurricular activities to participate in, how to use your leisure time, whether and where to worship, and who your network of friends will be. Out of all these concrete decisions, you will create a better sense of your authentic self and, inevitably, a public persona that can be an integral part of your life after graduation.

QUESTION 6

How can leaders have a lasting impact for the future?

There are many dimensions to this answer. First, it is important that there be **institutional fit**. One of the problems with using search firms for choosing upper echelon leaders is that they may know more about who is available in their rolodexes than about what is most distinctive and important about a business, a school, a not-for-profit, or a government agency. In the military, the Army, Navy, Marines, and Air Force all have particular cultures and traditions which have been honed over time. Someone not rooted in those will need to be brought up to date quite quickly. In higher education, there is a big difference between religiously affiliated institutions and those that are not, between all male or all female and co-ed institutions, between flagship state campuses and historically liberal arts colleges. Some people can negotiate the differences successfully and some cannot. (For nine years, I was on the Board of Trustees at St. Mary's College, an all-female college, and it was quite a learning experience about the importance of history and culture.)

Second, when moving into a leadership role, it makes a difference whether the institution is **thriving or under duress**. I was fortunate in inheriting the presidency of Notre Dame when it had a great degree of positive momentum. However, I have known many presidents who had to immediately deal with deficient enrollment numbers, financial crises, or public scandals. In those situations, a lot of energy goes into turning things around or, in some cases, sheer survival and, as a result, there is not a honeymoon period.

Third, the **core leadership group** that one inherits or quickly puts into place needs to quickly develop an **esprit de corps** and a level of mutual respect and confidence that bodes well for all the challenges that will be faced in subsequent years. One or two malingerers or troublemakers can cause significant harm. That is why I favor quick decisions about who to retain and who to let go in the central administration.

Fourth, there are certain businesses, agencies, not-for-profit organizations, or schools that do not have a **viable future**. Warren Buffett is well known for investing in businesses that provide products and services everyone will continue to need no matter what new technologies arrive. There are higher education institutions that may struggle for a while and keep the doors open but, in fact, their endowment is low or non-existent, their student population continues to decline, they are in the wrong location, their competition is too severe, or their past leadership has not been visionary enough. Many leaders may welcome a challenge, but it would be naïve to think that all challenges are legitimate opportunities.

With these four factors in mind, the final question is how important longevity of leadership is. Over the last 70+ years, Notre Dame has had only three Presidents (Hesburgh, Malloy, Jenkins). Historians will have to determine whether this has been good for the University. From my point of view, it has allowed for continuity but also significant change. (Almost all my top officers changed over my 18 years as President.) It has meant that each of us who has played that role can look back with a real sense that our leadership has had a lasting impact (of course, with a full acknowledgment that it has always been a team effort and it has depended on the generosity of many).

In my judgment, John Jenkins has done an extraordinary job in leading the institution. He has made many significant decisions, like keeping the University open during COVID-19, building the Crossroads Project, and, in addition, has been a great fundraiser. He has nurtured Notre Dame's Catholic identity and fostered the role of Holy Cross.

In most other institutional settings, there seems to be a natural lifespan of positive leadership outcomes. In higher education, it is often influenced by the length and rhythm of fundraising campaigns. Sometimes, health considerations or the aging process are relevant variables in the length of term of service. In some situations, poaching by rival companies or schools can have an impact.

Many new CEOs have five-year terms. Their impact would have to be gauged by the number of terms served and the fruitfulness of the leadership provided. For students, such reflections many seem irrelevant. But, eventually, those who aspire to future leadership will need to recognize that you cannot always control how long you serve, but you can still look back with gratitude for the opportunity when enough years have passed to make your mark. In today's context, most college graduates will have multiple jobs and live in different cities or parts of the world. It is important to aspire to live by one's highest values at whatever level of responsibility within an organization. At Notre Dame, people who serve as rectors or in Campus Ministry play an essential role. The same is true of athletic coaches, psychological counselors, and career directors. This is not to downplay the role of faculty or major administrators, but a modern university needs accomplished leaders in every structural unit. It is what we do together that makes Notre Dame such a distinctive and welcoming place.

QUESTION 7

What is the responsibility of a leader toward their community?

For me, this is an interesting question because I belong to multiple "communities," each of which has some claim on me. First, as a Holy Cross Catholic priest and an agent of the Gospel, I need to be faithful to my religious vows and my priestly obligations. When I celebrate Mass or preside at any of the other sacraments, I am a representative of a tradition and an active presence that goes back to the time of Christ. In this role, I have held various positions in the Congregation of Holy Cross: chair of various committees, chapter delegate, member of the

Provincial Council, college seminary director, and Master of Divinity Director. I have also been a priest-in-residence in Sorin Hall for over 40 years (separate from my academic and administrative roles at Notre Dame).

With regard to the broader Catholic community, I was involved for over 10 years with the *Ex Corde Ecclesiae* consultative process. I also served on the Bishops- Presidents Committee of the U.S. Bishops Conference. When invited, I have given talks for many Catholic institutions like grade schools, high schools, and higher education institutions, Catholic hospitals, parishes, homeless centers, and Catholic charities.

My involvement in broader higher education communities is described elsewhere. I always felt an obligation to be of service to other schools and their representative organizations, whether it be commencement addresses, advice to search committees, or service on governing boards.

But, perhaps, the most important drift of the question revolves around the so-called town-gown relationship or how the University community relates to the civic community that surrounds it. I have always been a student of cities—how they are established, how they grow, how they evolve over time, and how they undertake periodic reforms. Notre Dame is in St. Joseph County and abuts the twin cities of South Bend and Mishawaka. Our nearby neighbors include Elkhart, LaPorte, Michigan City, and Niles, Michigan. Our location on the Indiana Toll Road means that we have easy access to many small towns and farming communities. We have worked hard at strengthening those relationships by area promotion, charitable fundraising, and the provision of leadership for not-for-profit organizations. We have also been directly involved in the establishment of the South Bend Center for the Homeless, the Robinson Community

Learning Center, and have promoted neighborhood renewal, including the Eddy Street Project. Various units of Notre Dame have been active in the Chapin Street Health Clinic, Habitat for Humanity, Hannah's House, and many other charitable works.

The best answer to the question is that the leader needs to know the community, have positive relationships with its various elected and voluntary leadership groups, be supportive in terms of the mobilization of its own workforce (and/or students), seek appropriate financial support, and serve as a representative, when invited, of efforts to promote the community in a broader circle of identity.

There is no better preparation for such leadership than for students to volunteer early on for roles off campus which signal interest in the broader community and to bring their own personal skills, interests, and enthusiasm. The community leaders of tomorrow are being trained and motivated by their community-based activities in the present.

QUESTION 8

What has been the most defining impact of your leadership?

Like all newly elected presidents, in my inauguration address, I tried to lay out what I hoped would be my highest priorities and sought after goals. Many of these were consistent with the impact Father Ted Hesburgh had during his 35 years as President. We needed to pay close attention to our heritage as a

Catholic institution. We needed to continue our trajectory as a major research university. We needed to preserve our distinctive nature as a residential campus, particularly for undergraduate students.

Among other things, I promised to be a peripatetic president, always on the go both on and off campus. I intended to continue living in Sorin Hall and I hoped to return to teaching one course a semester after my first year as President. I did, in fact, become the only American higher education leader who both taught and lived in a student residence for my whole term as President. However, after I concluded my 18 years as President, I was frequently asked what I was most proud of as a lasting impact on the University. I always thought this was a good question, so I sought to refine my answer. Here is the latest version of what I came up with.

I am most proud that we were able to pursue multiple goals simultaneously, all of which were important dimensions of the University during these years:

The University paid close attention to and enhanced our **identity and mission as a Catholic university**. This included: undergraduate admissions, faculty hiring, new institutes and centers, Campus Ministry, Sacred Heart Basilica, the Grotto, dorm liturgies, and liturgical music. Each of these areas were, at least occasionally, the courses of dispute about Notre Dame's nature as a distinctive Catholic university. We had conferences and speakers on campus to address topical issues from a faith perspective. I, and several other administrators, became cofounders of the University of Notre Dame Australia, with four campuses. I served on the **Ex Corde**

Ecclesiae committee and its implementation committee in the United States context.

The University became **more fully coeducational,** with undergraduate enrollments approaching 50/50 and dormitories reflecting the new configuration. We had female vice presidents, deans, and other major administrators. The professional schools and graduate enrollments began to reflect our peer institutions. There were new investments in women's intercollegiate athletic teams. We celebrated a "Year of Women" with extensive programming spread across all units of the University. We had women elected as Student Body President and to leadership in other student organizations, including the Marching Band, *The Observer,* the yearbook, and hall government.

The University became **more diverse** both in census category terms and also socio-economically. We celebrated a "Year of Cultural Diversity" with an impressive array of speakers, panels, entertainment, and informal gatherings. We made key appointments to the faculty and administration. We sought a more diverse student body and put in place various support services.

The University became more precise in evaluating and being better informed about the **quality of teaching** at all academic levels. We took seriously the teaching records of faculty up for promotion. We put in place programming for graduate students and new faculty to be more systematic in utilizing state-of-the-art theoretical and practical perspectives.

The University promoted **graduate studies and research** with additional resources and new faculty positions. As part of this, we reduced the average teaching load of all faculty and upped the expectations for fruitful, peer-reviewed research results. As a result, the quality of our graduate students also improved. Finally, departments with strong research presence were highlighted in more public ways.

The University gave new emphasis to the **town-gown relationship**, or the dynamic between the University and its surrounding community. The most dramatic display of this was the creation of the South Bend Center for the Homeless, which has developed into a national model. We also created the Robinson Community Learning Center and cooperated with several other not-for-profits in the community. Various members of the administration served on the boards of many of these organizations and helped lead fundraising drives. We also cultivated a close relationship with the two mayors, the City Council, the County Council, and the State of Indiana. Over time, we became the leading employer in Michiana.

The University had **balanced budgets**, highly successful **fundraising campaigns**, and a major increase in the level of our **endowment**. Part of this was a great improvement in our **financial aid** resources.

All of this required a collective effort and the expertise, energy, and commitment of so many members of the Notre Dame family. I am thankful to have had some role in overseeing the development of each of these goals.

I should add that student support and enthusiasm was also a crucial component.

QUESTION 9

What is the best advice you have been given?

After I had been elected President of Notre Dame, I sought out advice from a broad cross-section of those who had carried similar responsibilities. Father Ted Hesburgh, my immediate predecessor, told me to "be myself." He went on to say that I should not pretend to be him or any other leader I might admire, whether in terms of style, public persona, priorities, or support structure. Implied in his wise counsel was a recognition that, as both Holy Cross priests, we shared much history and experiences together. We inherited a legacy from Father Ed Sorin and the Holy Cross brothers who were the founders of Notre Dame. We were both believers in the importance of a Catholic university and the role that it could play in society and the Church. We were both committed to the education of the whole person—body, mind, and spirit. We were both people who were part of a worldwide religious community and knew that Notre Dame had to have an international vision.

What Ted Hesburgh was really warning against for me as a new leader was a slavish devotion to the past. In his time, Ted had initiated coeducation and established a predominantly lay Board of Trustees. Both moves went against the grain of deep-seeded traditions and elicited a fair amount of opposition. He knew that I would need the courage to take on comparable decision-making moments, the content of which were unknown at the time.

Other people advised me to: get enough rest, keep present in the life of our local religious community, develop a regular exercise routine, keep living in a dorm (or move out as soon as you can), keep teaching (or leave behind your classroom involvement), take time for research and writing (or focus instead on administration exclusively), and be active in national and/or international higher education associations (or give Notre Dame almost exclusive priority).

From my family members, my mother promised to pray for me and hoped that I would visit her when I could (my father had died earlier). My two sisters wanted me to feel free to visit when I could. My Holy Cross peers urged me to relax and get away from the stresses and strains of my new job by enjoying common prayer, moments of relaxation, and meals with them (the expectation was that meals at Corby Hall were not the right place to talk business or ask nosy questions).

In some ways, the best advice I received was not one-on-one or face-to-face, but in my reading of institutional histories and reflective memoirs by former presidents or others in major leadership positions. The candor and honesty that I found there was a great preparation.

I knew I had a lot to learn and I was open to advice from whatever trusted source. My advice to you students is to do the same. The more questions you ask in times of leadership transition, the better. Eventually, you will have to sift through it. But, in the end, it is better to be over prepared than the opposite.

SECTION SIX

Leadership Practicalities

"Mentorship is about personal relationships, modeling from one generation to the next, exposure, and well-conceived experiences."

QUESTION 1

What are your favorite resources (books, organizations, etc.) for leaders?

There is nothing more important than being exposed to men and women who are inspiring and effective leaders. Such concrete experience is more important than theoretical explorations or solicited advice from sitting leaders. However, I have tapped into a variety of sources during my years of preparation and after I was entrusted with the presidency of Notre Dame.

As most people know, I am a prolific reader and I have always enjoyed historical accounts of the evolution of the modern university from the medieval schools like Bologna, Paris, Salamanca, Oxford, and Cambridge to the creation of the American university (Harvard, Yale), to the German model of graduate education and research, to the contemporary public and private, loosely-organized system of America's higher education, which has been adopted throughout the world. I have read many institutional histories and biographies of major educational leaders. I have also read books about general issues affecting higher education like admissions policies, tuition costs, financial aid, diversification, investment policies, fundraising, intercollegiate athletics, tenure, faculty and staff collective entities, academic freedom, federal research support, etc. I know other presidents who kept up by going to conferences, watching videos, and interacting with experts.

In addition to reading about leadership in higher education, I recommend benchmarking other institutions as a valuable practice. After my election as Notre Dame's 16th President in November of 1986, I did not assume the responsibility until July of 1987. That means that I had about seven months to travel around and visit other campuses and meet with their presidents.

A third helpful activity is participating actively in the various higher education associations. This I did right from the start and, eventually, I was chosen to head the board of most of them.

Finally, incorporate travel abroad into your yearly schedule. This was instrumental in promoting the internationalization of Notre Dame but also in giving me first-hand experience in all the continents except Antarctica. My involvement in the establishment of the University of Notre Dame Australia was particularly noteworthy. How many leaders have the opportunity to found a new Catholic university from scratch in this day and age?

It goes without saying that the mentorship of Father Ted Hesburgh, an iconic figure in American higher education, was a gift to me. He welcomed me into my leadership role and continued to be involved in the life of the institution in ways that were helpful.

In the end, all the preparation in the world will not make you a good president. But the various points I have recommended made my learning curve much shorter.

QUESTION 2

How do you continue to grow and develop as a leader?

Let me begin by acknowledging that when the Board of Trustees of Notre Dame asked Father Ted Hesburgh, the sitting President, to accept one last five-year term and to identify some Holy Cross priests with the potential to succeed him, I (and Bill Beauchamp and Dave Tyson) was given significant administrative responsibilities. I served as Vice President and Associate Provost, the #2 academic officer, and I was invited and encouraged, at the same time, to attend Officer, Board of Trustees, Advisory Council, and Alumni Board meetings both to familiarize myself with the work of each of these entities and to become better known by the members. We also visited the various academic, student life, and service units. In other words, we were given a lot of leeway to learn as much about the University in all its complexity as we could. The three of us maintained a good relationship during the four+ years before I was chosen as the next President.

I mention this because once my term of leadership began, I had already interacted regularly and comfortably with the other officers of the University, many of whom would be part of my new administration, including Tim O'Meara as Provost, whom I had reported to as Vice President and Associate Provost.

I did several other things during the preparatory period that would set precedents for my later activity. One, **I read widely** in the literature on higher education. Second, **I went to meetings** of the American Council on Education (the umbrella organization for higher education) and more focused groups like ACCU (for Catholic Schools) and NAICU (for private schools). These were great opportunities for networking and for listening in, as the various speakers discussed important issues of the moment. Later, after becoming President, I not only broadened the base of organizations that I became a member of but eventually served on the boards and often chaired the organizations for a period of time.

Third, I made it a habit to **visit other colleges and universities** when I was on the road. In the interval between when I was elected (November 1986) and when I took over as President (July 1987), I received very helpful advice from sitting presidents.

Other steps I took to continue to grow as a leader included **traveling abroad** to have a better grasp of the world, including the role of higher education institutions in other countries and cultures; **getting feedback** from alumni and learning how they viewed the University and what pleased them or made them anxious; **meeting with government leaders** who were essential in sustaining funding for scholarships and research grants; and **meeting with Church leaders** who had a special concern for the Catholic nature and identity of Catholic institutions (my participation in the many years of discussion of the *Ex Corde Ecclesiae* document was a big part of this).

My word of advice for you as future leaders is to keep well-informed, find sources of personal renewal, be active with other leaders in your sphere of influence and the associations that serve them, and, finally, keep enthusiastic about the importance of the leadership role that you play, whatever it might be. Learn from your mistakes, get good feedback, surround yourself with talented colleagues, and share the credit for the good things you collectively achieve.

Then, who knows what the future has in store for you as a leader, but it is sure to be exciting.

QUESTION 3

How important is mentorship for leaders today?

The word "mentor" may be too fancy for undergraduate students. It might be better to say "trusted older friend" or "inspiring teacher" or simply "someone who is there for me." The first challenge in establishing such a relationship is getting in the door, really or figuratively. Younger students or those who are a bit shy may be intimidated by important figures on campus. They may fear that they will be treated perfunctorily. In fact, faculty, rectors, counselors, campus ministers, and others are usually pleased when students take initiative. They do not expect you to bare your soul in a first meeting. But, over time, comfort may grow and a good dynamic achieved. It is, then, that real mentoring can take place. Sometimes, these sessions can be regularized or both parties may prefer that they happen spontaneously. The important thing is that you have access to a person or a set of people who can provide a degree of wisdom, experience, and human understanding that can become an invaluable asset to your future life as a leader.

When I was invited to serve as Vice President and Associate Provost of Notre Dame, I knew that I was a potential candidate to succeed Fr. Ted Hesburgh as President of the University. At the behest of the trustees of the University who had asked

Ted to serve another five-year term, I, along with Dave Tyson and Bill Beauchamp, had been identified as having potential for higher levels of responsibility. I was to work under the tutelage of Tim O'Meara as Provost and Ted Hesburgh as President. Over the next four+ years, I was provided the opportunity to learn as much as I could about the workings of the University (including the role of the trustees, advisory councils, and Alumni Board). I also met and interacted with a broad cross-section of the faculty, internal administration, and staff. I participated in University-wide planning processes, budget deliberations, and faculty evaluations. In the end, I (and Bill and Dave) was given access to just about every important event, process, and analysis. When I was finally elected President, I felt about as prepared as I could be as an internal candidate who had spent most of his adult life on campus.

My personal experience as a mentee was excellent and it took place over several years. When I became President, I tried to keep in mind that I now had a responsibility to prepare the next generation of Holy Cross and lay leaders. In order to pursue this goal, I first identified several Holy Cross religious whom I met with periodically in a group, placed them on University-wide committees and planning processes, and, eventually, gave some of them formal responsibilities. With regard to lay colleagues, I discussed with Tim O'Meara, Bill Beauchamp, and some of the other major administrators whom they should bring along as potential future leaders. Looking back, I think all this effort worked reasonably well. There was always some disagreement about using internal or external searches for replacements for leaders either retiring or moving to other institutions. Depending on the responsibility and available candidates, we used both internal and external search processes.

Here are some things I learned about mentorship:

→ Fostering talented **Catholic** administrators and leaders should always be a high priority at Notre Dame. If this is not attended to, we will end up looking like every other school in our category as a national research university.

→ We need to seek and hire **women** and members of **historically underrepresented groups** to more closely resemble the broader American population. They should be nurtured and mentored for various leadership roles.

→ Once people are part of our Notre Dame community, they deserve an equal opportunity to utilize and develop their leadership potential with appropriate levels of mentorship.

→ The Congregation of Holy Cross will continue to prepare some percentage of its members for potential leadership roles at Notre Dame and our other institutions of higher education. During my years as President, four future Holy Cross Presidents were part of my administration. John Jenkins became my successor at Notre Dame and Dave Tyson, Bill Beauchamp, and Mark Poorman served with distinction as Presidents of the University of Portland.

Mentorship is about personal relationships, modeling from one generation to the next, exposure, and well-conceived experiences. It never involves guarantees or the availability of sinecures. Individuals still have the responsibility to bring vision, enthusiasm, discipline, and hard work to the roles they are invited to play. Some will pass muster and some will not. But, if the numbers are sufficient, then the University will be well-served going forward (or any other workplace for that matter).

For young people who are zealous and highly motivated, you need to seek out opportunities for mentorship and, when available, enter them wholeheartedly. You never know where they may lead. Rectors of halls try to identify future resident assistants among the younger members of the dorms. Faculty are eager to find high quality students to assist with their research. Not-for-profit organizations are delighted when talented undergrads volunteer. All of these can be stepping stones to future leadership roles.

QUESTION 4

How do you surround yourself with good people?
What are important traits for new employees?

In my years as President and afterward, I have been involved in many leadership searches for CEOs (by whatever title), academic leaders, deans, vice presidents, athletic directors, and coaches. Some of these searches were done with internal sources and some with the use of search firms. In every case, we first described the nature of the responsibility, the strengths and weaknesses of the previous holder of the title, the highest priorities moving forward, and the set of personal characteristics that we considered either necessary or desirable for those being considered.

For boards, the CEO-selection is the most substantial and crucial. It is typical today to have a board search committee with representation from various constituencies of the institution. They, however, have only advisory authority. They do the grunt work with the assistance of a search firm, which identifies potential candidates, makes contact with them, goes through references, does background checks, and sets up the interview process. It is then up to the members of the board search committee to narrow down the number of candidates and, hopefully, recommend two or three to the board. Then, the board members (or a designated sub-section of the board) review the files, react to those nominated by the search committee, hold interviews (usually including both formal and informal interactions), and make a selection. An important outcome, after salary and other terms are negotiated with the selection, is that everyone gets behind the new leader.

Depending on the position, certain credentials are critical. Most college or university presidents have a Ph.D. or other terminal advanced degree (like a law or medical degree). Occasionally, presidents have been political leaders (like in state schools). Many candidates for presidencies have been provosts or presidents at comparable institutions in terms of quality and reputation.

In provost or academic vice president searches, a doctorate, a tenured faculty position, and a teaching/research profile are necessary. Many provosts are former deans or associate provosts.

Often, there is a heavy faculty presence in searches for provosts and deans, although the president has the last word in garnering the approval of the governing board.

The vice president of student affairs position is more flexible when it comes to the background of candidates. Some have advanced degrees from education departments with a specialization in student life. Others may have academic backgrounds or pastoral roles like rectors or campus ministry. In today's climate, a background in law or business might also respond to a recognizable need.

Executive vice presidents, who oversee the financial, physical, and personnel side of the institution, usually have an MBA or other financial degree. Other vice presidents who report to them (finance, investments, fundraising, physical plant, facilities, personnel, among others) normally have specialized backgrounds and successful career paths.

Perhaps the hardest choices are in the area of athletics (athletic director, head coaches) since the alumni of the institution may have a deep and sometimes emotional interest in these roles. The athletic director's responsibilities have evolved over time. In the present context, the job requires a background in athletics, management and business skills, and legal and personnel capacities. The individual also needs to be a savvy presence in the media and a solid representative of the institution to alumni, friends, and enthusiastic fans. The selection of head coaches, especially in the high-profile sports, is often accompanied by rumormongering, special interest advocacy, and false claims of interest. Background checks are important (as we found out in the George O'Leary situation). Competitive salary scales (which are rather astronomical) are another dimension of the search process.

No matter what position needs to be filled, there are certain characteristics that are desirable: proper credentials, a good level of experience, a positive evaluation from colleagues and key leaders in the reporting line, good health, a fitting age range and personal circumstances, and an enthusiastic interest in the job. On a more personal level, candidates should be persons of integrity, rooted in the values of the institution (whether Catholic or not), process-oriented, effective communicators, shrewd judges of people, and sufficiently self-confident to withstand criticism.

One of my favorite lines is, "Every search committee is looking for Jesus but they are lucky to find Paul or Mary." Students can experience the challenges of choosing leaders in student governing elections, in hall government, and in many important organizations on campus. While the level might be lesser, many of the same principles are operative.

QUESTION 5

How should leaders handle conflict?

The easiest way to answer the question is that leaders should seek common ground. Disagreements among members of the central administration or between the administration and various constituencies are to be expected. One wag suggested that the primary interest of alumni was tickets to athletic contests, of faculty was access to convenient parking, of staff was regular raises, and of students was a lively social life. This is a caricature, but it does remind us that the participants in the same enterprise can have significantly different perspectives.

College campuses are full of individuals who are bright and articulate and often have strong opinions. This means that there must be a forum in which there can be meaningful discussions. Some of these will be structural and some **ad hoc**. But, it is important to set some ground rules so that we get more than harangues and **ad hominem** arguments. This is where representative bodies and elected representatives can often break log jams and promote the development of consensus. In the end, everyone does not have to agree, but everyone does, in some sense of the term, need to be heard.

Let me provide some examples from my own experience. In athletics, it was important for us to maintain our independence in football and yet in most other sports to belong to a conference. For many years, we achieved this goal through our television contract for football and our membership in the Big East Conference. But, when the Big East began to lose members to the Atlantic Coast Conference, we faced a dilemma. The Big Ten and the Atlantic Coast Conferences both made strong pitches to have us join (as did some other conferences, less aggressively). There were good arguments for both alignments. Finally, after a long consultative process, I announced that we would be joining the ACC in all sports except football, hockey, and fencing. We would also play four or five football games each year against ACC opponents. Not everyone was happy with this outcome, but all the major players had a chance to share their perspectives.

A second example was the construction of the DeBartolo Performing Arts Center. In my first year as President, I announced that one of my personal priorities was to construct a new center for the performing arts. My main argument was that all great universities needed to have strong presences in the fine and performing arts. The Snite Museum gave us a good head start (and is now being superseded by the new Raclin Murphy Museum of Art). We hired an architectural firm that specialized in such facilities and they developed an attractive prospectus. Unfortunately, for years we could not find a donor and the project was put on hold. Then, after many years, I told the officers that we would complete a center before I stepped down as President.

Fortunately, we hired a new architectural firm who developed a much more ambitious scheme (with five separate performance spaces plus extensive offices for faculty and students). When the DeBartolo family generously agreed to fund the project, we were able to dedicate the facility in my last year as President. In the process of planning over the years, it was not so much that others were opposed to the idea but that they had other priorities, and I ended up being the critical advocate.

Finally, Fr. Ted Hesburgh was clearly the President when Notre Dame became coeducational at the undergraduate level (and implicitly more coeducational in the administrative, faculty, and staff ranks). However, with single sex dorms, each year we had to signal the Admissions Office about what percentage of male and female students they should choose for the incoming class. By the time I took over for Ted, there were petitions from student government and elsewhere to move to a 50/50 ratio of male and female students. At one particular meeting of the Student Affairs Committee of the Board of Trustees (a number of whom had daughters who either had been or wanted to be students at Notre Dame), the appeal was so persuasively delivered that they voted as a group to urge the administration to set some timelines for achieving the 50/50 goal. I was fully supportive of this priority and we began the process of implementing it after receiving encouragement from the Board of Trustees.

While these are three success stories, I have been involved in other conflicts that remained unresolved and were passed on to Fr. John Jenkins' administration. Students can learn from all of this that an open mind and effective processes of deliberation can usually achieve consensus. But, there are no guarantees, and leaders need to factor that into their notions of a successful administration.

QUESTION 6

How do leaders cope with stress?

The dictionary defines stress as a "constraining force or influence" or a "physical, chemical, or emotional factor that causes bodily or mental tension." In one sense, stress is an inevitable part of life in society. It can be precipitated by undue pressures, intense competition, an unexpected event or outcomes, a lack of confidence in some situations, being misunderstood, inexperience, illness, or a whole host of other factors.

Some people are worrywarts, prone to excessive fears about failure. They are preoccupied by imagined negative outcomes. All things being equal, they do not make effective or inspiring leaders. Others look forward to the adrenaline of challenging situations. They thrive in contexts of uncertainty or the need for rapid decision-making. They may make good leaders, especially if they have colleagues who can be a restraining force in charged situations.

As an athlete in grade school, high school, and college (and to a lesser extent later), I had to learn how to prepare well for the challenges of competition and then trust my coach and teammates for the active involvement in the game itself. In team sports, you have to establish a rapport and confidence level with your teammates. If you can shoot a successful foul shot with thousands of fans trying to distract you, if you can seek out the big play at the end of a close game, then other forms of active engagement will not seem overwhelming.

I have known both the thrill of victory and the agony of defeat. I have flopped and failed miserably on occasion, but this never became a characteristic quality. I was able to maintain my confidence level to pick up the pieces and start over.

Stress derives from emotional pressure and the absence of sufficient support structures. Some college and university presidents have found after their selection that they would have to deal with severe financial pressures, inadequate enrollment strategies, poor faculty and staff morale, and persistent rivalries among the administrative personnel. I was fortunate in not having to face such dilemmas. In addition, my religious community on campus was a ready source of encouragement both personally and in various campus structures, including the governing board.

I grew up in a family where my father suffered from ulcers during my whole youth. Ulcers were said to be caused by excessive tension, especially in the workplace. (This is disputed today). I learned from him to develop coping mechanisms and patterns of de-escalation. Here are some of the things I have learned along the way:

Those who advise getting enough **sleep**, **exercise**, and **relaxation** know what they are talking about. Of course, there are always situations where you cannot control any or all of these factors. In those cases, we need resilience and the ability to get back to these basics as quickly as possible.

All of us have a need for **quiet**, which is the best context for **prayer** and **reflection**. I like to walk (which is easy on a college campus) which I do without buds in my ears listening to music. While engaged in this way I plan homilies, prepare talks, think about the day, listen to the birds and other sounds, and otherwise slow down my metabolism.

Having **trusted friends** with whom you can share your life, seek advice, vent strong feelings, deal with disappointments, and receive reinforcement and understanding is a great gift. In fact, I have found that having multiple friendships enhances all these possibilities.

Having **reliable outlets** that are not connected to one's fundamental responsibilities are a real necessity. For me, I enjoy watching sports in person or on television (particularly, football, basketball, and the Olympics). For years I played basketball regularly with the students. I enjoy traveling and seeing new places and cultures. I am a committed reader with a wide-range of interests. I review books, cinema, and theatre performances. I am an experienced crossword puzzle solver. I often share lunch on the Notre Dame campus with faculty, staff, administrators, students, and alumni. I look forward to those conversations.

As I have grown older, I savor a late-afternoon nap which can last from 15 minutes to almost one hour. I do not set my alarm clock.

For most people, I think, dealing with stress is a learned skill but a critical one. It allows us to have calm in the midst of the storm, to be a center of healthy perspective for our colleagues and those entrusted to our care, and to model a style of leadership that is based on endurance and regular renewal.

For students, dealing with stress is well-learned early on in one's life. There are plenty of stressors in college life, but there are also many opportunities for fun, relaxation, and friendship. Finding the right balance is the key.

QUESTION 7

How do leaders deal with tragic loss?

In my first year as president, Father Bill Beauchamp's parents were murdered in their home outside of Detroit. Bill served as my Executive Vice President at the time. It came as an utter shock to all of us. Many of us attended the wake service and I concelebrated at the funeral Mass. Those responsible for the brutal attacks were unknown at the time so the police videotaped both events. Eventually, a man and woman who were drug addicts were arrested, tried, and convicted. But, as Bill and his extended family tried to cope with their sense of loss, the rest of us (new to our responsibilities) had to maintain our focus on our leadership roles at the University.

While this loss of life (close to me and all of us in the administration) was tragic enough in its own right, it was 9/11/01, which stands out as the most overpowering event during my 18 years as president. I have described in great detail elsewhere how the days during and after 9/11 unfolded. I will simply summarize them here: On 9/11 itself, we mobilized the campus, celebrated Mass for some 10,000 people on the South Quad, kept in contact with parents and alumni, had a blue Mass to honor first responders, honored the dead at the first home football game against Michigan State, raised money for the families, and delivered a new ambulance to St. Vincent's Hospital in New York City. I also spent two days at Ground Zero as a guest of the New York City Police and Fire Departments, which I then shared with the broader Notre Dame family in a variety of formats, including several talks and in my published diary.

Another tragic moment took place on January 24, 1992, when the Notre Dame Women's Swim Team was in a bus accident due to a blizzard on the Indiana Toll Road not far from campus after a meet in Chicago against Northwestern. I was in D.C. at a meeting when it happened. The campus community mobilized well in response. When I returned, I visited the 18 who were injured and helped plan for the funerals of the two young women who had died, Meghan Beeler and Colleen Hipp. I visited Haley Scott at Memorial Hospital. It was feared that she would be paralyzed for life, but later she miraculously recovered and swam again. Many years later, she was our commencement speaker.

While these three moments stand out in my memory, like any large community, we have known our share of illness, suffering, and death. The onset of COVID-19 has reminded us that all of us are vulnerable creatures of flesh and blood and even the young and healthy can discover that life has no guarantees.

We have had students die in car accidents, in falls, in trips abroad, and from illnesses. Occasionally, a student dies at his or her own hand. With faculty and staff, in addition to similar causes of death, the aging process is responsible sometimes for prolonged illness, lack of mental acuity, and death.

In my experience, Notre Dame is at its best in times of illness, family loss, personal disruption, and death. One of the reasons is our religious heritage, with practices of prayer, spiritual counseling, symbolic practices (like the use of crosses and the lighting of candles), and especially the celebration of the Eucharist. Hall chapels, the Basilica, and the Grotto of Our Lady of Lourdes are natural gathering places. Members of our community visit hospitals, write notes, attend wake services, and go to funerals and burials.

When each of my parents died, members of the extended Notre Dame family were present to me and my two sisters both in person and through various forms of communication. As a result, we felt supported and comforted. I personally have celebrated the life, death, and burial of students, faculty, staff, fellow Holy Cross religious, benefactors, advisory council members, and trustees. It is always an honor and a special opportunity.

For you students, the experience of COVID-19 and all the adjustments we had to make to our personal and collective lives stand as a reminder that we can be more resilient than we ever imagined. The regimes of testing, isolation, and quarantining taught us lessons about sacrificing for the common good. As future leaders, I hope you learned that when called to pursue a new emergency response academically, socially, athletically, and extracurricularly, we can bring out the best in people. Father John Jenkins did an extraordinary job in keeping us together on the Notre Dame campus and the results were better than many of us imagined were possible.

QUESTION 8

When is delegation more appropriate than direct leadership and why?

The best answer to this probing question revolves around what is called in the tradition of Catholic social teaching the Principle of Subsidiarity. This lays out that all decisions (and their concomitant implementation) should be done at the proper level of society. For example, the federal government should not do what the state or local level might more effectively undertake. Formal government agencies should not do what companies or voluntary associates can better assume responsibility for. In some cases, it is the family, or even the individual, who will have the best source of knowledge and the readiness, discipline, and skill to move forward.

Despite the antagonism that some have on ideological grounds to any level of government (and this can come from both the left and the right of the political spectrum), it is the case that large scale and complicated issues like national defense, food safety, weather forecasting, disease control, transportation systems, etc., are best dealt with by the federal government (through the power of the President, the Cabinet, Congress, and various federal agencies). In my experience, due to the standards for employment and the levels of remuneration, federal employees are usually excellent public servants who perform their roles with dedication and commitment no matter which political party is in control and, with some noteworthy exceptions, the smaller and the more local the government might be, the less competence we can take for granted.

There are many not-for-profit agencies whose record of achievement is high. This is usually because of the quality of their leadership and the dedication and consistent involvement of their governing boards. This is especially true in higher education, hospital systems, and national organizations like the Boys and Girls Clubs of America, the American Cancer Society, and the American Heart Association.

Most boards today choose leaders who are process-oriented, consultative, and comfortable making information available to multiple constituents. They also do not try to interfere with the appropriate decision-making authority of the CEO or the top administrative team. The more that each unit, within a broad system of decision-making, feels that its role is respected, the better the overall morale.

Sometimes complicated personnel matters require a greater degree of confidentiality or a more intrusive involvement of the CEO or other top administrators. That is simply part of the human condition. Every effective system of accountability entails the preservation by the final decision-maker(s) of sometimes emotional interventions that otherwise would not be warranted.

In my years as President, I had to deal with theft, social misconduct, failure to properly oversee a unit of the University, unhealthy ambition, nepotism, and incompetence. Thankfully, these were unusual occurrences. Subsidiarity is about shared responsibility with each person, echelon, and group playing its proper role. At the same time, there is a need for a system of checks and balances that goes both ways. I was reviewed annually by the Board of Trustees and I met with all of my direct reports each year to do the same. At their best, such processes cultivate personal growth and higher levels of performance.

It would be wise for students to embrace the Principle of Subsidiarity in student government and across the range of student activities. This will prepare the participants well for their later involvements in more sophisticated organizational structures.

QUESTION 9

How do leaders best prioritize?

I will answer this question in three parts—in my own life, in my leadership role, and in the life of the institution. All three are relevant to a variety of leadership contexts.

In **my own life**, I have always sought a sense of balance. That means, as I have already disclosed, that my routines need to include, all things being equal, sufficient sleep, a balanced diet, regular exercise, a pattern of prayer, social time with colleagues and friends (and especially the Holy Cross community), habits of reading, study, and writing, and quiet time. On an ideal day, I get all these in.

But, as most leaders can reveal, few days are ideal and

sometimes the very busyness of our lives puts a strain on desired schedules.

This is where the academic calendar is helpful. Few other leadership roles have breaks and vacation built in. At Notre Dame, we have Fall and Spring breaks (one week each), three weeks to a month between Fall and Spring semesters, and about three months of Summer vacation. Obviously, much is still going on administratively, but the pace is different and there is more freedom for business and personal travel. Since I have taught a class every semester (where I had to correct papers and assign grades), the breaks provided more leeway for other activities.

When it comes to **my leadership role**, I am always a big fan of consultative processes and collaborative decision-making. When preparing for any major decision, I sought the input of the other major administrators and my own staff. Sometimes decisions need to be made quickly and, then, I may have relied on one or two others. In times of crisis, my tendency was to reconfigure my schedule in order to make sure that the most important things were attended to first. When I was traveling abroad, I empowered the next level of administrators to act on my behalf unless they thought it necessary to directly solicit my own opinion. Depending on the significance of the issue, I would usually consult with the leadership of the Board of Trustees (or sometimes the Holy Cross community, if it was pertinent) both to keep them informed and to make sure I had their backing.

When it came to the **life of the institution**, I used preexisting entities (such as the Officers Group, the Academic Council, the College Councils, the Alumni Board, and most of all the Board of Trustees) for various matters of long-term planning, budget priority setting, and changes to appropriate regulatory documents.

The most important group that I established was the 10-year Review and Priority Committee, which was a necessary part of the every 10-year University-wide accreditation process. This rather large group deliberately included representatives from the administration, faculty, staff, and student body. It was divided into various committees which looked at every part of the University and, then, having received widespread feedback from every source, created a series of priorities. This was then taken by the Executive Committee, further refined, and given to me to write the final document, which I then presented to the Board of Trustees for their final approval. Once all of this took place, we presented the report to the accreditation group for their feedback. Internally, we also put dollar figures on each of the priorities in preparation for the next fundraising campaign.

While the accreditation process warranted the most extensive consultation and time commitment, there were other small efforts that also required a lot of process, including constructing the annual budget, dealing with college-wide accreditation visits, and responding to student and staff concerns as they emerged.

Every leader has to set priorities—personal, process-wise, and in terms of broad-based decision-making. Student leadership efforts ought to reflect the same types of concern. Although the areas of involvement may be less complex and the number of actors more limited, one's own leadership style can emerge early on and serve as a good preparation for the future.

In student life, the academic calendar also plays a big role. No one looks forward more to vacation and holidays than undergraduate students. Presuming these built-in breaks, the rest of the calendar tends to be structured, at least academically, by course and testing schedules. When it comes to extracurricular activities, there is a difference between practice sessions and actual performances. This is true of athletic teams, the Marching Band, the theater group, the student newspaper, student government, intramurals, and the whole range of voluntary student involvements. When the latter have a non-student coach, it is easier to presume a necessary discipline and an effective use of time.

I always found keeping a schedule, even for social events on the weekends, a helpful structure. Then, if I eventually felt overloaded, I could adjust accordingly. I never felt a prisoner of my schedule. On the other hand, some prefer a more spontaneous path through college. There is nothing wrong with this as long as it works for a given individual. Some first-year students want to do everything, join every club, take course overloads, attend every event, and run for every office like they did in high school. For the vast majority of college students, this is a very bad idea.

The big challenge for all students (and adults for that matter) in setting priorities is finding a sense of balance. Living away from home, developing one's own schedule, trying to create a network of friends, being happy, enjoying learning, worshipping God, and serving generously are all components. But, hopefully, like me, you will learn from your mistakes and become more confident and self-assured with the passage of time. Later, you will discover that life is always complicated and that setting priorities is never easy, but by beginning the search for a meaningful life in college, your future can be more assured. And you can be confident that you will adapt well to all the changes that life brings.

QUESTION 10

How does a leader best listen and remain open to the ideas of subordinates and colleagues?

One of the first lessons you learn when you become the president of a contemporary university is that there are whole areas of activity and centers of scholarship about which you know very little. This means that you constantly need the expertise and advice of others—the provost, the executive vice president, various vice presidents, deans, institute and center heads, and so on. My starting principle was that if those leaders could not explain a priority, policy, or practice to me (a relatively well-educated individual), they probably did not know it as well as they thought.

Let me provide some examples. I am by background and interest more of a word person than a number person. This meant that in discussions about budget priorities and goal setting, I relied on others to do the grunt work. But I always wanted to be involved in the final distribution of dollars across the University from salary levels and benefit packages to financial aid availability, maintenance costs, and expenditures for construction and renovation of facilities.

A second example is faculty hiring and periodic evaluation of faculty performance. The provost, academic vice presidents, deans, and representative faculty groups all played important roles in these processes, but I was the final decision-maker for faculty hires and faculty promotions, especially the granting of tenure. No one would claim to have mastered all the fields that our faculty represented but, occasionally, I had to adjudicate some internecine battles within academic units in order to be fair to those being reviewed. In the few cases where I intervened in hiring or tenure decisions, it was in a positive rather than negative direction.

A third area where I clearly needed the assistance of experts from among my colleagues was in our investment policies and their implementation. This was an area where experienced trustees could be of great help to our internal investment team. Like fundraising, investment success or failure was relatively easy to track in a comparative way. We were indeed fortunate that in both areas we knew excellent results during my years of service as President.

One way to assure good counsel and advice from the administrative team was to structure our various meetings in an effective way. I regularly sought feedback from the other officers and the next level of administrators. I also met with all of them during the course of the year and, for those who reported directly to me, this included a one-on-one annual review.

It is also important to note that our annual four- or five-day meetings at Land O'Lakes with officers and spouses, the local Holy Cross Superior, and those who served in my office were an effort to integrate new members, review the successes and failures of the past year, and plan for the coming year. These days included daily Mass, meals, and relaxing time together, all intended to promote our group morale and sense of common purpose. We asked a lot of these individuals (including spouses) during the academic year, especially during home football weekends when our trustees and various advisory councils met on campus, so they deserved some time for fun and relaxation.

In general, I think a willingness to listen to subordinates and colleagues is part of a team concept of leadership.

QUESTION 11

How should leaders bounce back from failure?

One of the emotionally challenging moments of my Presidency was when the NCAA rendered a decision that claimed we had a major violation in our football program. A woman provided extra benefits for some of our players, several of whom she had a personal relationship with. Her only relationship with the University, other than being a fan, was a relatively inexpensive membership in one of our booster clubs.

This led to a wide-ranging conversation among the administration, our athletic leadership, and the leadership of the Board of Trustees. We needed to develop a response that was consistent with our value system and heritage, sufficiently humble, and directed at the future more than the past. We brought in outside consultants who were specialists in damage control. After much deliberation, it was decided that I would be the main University spokesperson, that we would have a press conference at which all media outlets could be present (either on the spot or over the various delivery systems), and that we would announce a series of steps we would be taking to assure that nothing like that would happen again.

We could have fought the severity of the decision or sought to influence the court of public opinion. Instead, we chose to acknowledge that things had taken place that were incompatible with our legacy in intercollegiate athletics and the important thing was to clearly lay out the reform steps we would be taking.

The result was a period of bad publicity that soon dissipated. The media moved on to other concerns. And, I never received another question about the penalty in my remaining time as President. By addressing this issue head-on, we were able to redefine what was at stake and reassure our multiple audiences that we were taking the NCAA decision with the utmost seriousness.

A second example was the priority that we gave to financial aid for undergraduate students. Over time, we learned in our fundraising efforts to make the case for financial aid more effectively and began to build momentum for this effort. Many of our benefactors were thrilled when they received thank you letters and life updates from students who benefited from their generosity. As a result, our socio-economic profile and diversity have changed for the better.

One of my examples of failure was a severe negative crisis of reputation. The second was a challenge to deliver on a promise. I think most failures are like that—unexpected, public, and demanding in time and emotional energy. I was fortunate in having such a great group of advisors and the institutional capacity to pursue better options. As a leader, I think the important thing is not to allow yourself to get overwhelmed by events (especially those outside your direct control). We can all muster a good degree of resiliency and learn from our mistakes and failures. Most people will give a leader the benefit of the doubt if one is forthright and honest and committed to moving forward with new insight and determination.

For students, failures might be academic or social or aspirational. Whatever the cause or degree of difficulty, such moments can prepare you for the real world. I flunked the first semester of freshman math but went on to become the president of the same institution. Students may discover in retrospect that they were in the wrong major or had poor study habits or were affected by events at home. Whatever stood in the way of success can also be an opportunity for more decision-making and a clearer picture of one's life goals. In the end, one should never give up hope.

QUESTION 12

How does it benefit leaders to have a "thick skin"?

Leaders are inevitably public figures. Even if their primary responsibility revolves around a few people, there are dynamics of publicity, the interpretation of decisions, hiring practices, fairness, and morale. And, the larger the activity, the more challenging the social dynamic will be.

Leadership requires a clear sense of identity, good working habits, a sense of balance between the public and the private, and a willingness to articulate, inspire, make judgments, and respond appropriately to success and failure. Each of these actions can generate negative responses by either individuals or groups of the like-minded.

By a "thick skin" I mean the ability to focus on key actions and large-scale processes even when what happened yesterday or in the past is dominating the present conversations. Leaders cannot allow themselves to be overwhelmed by rumormongering, bad public relations, or implicit or explicit hostility by a few.

Most of the time leaders can draw comfort from regular routines and trusted colleagues. In fact, leaders (especially at the upper ranks) tend to know more about the big picture than most of those who make up the work group responsible for one part of a collective operation. Sometimes, leaders have to make difficult decisions about future prospects or required personnel or methods of repositioning. Inevitably, some lives will be negatively affected and the feedback from them (and other sympathizers) may be difficult to tolerate.

However, effective leaders need to be open to legitimate criticism and recommendations for improved performance. Governing boards must be both supportive of those they have chosen for leadership roles and committed to providing honest feedback that may be obtained from multiple sources.

Leaders may be credited with accomplishments for decisions and actions that they were not directly responsible for and blamed for others about which they were ignorant. But, hopefully, over time, public accolades will be accepted with humility and public critiques with an appropriate level of self-confidence. No one is perfect, but no one is as bad as some hostile forces might assert.

The building of self-confidence in the face of adversity and social hostility is probably a life-long process. We all want to be liked and accepted by our peers. But, if we develop strong friendships and vigorous support structures, we can focus on what is most important. Student life can be tricky in this regard yet I assure you that you can develop a thick skin and still remain socially active and reliant on those who bring out the best in you.

QUESTION 13

How did continuing to teach during your presidency impact your leadership?

When I was accepted into the Congregation of Holy Cross, when I was ordained, when I was hired at Notre Dame, and when I gained tenure in the Notre Dame theology department, my main attraction and attention was to become a successful priest/teacher/scholar. When I taught six sections of a theology course in my deacon year, my experience convinced me that I not only could be a committed and effective teacher but that I also really enjoyed that role at a high-quality institution like Notre Dame.

During my years of graduate work at Vanderbilt, I often hearkened back to that pivotal year to motivate me to complete my degree work on time. In that spirit, I also taught a course at Aquinas Junior College in Nashville in my third year of residence at Vanderbilt. When I returned to Notre Dame to complete my doctoral dissertation, I kept my hand in by giving some lectures in courses taught by Stanley Hauerwas and John Howard Yoder, among others.

From the time I joined Notre Dame's theology department to when I become President, I combined teaching and scholarly publication with a variety of administrative responsibilities. I was director of the undergraduate seminar program for four years, Master of Divinity director for four years, director of undergraduate theology for one year, and Vice President and Associate Provost for four+ years. During these responsibilities, I never stopped teaching.

Being an educator has become part of my self-definition. I have enjoyed all of the formats that I have taught in small graduate seminars, graduate lectures, undergraduate introductory and advanced courses, and, more recently, University seminars. I have also done my share of guest lectures and Q&As in others' courses.

When I was going through the interview process for the presidency, I made it clear that I intended to continue teaching as President (and also continue living in a residence hall). I implicitly knew that amidst my formal responsibilities as President, I needed to keep grounded in the life of the campus as a teacher and priest-in-residence. I also suspected that I would have more credibility with other faculty if I shared a vocational calling with them. Over time, I had challenges to fit it all in yet, somehow or other, I was able to mesh decision-making, public presence, required meetings, outside presence, and domestic and international travel with my teaching schedule. I think I was the only President in my era who combined teaching a class both semesters, living in a dorm, and serving as President. I did it because I enjoyed it. I did it because it was connected to the role that Holy Cross had traditionally played at Notre Dame. I did it because I was inspired by our students and all the hope and possibility that they represented.

Now, I would like to urge your generation of students not to be unnecessarily constricted by cultural expectations when you move on to your own careers. Maybe you will become a physician who has time for opera or an investment banker who leads the board of a homeless center or a lawyer who works on the side with immigrants. Do not fall into the trap of conventionality. May the balance you achieve be a true reflection of your strengths, your needs, and your opportunities for service.

QUESTION 14

How important is remuneration for leaders today?

When I was elected President of Notre Dame, I received the equivalent salary that Fr. Hesburgh had. I knew that I would never get it directly since all the Holy Cross salaries at Notre Dame go into a common fund that helps to pay for the expenses of the community around the world and I would simply live on a specified budget as an individual religious. But, philosophically, I felt that the President of the University should receive the top salary directly from the institution. I knew that some of the athletic coaches had enhanced salaries from various deals that they had put together with television programs and other sources of funding. That philosophical principle did not last long.

As we became more sophisticated in our investment work and in our fundraising and, as the world in collegiate athletics became more expensive, I was soon left behind when it came to my direct salary. The same thing was going on in other higher education institutions. The funny thing is that *The Chronicle of Higher Education* has its annual edition in which they complain about how presidential salaries have escalated and far exceed faculty salaries, even those who are chaired professors. My question is why don't they examine the really high salaries if they want to be critical?

I did not become a priest or an administrator in order to become rich. I realize that in for-profit activities, like companies, the expectation is that the CEO will receive a rather large salary and other kinds of benefits. In my experience, in higher education, most faculty and administrators are attracted to the work because of its inherent value rather than because they will become rich. On the other hand, they believe that they deserve proper remuneration.

In addition to direct salaries from the University, our faculty and staff receive medical benefits, tuition, support for their children, and healthy and good working conditions. The aspiration to live as a community of work and mutual support is also a great attraction for many.

I have no objection to corporate leaders receiving relatively high salaries, but the concern expressed by many that the differential between that level and the salaries of the lowest employees is a matter of concern. Some campuses are unionized, as are some corporations. This has an influence on the amount of money available to the different participants in the collective effort. It is also a function of competitive pressures between different participants in the same field of endeavor. If one company does one thing, the rest tend to follow in their train.

Those who work in not-for-profit settings, generally, expect a lower salary scale. But, with regard to some of the not-for-profits that I have been engaged in, it is clear that the top leadership has a major level of responsibility and deserves appropriate levels of compensation. For example, I have been on the Board of Governors of the Boys and Girls Club movement for many years, and it is a very large and complex institution. Those who work at the top level in Atlanta need to have a comparable level of skills to comparable individuals from other walks of life. I could easily make the case that primary and secondary school teachers should be rewarded in a significant way for the very important responsibilities they bear. The same thing would be true with nurses, as we have discovered again during the COVID-19 crisis. You could say the same about police officers and firefighters who put their lives on the line, as do first responders, and in the contemporary context, they are often under-appreciated and much critiqued. I have great respect for those who serve in various levels of government. I have seen in my experience that federal government leaders are often well-trained and have a very important role to play in the broader society. The same thing would be true at the state and local level with a lesser level of complexity in the operation.

Probably those who have the greatest control over their level of remuneration are those who have founded their own businesses, especially if they are successful.

Another dimension of remuneration for leaders is to what extent they manifest a spirit of generosity in their financial donations. Many long-time leaders of the corporate level have started their own foundations and are often quite generous in the level of their gift-making and in their willingness to take on important contemporary areas of deeds. As the University President, I was often very impressed with the willingness of members of our Board of Trustees and Advisory Councils and others who believed in our mission and were willing to give substantial gifts to enhance our capacity to fulfill it. We indeed expect trustees to conform to the standard of time, talent, and treasure and the willingness to be of assistance in supporting the grand visions that I and other University leaders have conveyed. Leadership by example is an important part of the role that all of us can play.

QUESTION 15

What role does public relations play in leadership?

Public relations (PR) is the effort to induce the public to have a positive understanding of a firm or institution and a feeling of goodwill about it. In contemporary life, PR has become a critical and expensive function, often entrusted to a specialized office and group of highly trained individuals. In an era of instant communication and in a time of preoccupation by the media with scandals of various levels of severity, it is crucial to respond quickly to stories, legal suits, and rumors that call into question the integrity or proper oversight of those who lead the organization.

As President of Notre Dame, I was often the chief spokesperson of the University. Sometimes my role was simply to acknowledge that we had an issue that we were exploring and would eventually make public what we had discovered. When the NCAA ruling came down, I spent about four hours in 15-minute increments with representatives of print, radio, and television media responding to questions. The important thing was not to be defensive, to acknowledge that unacceptable things had taken place, and to assure the audience that we would do everything we could to prevent a recurrence.

On other occasions, I celebrated positive things like the successful completion of fundraising campaigns or the way we had responded to 9/11/01 or high rankings vis-à-vis our peer higher education institutions. Much PR at Notre Dame is concentrated in our Media Relations Office or the comparable area of the Athletics Department.

We have become more effective in telling the Notre Dame story in video, in written publications, and on the internet. Crisis management is only one small part of our outreach efforts.

The leaders of the Catholic Church have been bedeviled by the so-called sex abuse crisis. Many missteps were made both in properly responding to victims and in dealing with offending religious, priests, bishops, and lay people. Many Catholics (and others) have been scandalized by the extent of the problem. Yet, much progress has been made and more people are recognizing that all youth service organizations have had similar problems. A lot of money has changed hands, but it is not clear that this, in itself, has made the world safer for children.

The disputatious nature of American society has led to a reluctance by many leaders to speak candidly lest their comments come back to haunt the organization in legal suits.

The best PR is honest, well-thought out, and focused. It allows the organization to manifest its pride in the good things it has achieved (and those who made them possible) and, in some cases, to seek financial support for a continuance of the good work. PR is also about personal relationships between leaders, media representatives, and the general public. When solid bonds have been created over time, challenging situations are more easily gotten past.

SECTION SEVEN

The Fun Stuff

"People in leadership positions need to know when and how to laugh."

QUESTION 1

Do you have a set routine that helps start your day?

I am without a doubt a night person. From my family upbringing until today, my natural instincts continue this way. Even my years in seminary formation, when early rising for morning prayer was required, did not affect my later habits in ministry.

Living over 40 years in a student dormitory at Notre Dame (when late night hours are not unusual, especially on the weekends) has reinforced my propensities toward being a night owl. In my early years in Sorin Hall, I often stayed up until 2:00 or 3:00 in the morning. I did this to be available to students but also to get my academic work done. To offset sleep deprivation, I often took power naps when I could.

From my earliest years as a Vice President and later as President, I deliberately made a shift in my schedule. I began to get up at 8:00 a.m. and go to bed at midnight. The only exception was when I was jet-lagged and often rose at 4:00-5:00 a.m. when I first arrived back from other continents. Within the U.S., I usually try to sustain an East Coast schedule.

When I rise at 8:00 a.m., I often watch ten to twenty minutes of T.V. news before showering, shaving, and dressing. I have some morning prayers that I like to recite and I may work on a homily in my head for a Mass later in the day. On weekdays, I get to my office around 9:00 a.m. Then, I have a diet soft drink and an energy bar. Normally, I do not eat breakfast (except when I am abroad). I chat with Carri Frye, my assistant, and read the morning mail, email, newspapers, and magazines. If I have morning meetings (in-person, via Zoom, or on the telephone), I factor those into my schedule. I often meet with University faculty and administrators or Holy Cross religious or visitors over lunch.

If I have lunch at Corby Hall, I customarily get my walking exercise in afterward. I have both indoor and outdoor routes depending on the weather. When I eat at the Morris Inn or elsewhere on campus, I exercise when I leave the office around 3:00 p.m. I usually take a late afternoon nap which lasts 20 minutes or more. I wake up refreshed.

On some mornings, I will be on Zoom or conference calls or I will attend meetings on campus or in the area. When I travel to meetings around the U.S., I normally have morning committee or full board meetings. I am not always at my best on those occasions.

Somewhere in the Psalms it suggests that morning is God's time and evening is the time of the evil one. For me, it has always been the opposite.

QUESTION 2

What is the role of humor in leadership?

I am terrible at telling jokes to audiences. In fact, I usually forget jokes that others tell almost as soon as I hear them. I am personally best at telling stories that have a humorous content and/or a surprising or upbeat ending. In one of my books, *Monk's Notre*

Dame (recently republished by Notre Dame Press), I recount many rather funny stories from my personal experiences or knowledge of the lore of Notre Dame. A simple example highlights Brother Conan Moran, C.S.C., the long-term Director of the Notre Dame Bookstore. He was a much-beloved and highly visible figure on campus. He was famous for never allowing **sales** at the bookstore since he wanted to magnify the profits to help subsidize student scholarships. When I used to ask him about it, he would claim that only over his dead body would there be a sale. It so happened that I celebrated his funeral liturgy and, in my homily, I recalled his old line and thereby declared as President a day of sales at the bookstore.

Some leaders are good joke tellers or can engage audiences with quick wit. I have appeared on programs before live audiences where some speakers had us all rolling in the aisles. In these cases, you either have it or you don't.

Some people seem to have a knack for recognizing the incongruities of life, those situations where rational patterns break down, where the ludicrous or the absurd seem to prevail. Sometimes humor revolves around people—how they dress, how they act, how they speak. Other times, it is the uniqueness or confluence of certain factors that touches our funny bone, so to speak.

Comics and comedians make a living concocting strange stories or imitating famous people (like politicians or entertainers). Some humor revolves around mocking the pretentions of public figures. By consensus, puns are thought to be the lowest form of humor, but there are plenty of other contenders. I once knew a young man who was an unredeemed punster but, when I met his father, I knew why.

People in leadership positions need to know when and how

to laugh. Better to be moderate in such reactions than to inadvertently offend someone or seem to enjoy too much caricature, implicit critiques, or straightforward attacks on others in thinly disguised ways. It is important to laugh or enjoy oneself only if the performance or repartee actually seems funny. Phony responses are easily discovered.

Leaders with no sense of humor come off as uninteresting, excessively earnest, and somehow lacking in a prized human quality. But, every leader has to be true to him or herself in incorporating humor into their public persona. Students have a great propensity to imitate their teachers, rectors, and administrators. The first time you witness this it can be a shock, but later you go with the flow and laugh along.

A couple of caveats for those of you who are young and aspiring to become leaders. First, acceptable humor is quite context-dependent. What might pass as acceptable among one's peers and friendship group may be offensive in other settings. The sensitivities at this point in American history about race, gender, religion, ethnicity, and sexual orientation should loom large in deciding what types of humor can pass muster (and keep you out of trouble).

Second, acceptable humor needs to be lighthearted and welcome and not mean-spirited or thinly disguised one-upmanship, especially for those new to a company, organization, or activity. The powers that be are on the alert for those who are inept in social situations or just don't get it.

One final reflection. Just think what it is like to be a late-night T.V. comic and have to be funny every day. That is not the role of the leader elsewhere. So just relax and have fun.

QUESTION 3

How important are vacations, sleep schedules, outside activities, and preoccupations for leaders?

Contrary to what some gurus about leadership proclaim (or biographies of a subset of extreme type-A leaders), endless and unceasing work for its own sake is a path to an ulcer, an emotional breakdown, or absent spousal and parental presence. Buckminster Fuller, a famous scientist, supposedly trained himself to get by on three hours of sleep a night. In Japan, there is a name for a syndrome where workers die at their desks after working long hours and taking no vacations. A former president of Harvard University collapsed after taking no breaks and had to be weaned back to health.

After I was elected President of Notre Dame but before I took over officially, I visited various sitting or former presidents of academic institutions to solicit their advice. One went after the sleep issue. He pointed out that when you physically appear tired, distracted, or overwhelmed in public, various constituencies then interpret that as a manifestation of how the organization is doing. And, vice-versa, when you appear energized, enthusiastic, and fully focused on the matters at hand, it inspires confidence in the same audience. Everyone can have a bad day or a challenging week, but over the long term, each leader must recognize that sleep is essential and, depending on one's personal needs, long periods of personally enforced sleeplessness can be a fatal trend for the organization and for oneself.

People who have heavy responsibilities often get by with too little sleep. This is true of parents of young children and those beginning their careers in medicine, law, business, the military, or other professions. Sometimes, there is nothing that can be done in the short term. Individuals working two or three jobs just to pay the bills face a similar dilemma.

Most scientific studies have shown that the average person needs around eight hours of sleep a day to function at their top level. Some cheat with regular bursts of coffee or other uppers which become an essential part of their daily diet. Like any norm, there are those who can get by with five or six hours of sleep and others who need much more than eight.

All of this is to say that when leaders of organizations work out their daily and weekly schedules, assuring a decent amount of time for sleep often is a low priority. The sheer adrenaline rush of new responsibilities may sustain you for a period but, in the end, the thrill will wear off and scheduling decisions will need to be made.

There is no group of individuals more prone to push the limit on sleep deprivation than college students like yourselves. The combination of academic requirements, extracurricular activities, parties, athletic events, late-night gabfests, and social expectations can generate a perpetual battle with too little sleep and the accompanying emotional distress and inability to focus and set proper priorities.

Good leadership preparation needs to, at least, ask the question of whether there are natural limits to one's energy and attention span. Learning to say "no" and being able to take on the most important tasks are part of the same disciplined approach to one's life. The first bit of advice—"Get enough sleep."

A second related area of concern for leaders is the role of **vacations** and other breaks from one's normal routines.

Everyone, no matter their situation, needs to periodically

have time off to refresh, renew, and put things into perspective. Many European countries have weeks of expected vacation time for just about everyone (up to a month or more). Some professions, like teaching, professional sports, or government service, have clear periods of time away, normally subsidized.

It is the leaders of organizations who are often tempted to skip such periods of leisure because they either think themselves indispensable to the overall activity and decision-making or there is pressure from various sources to skip such times of relaxation and refocusing. There are those, who in a post-cell phone era, might as well have stayed at home because they feel compelled to keep on top of everything back at the workplace.

For those who recognize the need for vacation time, either alone or with family or friends, there are various ways of achieving the intended purpose of a vacation. Instead of taking two, three, or four successive weeks off, they can divide time into smaller increments—Christmas, New Years, Summer. Others will extend business travel by adding a day or two or more for sightseeing or just vegging out. Still others will attend convention meetings of affiliated groups and find the off time quite helpful.

Those of us who operate in the academy have times of breaks built into the regular schedule. Most colleges have a Fall, Spring, and Summer break. Research trips may include international travel. For presidents of major research institutes, one of their responsibilities is to make their institutions better known around the country and world or to sign exchange agreements or promote mutual research efforts.

I have always been a calm flyer and enjoy visiting new places and experiencing different cultures. The challenge then is to have a balanced schedule and not simply go from one meeting to another. This is even more important if jet lag is involved.

All things being equal, every leader needs to take vacations according to schedules that fit their own personal needs and lifestyle.

A second bit of advice to students is "take vacations and other breaks in order to find balance between the workplace and one's personal life." Most upwardly mobile college graduates must start all over, especially in business, the military, the academy, and the professions in earning time off from one's labors. Billable hours, performance reviews, and opportunities for travel all come at a cost. It is important to keep alive the desire for balance and equanimity of spirit.

Finally, there is a need for various **forms of relaxation and fun**. I, for one, enjoy reading, theater, cinema, and museum exploration. I am an avid crossword puzzle solver. I prefer big cities to rural settings. I am also fond of traveling to new places both in this country and abroad.

As a former athlete, I follow collegiate and professional football and basketball. I watch the summer and winter Olympic games and often favor the least known sports, where I feel the competition needs at least some recognition. At one time in my life, I enjoyed baseball, but now I find it too slow to sustain my interest. I never played soccer, lacrosse, rugby, or cricket so I do not really understand the strategies involved. I particularly enjoy women's basketball, softball, and volleyball. I have only occasionally played golf and I have no particular skills in it, even though some think that it is the sport where leaders can hobnob with other leaders and potential benefactors.

For some leaders, travel to exotic places fulfills a need. Having been to 90 countries myself, I can understand the allure of travel or encountering the unknown. Some travel, of course, is about recognizing the diversity of the world's cultures or the great discrepancy in quality of life and economic resources from one country to another.

In the same way that exercise, quiet time, and regular vacations are important, so are the wide range of activities, enjoyable leisurely pursuits, and familial pursuits that give balance to our lives and a greater inner peace than we might otherwise enjoy.

College is a great time to find forms of engagement that one enjoys. Bill Clinton was a master crossword puzzle solver. George H.W. Bush once said that he never lost a golf game while serving as President. Teddy Roosevelt was an outdoorsman. Condoleezza Rice played the piano. Winston Churchill was a prolific reader and author. Barack Obama played basketball on a special White House court. Notre Dame's President, John Jenkins, is a swimmer.

For sure, retreat participation and prayer and meditation are essential elements in their inner life and a source of stability and resilience in challenging times. At a school like Notre Dame, the opportunities to practice various forms of reflection were, for me, one of the great benefits of my college years.

QUESTION 4

How do leaders incorporate serving in organizations outside their own?

When I became President of Notre Dame, I was fortunate to be following Father Ted Hesburgh who, for 35 years, had, in addition to leading the University, been extraordinarily involved in service of Presidents of the United States and Popes as well as higher education associations and a whole list of Church organizations. It was just taken for granted that this was what Notre Dame Presidents did.

In the course of my 18 years as President, I was involved in serving:

On the boards of various academic institutions—Notre Dame, Notre Dame Australia, St. Thomas University (MN), Vanderbilt University, St. Mary's College, Our Lady of the Lake University, and the University of Portland;

On the boards of higher education—American Council on Education (ACE, the umbrella organization), Association of Catholic Colleges and Universities (ACCU), Association of Governing Boards (AGB), the Business/Higher Education Forum (BHEF), Campus Compact (CC), Indiana Campus Compact, Indiana Independent Colleges and Universities, International Association of University Presidents, International Association of Universities (IAU), and International Federation of Catholic Universities (IFCU);

On not-for-profit boards—Board of Governors of the Boys and Girls Clubs, Riley Children's Hospital, Riley Regional Committee, Center for Addiction and Substance Abuse (later named Partnership To End Addiction), Commission for a Drug-Free Indiana, Community Anti-Drug Coalition of

America, Corporation for National and Community Service,
President George H. W. Bush's Drug Advisory Council,
National Advisory Council on Alcohol Abuse and Alcoholism,
National Institutes of Health Advisory Committee on
Alcohol Research, NCAA Foundation, and Points of Light
Foundation;

Church-related—Bishops and Presidents Committee, Ex
Corde Ecclesiae Committee, Ex corde Implementation
Committee of National Conference of Catholic Bishops,
Sister Thea Bowman Black Catholic Education Foundation,
and Partnership for Children's Health.

In addition, I traveled the world for Notre Dame. I made many
visits to Australia as part of being a cofounder of Notre Dame
Australia, the Holy Land as part of overseeing the Tantur
Ecumenical Institute, various parts of Asia, Africa, Europe, Latin
America, and Australia/New Zealand for meetings and some of
my board meetings and exploratory meetings with academics,
government leaders, business leaders, and papal and American
representatives, and to Rome to visit with Vatican congregations
and for Ex Corde meetings.

In this country I visited a good percentage of our Notre
Dame local alumni clubs as a part of fundraising campaigns, to
give invited talks, and to give commencement addresses. All of
this was facilitated by having a University plane and a system of
administration that I could count on when I was missing.

All things being equal, I think it serves the best interests of
a university (or any other major institution) to have leaders who
are not prisoners of their home location or work places. For me,

my travels were opportunities for constant learning, networking, and enhanced visibility. When, for example, as President I contributed to the *U.S. News & World Report* rankings of higher education institutions, I was inclined to rate higher those places that I had seen first-hand or knew their leadership group from our mutual service on the boards of higher education associations.

I had an internal sense for how many boards I could serve on at any one time. When I felt I had made my contribution, I retired from service. The same was true with invited talks and other one-shot involvements.

It is true that some leaders are elected at times of crisis and the initial focus needs to be on the home front and achieving a degree of equanimity and collective confidence. In that sense, I was lucky. But, I was also able to sustain a long presidency because I never grew bored and I was always learning from my peers from outside the institution.

QUESTION 5

Do you have a favorite prayer?

My first answer to this great question might seem like a cop-out, but my favorite prayer is the Mass or the Holy Eucharist. I realize that this is a compilation of prayers, some of which change according to the liturgical seasons. The Eucharist at its simplest is: the introductory rites (which include a greeting, a penitential act, the collect), two readings (including a responsorial psalm and a Gospel), a preparation of the gifts, a prayer over the offerings, the Eucharistic Prayer (which includes a preface, one of the Eucharistic prayers, the consecration, an acclamation, the Lord's Prayer, a sign of peace, the fraction of the bread, the Communion prayer), reception of Communion, the concluding rite, and the dismissal. This could all be recited in 15 or 20 minutes. If hymns are sung or the Gloria and Creed are recited, the Mass will take longer. In addition, Sunday Masses are usually longer and more elaborate and the liturgies of Christmas and Holy Week and special feasts are sometimes considerably longer.

My main point in describing the Mass as my favorite prayer is that long before I became a seminarian and later a priest, I found participation in the Eucharist as the heart of my spirituality. From fifth grade on, I was an altar server. In that role, I was physically close to the priest who celebrated Mass. I also was more attuned to the rhythms of Mass and the significance of the words, especially after Vatican II when the liturgy was celebrated in English.

At Mass, the responses can all be seen as prayers. The reception of the Eucharist, when properly prepared for, can be seen as an act of faith and a reinforcement of our sense of God's presence in our lives.

As a priest, I have celebrated Mass all over the world in famous churches, in monasteries, in the Holy Land, at the Vatican, in Marian shrines, and in all the chapels of Notre Dame (as well as the Basilica, the Parish, and the Grotto). When necessary, I have celebrated on ships, trains, planes, and other forms of transportation and also in various outdoor settings from seashores to mountain tops. As an inveterate traveler, I have celebrated Mass in hotels, airports, train stations, and wherever I might be staying for the night, from hotel rooms to private residences.

I firmly believe that in the Eucharist we receive the very body and blood of the Lord. It is food for the journey and the central act of the Christian community. In that sense, it is the prayer above all prayers.

A fuller answer to the question would be to say that I have many favorite prayers, depending on the circumstances. In the morning, I pray in thanksgiving for another day of life and for all my family and my religious family and those entrusted to my care. Before I preach or give a talk, in imitation of Fr. Ted Hesburgh, I pray "Come Holy Spirit." Other prayers that I like include: the Memorare (a Marian prayer); the Canticle of Brother Sun and Sister Moon and Lord, Make Me an Instrument of Your Peace (both attributed to Saint Francis of Assisi); and the Canticle of Mary (Luke 1:46–55).

Finally, at meals, I usually pray a blessing and, before my seminar classes begin, I read a prayer from various collections I have, some of which have been composed by Notre Dame students from the past.

I am always inspired by the active prayer lives of people I meet in my ministries. They are my models and sources of encouragement.

QUESTION 6

Why are athletes good leaders?
How did athletics help your leadership?

From an early age, I was involved in various sports—baseball, softball, basketball, football, tennis, and a little bit of golf. I grew up near the Turkey Thicket Playground in Northeast Washington D.C., near Catholic University, which was a quite large area with multiple basketball courts and tennis courts, a baseball diamond, three softball fields (the area in between could be used as a football field), a clubhouse, playground equipment for little kids, and plenty of open space where we could invent games of our own, like 3-on-3 touch football, nerfball, and endless 3-on-3 or 5-on-5 half-court basketball games.

I was always tall and rather athletic so I knew a fair amount of success in sports competition at an early age. The Turkey Thicket summer teams won the recreation department championships in both softball and baseball. In fact, we played the championship game at the Washington Senators Major League Park. Our teams at St. Anthony Grade School also did well.

However, it was at Archbishop John Carroll High School that I was part of what became a mythical national champion high school basketball team. We won national tournaments in D.C. and Rhode Island. The Carroll team was also undefeated the following year ending that season (and my senior year) with a 55-game, two-year, undefeated streak against high school competition.

At its best, athletic competition can teach many valuable lessons. For me, one of the most important learning opportunities is

teamwork. In team sports, everyone has a role to play. Opponents are always probing (and scouting) for weak links. On our Carroll basketball team, George Leftwich, our point guard, was our most important player. He got the other four players involved, broke the press, played solid defense, and found his own openings on offense. We had a lot of great players but no selfish egos. I was primarily an outside shooter (before the 3-point shot went into effect). John Thompson (later national championship coach at Georgetown) was our best inside threat. Tom Hoover, at 6'9" and 230 pounds, was a master rebounder and shot blocker. Walt Skinner was our jack-of-all-trades and an excellent defender.

A second lesson revolves around the importance of **preparation**. You eventually learn that the team that practices well usually plays well. In my day, most of our physical fitness drills revolved around wind sprints and calisthenics. Even at Notre Dame, we did almost no weight training or aerobic exercises. Neither were we particularly concerned about diet or dietary supplements. At Notre Dame, during the season, we had access to a training table and pre-game meals, but I never considered any of that to be special.

A third opportunity for learning revolves around the **thrill of victory** and the **agony of defeat**. No matter what sport you compete in, odds are that you will eventually lose, because the other team is better, or luck did not go your way, or due to the home court advantage or bad referees. Whatever the reason, you have to accept the reality of defeat (at least occasionally). But, there is also a proper way to accept victory with due modesty and respect for one's opponents.

There are many other lessons to be learned—the role of **discipline**, the importance of **playing by the rules**, developing the skill to **pace oneself** over a long season, **coping with injuries** of various levels of severity, handling **coaching changes**, using one's **summers** productively, balancing the **academic and the athletics**, and for some, using good judgment in the **recruiting process** from high school to college.

I think I was fortunate in coming along when I did, before the nature of high school and college athletics changed so drastically under the influence of television and the media and with large sums of money being vied for.

Many of the lessons learned from athletics can be derived from other forms of activity—band, theater, student government, the student newspaper, and various forms of not-for-profit service. But, for me, athletic participation was a great preparation for the roles I later played as a leader.

SECTION EIGHT

Examples of Successful Leadership

"Some of the individuals we study simply have _inspiring stories to tell_."

QUESTION 1

Can you give us some examples of excellent leadership that may be less generally known in the broader society?

In this last section, I will provide the contributions of a cross-section of leaders that I have known personally or have learned about through my board service or my reading. I could have included well-known figures like Abraham Lincoln, Nelson Mandela, Mahatma Gandhi, Mother Teresa, Winston Churchill, Queen Elizabeth, Knute Rockne, and a whole host of others. Or, I could have focused on some of the extraordinary people I have worked with at Notre Dame like my two Provosts, Tim O'Meara and Nathan Hatch, my Executive Vice Presidents, Bill Beauchamp and John Affleck-Graves, or some of my Vice Presidents—Bill Sexton, Jim Lyphout, Dave Tyson, John Sejdinaj, Mark Poorman, Scott Malpass, Jim Merz, Jeff Kantor, Bob Gordon, Chris Maziar, Roger Schmitz, Phil Faccenda, and John Jenkins. Or, I could have included some of those overseeing Notre Dame's athletic activities—Dick Rosenthal and Gene Corrigan or many others like the women I have highlighted in Section Four, Question 5, or those who have served on my immediate staff like Roland Smith, Mark Poorman, Lou Nanni, Chandra Johnson, Matt Cullinan, and Father Pete Jarret. I could have included members from the Notre Dame Board of Trustees, of which we have had established leaders from across the country and around the world, so, I was forced to choose just two as representatives of the whole.

I have been teaching a seminar on biography/autobiography for around 20 years. The course is designed around eight books and two movies each semester. The students write a paper on each book or movie and later we discuss it in class. In choosing the material for the class, I have sought to include a wide range of cultural, social, and political contexts. Some of the individuals we study simply have inspiring stories to tell. But others are good examples of leadership in a variety of settings.

I will now share some of the accounts in order to argue that there is no one form of leadership that can bring out the best in others. In fact, it all depends on concrete situations over time and the background, motivation, and skills of the leader.

I have divided my examples of successful leadership into subcategories:

→ EDUCATION

→ COURAGE IN ADVERSITY

→ BUSINESS

→ PROFESSIONAL

→ MENTORSHIP

EDUCATION

CAROLYN WOO

Carolyn Woo was born and raised in Hong Kong. Under the influence of her nanny and the Maryknoll Sisters, she had deeply rooted values at a young age. Despite being born into a family of traditional cultural expectations, her father and other family members supported her desire for an American college education. Carolyn chose Purdue University, where she received financial aid after her first year and went on to a Ph.D. in Strategic Management.

While at Purdue, Carolyn was given a series of administrative responsibilities and was expected to eventually be promoted to a top level of administration. Then, when I was serving as president of Notre Dame, we offered her the Deanship of the Mendoza College of Business. After considerable prayer and consultation, she accepted our offer and went on to lead the undergraduate program to #1 national ranking. She held the position of Dean from 1997 to 2011.

Then, in 2012, she accepted the offer to become Chief Executive Officer and President of Catholic Relief Services, the Catholic Church's vehicle for the provision of short-term and long-term assistance around the world. In this position, Carolyn was transformative at both the strategic and practical levels. She continued at Catholic Relief Services until December of 2016. Throughout her career, she has served on corporate and not-for-profit boards as well as in a variety of Church-related organizations.

Carolyn has published two books providing reflections on her life and work, *Working for a Better World* (2012) and *Rising: Learning from Women's Leadership Experiences in Catholic Ministries* (2022).

Carolyn Woo is an example of faith-filled leadership in multiple settings with an emphasis on mission and strategic planning.

MUFFET MCGRAW

Muffet McGraw was born outside of Philadelphia and attended Saint Joseph University, where she played basketball. For 33 years, she served as head basketball coach at Notre Dame. When she began, the women's program had low levels of success and small spectator groups. In subsequent years, she won 848 games at Notre Dame, including national championships in 2001 and 2018, becoming the sixth women's basketball head coach to win multiple NCAA titles. Her teams also appeared many times in the Sweet Sixteen, Final Four, and and National Championship game". In response to this regular success, the fan base grew exponentially and many of the players went on to compete in the WNBA.

Among the honors that Muffet has received are: Women's Basketball Hall of Fame (2011), Indiana Basketball Hall of Fame (2014), and Naismith Memorial Basketball Hall of Fame (2017). I recommend two of her books, *Expect More: Dare to Stand Up and Stand Out* (2021) and *Courting Success: Muffet McGraw's Formula for Winning* (2003).

Muffet remains active in the South Bend community with involvement in food drives and teaching a Sports Leadership class in the Mendoza College of Business. For several years, she has worked for the ACC Network as a basketball analyst. Muffet McGraw is an example of someone pursuing opportunities for women in spirit and, derivatively, in the broader society.

PETER TANNOCK

Peter Tannock (along with Denis Horgan) solicited us at Notre Dame to assist them in founding the first private Catholic lay-led university in Australian history. We readily agreed and in my first year as President, Tim O'Meara, Bill Beauchamp, and I were among the cofounders of what became the University of Notre Dame Australia. It is a lay-run, Catholic institution with strong ties to the Archdiocese of Perth and Sydney and the Diocese of Broome. Presently, Notre Dame Australia has over 12,000 students on four campuses: one in Fremantle (the original campus), one in Broome, and two in Sydney. It has established itself as a major force in higher education in Australia.

Peter Tannock was educated at Christian Brothers College, the University of Western Australia, and Johns Hopkins University. In his professional career, he served as professor of education and dean of the faculty of educators at the University of Western Australia, as civil servant in the federal government in Canberra, and as an administrator of primary and secondary education programs for the archdiocese of Perth. In 1992, he became the second Vice Chancellor (or President) of the University of Notre Dame Australia. He served in the role until 2008.

Peter has been a visionary leader, a strong administrator, and a respected voice of Catholic education. In his leadership role, he negotiated effectively with both the state and federal government as well as the episcopal leadership of the various dioceses. In my personal experience, he has been one of the most effective leaders I have ever encountered. May other such lay leaders emerge in the next generation.

COURAGE

KAMILA SIDIQI

Kamila Sidiqi is a young female entrepreneur in Afghanistan who, during the first period of despotic rule by the Taliban, developed a dressmaking operation, and later, a school, to help provide income for families suffering from the absence of their usual male providers.

Kamila received her teaching certificate while the Taliban arrived in Kabul. The Taliban sought to completely isolate women under sharia law. With the help of her sister, Kamila soon mastered the art of dressmaking. Despite the risks, she approached the owners of local dress shops and gained their business. As the business activity grew, Kamila opened a tailoring shop to help train other women desperate for a source of financial support. Along the way, Kamila accepted an order for dresses for a wedding according to a tight timeline. When she successfully completed the order, she learned that it was for a Taliban wedding.

In 2001, the Taliban withdrew from Kabul. By 2005, Kamila had become an official in Mercy Corps, a global organization, with a focus on helping women to be self-supporting.

Kamila's story is told in the book *The Dressmaker of Khair Khana* by Gayle Tzemach Lemmon (2011). Kamila is a fine example of leadership in a time of crisis. She displayed both ingenuity and bravery. She used her own education to share opportunity with other women. Condoleezza Rice invited her to visit Washington, D.C. as a woman worthy of emulation.

ERNEST SHACKLETON

In 1914, at the beginning of WWI, Ernest Shackleton received permission from the British government to begin the Imperial Trans-Antarctic Expedition, which intended to traverse Antarctica from west to east by dog sleds. While the South Pole and already had been explored (as had the North Pole), Shackleton considered his proposed journey even more impressive. He purchased a boat and renamed it *Endurance.* He chose 27 seamen for the trek (plus one stowaway). Unfortunately, the expedition had endless bad luck and in November 1915, the ship sank. The crew was able to retrieve three boats, a good number of sled dogs, and essential supplies.

Eventually, Shackleton led the crew on a journey to the open sea, dragging the three boats behind them. They faced consistently severe conditions of ice, wind, and weather. Eventually, they were forced to subsist on a diet of penguins and seals and a few items from the ship. The most important factor for Shackleton was maintaining the crew morale, which entailed understanding the strengths and weaknesses of each sailor. In the spring of 1918, the crew entered the waters in three open boats. After a perilous journey in the most dangerous waters in the world, they made it to Elephant Island, where they established a camp.

In the last crucial stage of the journey, Shackleton and five crewmembers headed for South Georgia Island, the site of a whaling station. Despite the heavy winds and huge waves, they made it to one side of the island. Then, Shackleton and two crewmembers climbed a glacier and slid down to the whaling station on their rear ends. Later, after a period of revival, Shackleton led a whaling ship to Elephant Island where all the other crewmembers were rescued. In the end, Shackleton brought all members of his crew home safely.

Ernest Shackleton is a spectacular example of leadership against the odds. He was valiant, persistent, and confidence inspiring. Few could claim a more amazing result of the role he played. His story is told quite excitingly in Alfred Lansing's book, *Endurance: Shackleton's Incredible Voyage* (1959).

FATHER GREGORY BOYLE

Father Gregory Boyle is a Jesuit priest and has spent most of his priestly ministry in Los Angeles working with gang members. First, he provided a welcome for gang members to his church. Then, he founded a school program for gang members who had been kicked out of public schools. Finally, he founded a not-for-profit called Homeboy Industries.

The new entity provided tattoo removal, psychiatric counseling, and most of all, jobs. Boyle celebrated Mass and visited prisoners in various jails around Los Angeles. Perhaps his most difficult pastoral role was burying the dead (well over a hundred) with dignity and respect.

By putting members of difficult gangs in each other's company in the various moneymaking operations of Homeboy Industries, he attempted to break down barriers. Amidst some of the tragic stories, there were also examples of lives transformed. Boyle worked with "outcasts," following the example of Jesus. In the early 2000s, Boyle came down with leukemia but, since his recovery, he has spent much of his time on the road giving speeches and often bringing along gang members that he has befriended. In 2017, he was awarded the Laetare Medal by Notre Dame.

Father Greg Boyle is a religiously-inspired example of leadership working on the margins of society to provide positive alternatives for young people living within a culture of violence. A description of his work can be found in his book, *Tattoos on the Heart* (2018).

HALEY SCOTT DEMARIA

Haley Scott DeMaria was born and raised in Phoenix, Arizona. She came to Notre Dame in 1991 and was a member of the women's swim team when the bus carrying the team home from a swim meet overturned in a snowstorm. Two of her teammates were killed and a good number were injured. The accident left Haley paralyzed from the waist down. After two emergency surgeries, she was told that she would never walk again. Over the next several months, Haley endured hours of exhausting physical therapy, painful setbacks, and three additional life-threatening surgeries. In October 1993, she returned to Notre Dame's swim team and won her first race back.

Haley graduated in 1995 with a bachelor's degree in history and returned to her alma mater, Xavier College Preparatory in Phoenix, to teach and coach swimming. She later received several national awards. In 2008, she published *What Though the Odds*, which recounts her inspiring journey. Today, married and the mother of two sons, she travels the country to speak to businesses, schools, churches, and civic organizations. In 2012, she was the commencement speaker at Notre Dame.

Haley has become a leader through sharing her story at the national level. It is hoped that soon a major motion picture adaptation of her book will further increase her positive, inspiring influence.

BUSINESS

JIM MORRIS

Jim Morris, who received an honorary degree from Notre Dame in 2005, is a superb example of someone who has been a successful leader in a variety of contexts. A graduate of Indiana University with a master's degree from Butler University, early in his career he served as Chief of Staff for Indianapolis Mayor (later Senator) Richard Lugar. Subsequently, he served for six years (1983–1989) as President of Lilly Endowment, a role in which he oversaw highly effective plans to revitalize downtown Indianapolis. In 1989, he became Chairman and CEO of IWC Resources Corporation and Indianapolis Water Company. In 2002, Morris became Executive Director of the United Nations' World Food Programme. In that position, he oversaw food aid distribution to more than 110 million people each year in about 80 countries. In 2008, he became President of Pacer Sports & Entertainment (home of the NBA franchise).

Jim Morris has been heavily involved in the Board of Trustees of Indiana University, the Boy Scouts of America, the U.S. Olympic Committee, the Riley Hospital Children's Foundation, and the American Red Cross. He has served on several for-profit boards. He has also played a leadership role in his church community. He and his wife, Jackie, have three children and eight grandchildren.

Jim Morris is a leader whose energy and enthusiasm knows no bounds.

PROFESSIONAL

DR. DILAN ELLEGALA

Doctor Dilan Ellegala was born in Sri Lanka but attended medical school at the University of Washington, followed by eight years of research and residency at the University of Virginia and a vascular fellowship at Harvard's Brigham and Women's Hospital. After all that training, he felt in need of a break and decided to go to a small, rural hospital in Tanzania where he hoped to stay for six months.

When he arrived in Tanzania, he soon discovered that there were only three practicing neurosurgeons in a country of 40 million and all three were in the capital city, Dar es Salaam. Although a number of American and European doctors came as short-term volunteers, they tended to assume a spirit of self-importance and were not a solution to the problem of neurosurgery care in the long run.

Dilan did identify some local paramedics who had real ability and he began to explore the possibility of significantly shortening their training and teaching them individually the skills of particular forms of surgery. A man named Emmanuel Mayegga became Dilan's first student. Later, a pediatrician named Carin Hoek from Europe (whom he would later marry), joined him at the hospital. Dilan decided to set up a program to help doctors teach in East Africa with "teach first" as its guiding philosophy. As Mayegga learned brain surgery, he decided to go to medical school. But first, he taught another Tanzanian to do what he did.

After Dilan took a job in South Carolina, he and Carin alternated their residences between Tanzania and the U.S. Eventually, Dilan formed Madaktari Africa with an emphasis on teaching rather than treating. Gradually, one person taught another and neurosurgery became possible in rural Tanzania.

Dilan Ellegala is a fitting example of a world-class doctor who used his ingenuity and entrepreneurial skills to create a not-for-profit organization to localize medical training in a highly specialized field and to foreshorten the period of preparation in order to serve the common good. His story can be found in Tony Bartelme's book, *A Surgeon in the Village* (2017).

JUDGE ANN WILLIAMS

Ann Williams was born in Detroit, Michigan, and received a bachelor's degree from Wayne State University and a master's degree in guidance and counseling from the University of Michigan. After teaching for a period in Detroit public schools, she graduated from the Notre Dame Law School, where she also served as an assistant rector in one of the dormitories.

After graduating from law school, she worked as a law clerk for Judge Robert Sprecher of the U.S. Court of Appeals for the Seventh Circuit. Later, she worked as an Assistant U.S. Attorney in Chicago for nine years, trying major felony cases. In 1983, she became the first chief of the Organized Drug Enforcement Task Force.

Ann has also taught at Northwestern, John Marshall, and Harvard. During her legal career, she taught in more than 150 trial advocacy and deposition programs with the National Institute for Trial Advocacy in the United States, Europe, and Africa.

In 1985, she was confirmed by the U.S. Senate as a district judge for the Northern District of Illinois. In 1999, she was confirmed as the first judge of color on the U.S. Court of Appeals for the Seventh Circuit. In 2017, she assumed senior status on the Court and retired in 2018.

Ann began serving on the Notre Dame Board of Trustees in 1988 and as an Emerita Trustee in 2022.

Ann Williams is an example of distinguished leadership in the field of law both at the prosecutorial and judicial levels and as a faithful graduate of Notre Dame.

JUSTICE ALAN PAGE

Alan Page was born and raised in Canton, Ohio. He attended Notre Dame after being recruited to play football. He graduated in 1967, when he was chosen as a consensus All-American. He was drafted by the Minnesota Vikings, where he earned Pro Bowl honors in his second season. He led the Vikings' "Purple People Eater" defense to four Super Bowl appearances. During his career, he was named to six All-NFL teams, nine straight Pro Bowls, and was the NFL's Most Valuable Player in 1971. After eleven years with the Vikings and three years with the Chicago Bears, he retired in 1981.

While playing professional football, he attended law school at the University of Minnesota and completed his J.D. in 1978. Then, he worked in a law firm before working in the Minnesota Attorney General's Office.

In 1992, Page was elected to the Minnesota Supreme Court and twice more re-elected and became the first African American to serve there. He spent much of his legal career fighting racial bias in the justice system and working to give students of color access to post-secondary education through the Page Education Foundation he founded with his wife, Diane.

In 2004, Justice Page gave the Notre Dame Commencement Address, where he eloquently advocated for the continued quest for racial justice in our country.

Justice Alan Page is a wonderful example of a former Notre Dame athlete who utilized his God-given talents on multiple athletic teams, in a major law firm, and through his membership on the Minnesota Supreme Court to be an advocate for justice and a benefactor of minority children seeking a college education. I recommend reading *All Rise: The Remarkable Journey of Alan Page* (2010).

MENTORSHIP

DONALD KEOUGH

Don Keough was born in Maurice, Iowa and later graduated from Creighton University. He and his wife Marilyn had five children, all of whom attended Norte Dame. In 1950, Don began working for the Coca-Cola Company. Through the years, he rose to progressively higher positions of leadership. In 1981, he began his service as President, Chief Operating Officer, and Director of the company, a position he held until 1993. During his years with Coca-Cola, he traveled around the world and developed a special interest in Ireland, the land of his forebears. In 1993, Don became Chairman of the Board of Allen & Company LLC, a New York investment-banking firm.

My direct involvement with Don came with his role as Chair of the Board of Trustees of Notre Dame, a role he played when I was elected President in 1987. He became a trusted mentor. Don and his family became one of the major donors in the history of the University. This included buildings, professorships, student scholarships, and the Keough-Naughton Institute for Irish Studies.

In 1993, he was awarded the Laetare Medal, Notre Dame's highest honor. He received many honors from higher education institutions and not-for-profit organizations, and in 2007, he was made an honorary Irish citizen by President Mary McAleese.

Don Keough is a great example of a successful business leader who brought expertise and great enthusiasm to multiple institutions, most especially his beloved University of Notre Dame. His Catholic faith was manifest in multiple ways as a devoted lay leader. His book, *The Ten Commandments for Business Failure* (2011) has an interesting twist of advice to young leaders.

SHANNON CULLINAN

Shannon Cullinan lived in Sorin Hall with me as an undergraduate student. He was a fine athlete (won the ND Bookstore Tournament and was voted Mr. Bookstore), received a bachelor of business administration degree (1993), and served during his senior year as a resident assistant. He spent 14 months doing post-graduate work at City Year, a nationally renowned youth service program. He led a team of 12 young adults in urban service initiatives. In 1993, he received his MBA degree from the Wharton School. From 1997 to 2000, he served as Associate Executive Director and Controller of the South Bend Center for the Homeless (where he was a colleague of Lou Nanni).

From 2001 to 2013, he served Notre Dame as Assistant Vice President of University Relations and Public Affairs and Communication. He was then promoted to Assistant Vice President of University Relations from 2005–2009. Later, he became Associate Vice President of Campus Service and Continuance Improvement followed by Associate Vice President of University Relations. Lastly, he became Vice President of Finance from 2016–2019.

In 2019, Shannon Cullinan was elected as the Executive Vice President of Notre Dame, the #3 officer. Today, he oversees the University's operating budget and leads the divisions that operate Campus Safety and Operations, Economic Development, Facility Design and Operation, Finance, Human Resources, Information Technologies, Investment, and University Enterprises and Events.

Shannon is married and is the father of four children. Shannon succeeded John Affleck-Graves as Executive Vice President. John was a strong mentor and guide to Shannon as he excelled at various levels of administration. Shannon is part of a new generation of senior administrators. He is energetic, team-oriented, and very smart with a strong emphasis toward mission.

LOU NANNI

Lou Nanni was born in upstate New York and received his undergraduate degree in government and the Program of Liberal Studies at Notre Dame. After graduation, he spent over two years as a Holy Cross Associate, and among other things, worked with women political prisoners under the Pinochet regime in Santiago, Chile. He then returned to Notre Dame for a master's degree in Peace Studies. In 1988, he moved to Orlando, Florida, where he headed the World Mission Office for the Catholic Diocese.

In 1991, we recruited him to become the Executive Director of the South Bend Center for the Homeless, which, under his leadership, became a model for communities across America in breaking the cycle of homelessness. After eight years in that role, I recruited him to become my Executive Assistant. In 2002, he was elected as a Vice President of the University and soon after became Vice President for University Relations.

Lou and I have been friends from his days of residence in Sorin Hall, where he later served as a resident assistant. I had the privilege of celebrating his wedding to Carmen Lund (also a Notre Dame graduate) and baptizing several of their five children. From early on, it was clear to me that he possessed superb public speaking skills and a native gift for leadership. He has been a transformative agent in all of his roles. As Vice President for University Relations, he has overseen successive fundraising campaigns that achieved success in multi-billions of dollars.

Lou Nanni is a good example of the importance of mentoring in the development of leaders of character and vision. All of us who have served in major leadership roles have an obligation to prepare the next generation.

KEVIN WHITE

Kevin White served as Notre Dame's Athletic Director for 8 years during my time as President. He was educated at St. Joseph College, Central Michigan, and Southern Illinois, where he received a Ph.D. in 1983. Subsequently, he served in Athletic Administration at Loras, Maine, Tulane, and at Arizona State before coming to Notre Dame. He finished his career at Duke. He and his wife Jane have five children, four of whom work in college athletics, and 14 grandchildren.

Kevin has been active in athletic conferences and in the NCAA. He has also created summer courses for the next generation of athletic administrators. Kevin has been a successful fundraiser and a powerful voice on athletic issues.

During his time as Athletic Director at multiple institutions, he mentored many male and female administrators from diverse backgrounds who have gone on to serve as athletic directors at institutions across the country and one to serve as a Conference Commissioner. The Kevin White legacy has been a golden credential for so many who have aspired to become athletic directors themselves.

Kevin is a fine example of a generous mentor who has prepared others for significant careers in intercollegiate athletics.

CONCLUSION

To be elected or appointed to a position of leadership is always an honor and a privilege. It represents a sense of others' confidence in one's capacities to take the organization forward. Inevitably, this entails a newfound sense of responsibility for the common good.

Some leaders come to their new positions with many years of experience and a full portfolio of previous job-related difference-making. This is usually true at the highest levels of government, education, the learned professions, religion, business, the military, and larger not-for-profit organizations. Some of these leaders have advanced degrees appropriate to the roles they have played. Others have learned from experiences or various types of mentoring relationships. This is to suggest that there is no one path to successful leadership preparation. Raw ability, refined interest, enthusiasm, and inner drive also count.

In this book, I have offered a series of reflections on different aspects of leadership in a manner that might be of interest, first, to undergraduate college students but also to their parents, teachers, and others who recognize the importance of this topic. I have drawn heavily on my own experiences as a leader, my reading and reflection, and on some of the amazing leaders that I have met along the way.

In the first section, I discussed what makes a good leader. The characteristics that come to the fore were: a willingness to learn from others, adopting a style that fits one's own personality and talents, the courage to live by one's own convictions even in the midst of criticism, utilizing means of communication that one is compatible with, dealing straightforwardly with differences of opinions, the willingness to take risks when called for, and looking to the future with optimism and hope.

In the second section, I carried the discussion to a higher stage. This entailed taking into account: the shifting nature of the world order, particularly the struggle between democratic and authoritarian forces of government, the persuasiveness of social media, the search for a greater degree of diversity and inclusion, discerning the most reliable sources of information, and recognizing the threats that principled decision-making can elicit.

In sections three and four, I turned to some of my training in moral theology to pursue the analytical insights provided by the Catholic Christian tradition. Thus, leadership could be seen relative to the seven deadly sins, the corporal and spiritual works of mercy, the cardinal virtues, the practice of prayer, the gifts of the Holy Spirit, the impact of demagoguery, the need for compromise and interaction, and the code of loyalty in governance dynamics.

In section five, I centered in on how inspiration and modeling work in leadership formation and practice. This included: which leaders inspired me and/or impressed me, what responsibilities leaders have toward their community, and what impact I hoped to have had in my various roles, particularly as President of Notre Dame.

The next two sections were concerned with practical and everyday aspects of leadership. This included: the role of mentorship, how to hire and inspire good colleagues, dealing with conflict, stress, and tragic loss, setting priorities, bouncing back from failure, and properly engaging colleagues in the decision-making process. I also discussed: the importance of good scheduling, a proper sense of humor, and how my athletic background helped prepare me for the vigor of the responsibilities that I have borne.

In the final section, I provided examples of people who have impressed me with their outstanding leadership skills, some from my years at Notre Dame and some from other involvements and my general reading.

My 18 years as President of Notre Dame were a real gift and a special time. I was able to be involved in a collaborative effort as a Holy Cross priest to help further develop a great Catholic university with all that it involved. I saw Notre Dame become more inclusive and more diverse and be a better neighbor to the surrounding communities, become more intentional in pursuing excellence in teaching and research at all academic levels, inspire great generosity from a host of committed benefactors, become more structurally international, expand the physical side of the campus according to a set of institutional priorities, continue to be a model of athletic success with integrity of purpose, have balanced budgets and productive investments, and be faithful to our mission and character as a Catholic university with a continued vital role for the Holy Cross community.

I received from Father Ted Hesburgh responsibility for a university that had a quite positive momentum, great loyalty from its graduates, a distinguished faculty, outstanding students, a talented and committed central administration, and impressive financial realities. Unlike many new presidents, I did not have to make drastic cuts or lay off groups of people. As a result, my administrative colleagues and I could focus on positive growth over time in each of our defined areas of involvement. In fact, the good that we were able to achieve was rooted in a collective effort that I was only partially responsible for.

I enjoyed being President of Notre Dame. Not every moment was sheer bliss, but in my 18 years of service, I traveled the world and the country, met popes and heads of state, encountered some of the richest and poorest communities, celebrated Mass in elegant churches and in humble chapels, and served on boards with an impressive cross-section of leaders from every area of life. I also continued to reside in Sorin Hall and teach first-year seminar. Who could ask for anything better?

I say to you students, members of the next generation of leaders in every walk of life, I am confident that you can be real difference-makers, agents of transformation, wherever

God may lead you. If you give priority to people above all, your impact as a leader will be profound. Someday, I hope you can look back in a spirit of thanksgiving and gratefulness, as I have, for the opportunities you have been given and the sense of satisfaction that best characterizes all that has been.

—Monk Malloy

ABOUT MONK

Edward A. "Monk" Malloy, C.S.C., is president emeritus of the University of Notre Dame, where he served from 1987 to 2005 as the sixteenth president and where he is currently a professor of theology. He serves on the board of directors of several universities and national organizations and is the recipient of 25 honorary degrees. He has published 12 books, including a 3-volume memoir, and most recently *Monk's Musings* and *Monk's Notre Dame: People, Places, and Events.*

Professor Malloy in the classroom; Photo by Matt Cashore

TAKING
ON Constitutional Rights
in Conflict
THE
PRESS

Beyond a Reasonable Doubt:
Inside the American Jury System

Call the Final Witness:
The People v. Darrell R. Mathes as Seen by the Eleventh Juror

TAKING ON THE PRESS

Constitutional Rights in Conflict

MELVYN BERNARD ZERMAN

Thomas Y. Crowell   New York

The author would like to extend deep appreciation to Peter Nadler, Michael Thomas, Leonore Zerman, and, especially, Wayne Stanton.

Picture credits: AP/Wide World Photos: pages 40, 46, 59, 79, 116, 117, 128, 141, 169. Cornell Capa, Life Magazine, © 1955 Time Inc. and Philadelphia Daily News: page 26. The Granger Collection, New York: page 15. Copyright © 1971, 1976 by the New York Times Co., reprinted by permission: pages 101, 160. Copyright © 1979 by Richard Pryor for an advertisement © 1979 Gannett Co. Inc.: page 151. Stanford Daily News: page 67. UPI/Bettmann Newsphotos: pages 163, 176. © 1978, 1979, Washington Star, reprinted with permission of Universal Press Syndicate, all rights reserved: pages 69, 183.

Library of Congress Cataloging-in-Publication Data
Zerman, Melvyn Bernard.
    Taking on the press.

    Summary: The conflict between the first amendment
rights of the press and the rights of individuals and
the government is explored through actual, well-known
cases.
    1. Freedom of the press—United States—Juvenile
literature. 2. Press law—United States—Juvenile
literature. [1. Freedom of the press—Cases. 2. Press
law. 3. Journalistic ethics] I. Title.
KF4774.Z9Z47 1986   342.73'0853   85-47896
ISBN 0-690-04301-5   347.302853
ISBN 0-690-04302-3 (lib. bdg.)

To the memory of my wife

Contents

Author's Note

About two hundred pages from here I remark on how difficult it is to maintain complete objectivity in reporting. Since I most certainly do not exempt myself from this observation, it seems only proper that I prepare the reader for my bias at the outset, before evidence of it comes creeping into the text.

I am usually inclined to stand at the side of the press when it opposes efforts to punish or restrain or—worst of all—silence those who would report or comment on the news. Note that I say "usually," not "always," for I do believe that the press must operate within boundaries of decency, compassion, and responsibility. Because these boundaries sometimes are clouded over and hard to define, and because on occasion they are unquestionably breached, my sympathy for the press has been known to fade into ambivalence or even turn into outright hostility.

But such lapses in allegiance are rare, and I confess my bias so that readers, aware of it, can better make up their own minds about the controversies that churn through the pages ahead. Feel free to question and doubt and disagree. Feeling free to criticize is really what this book is all about.

Melvyn Bernard Zerman
November 1985

Foreword

This is a book about one of the wonders of history. It is about a treasure given to you and to me by our forefathers and -mothers.

The First Amendment to the Constitution of the United States has only forty-five words. They are forty-five words that changed the world and are an important part of what makes our still young country a new thing in history. When Abraham Lincoln called America "the last best hope of mankind," he had the First Amendment—its content and meaning—in mind.

These forty-five words guarantee to you, and to every other American, freedom of religion, freedom of the press, and the right to assemble peaceably. In years past these words have been interpreted by the Supreme Court of the United States to include also certain rights of privacy, freedom of association (such as the right to join politically motivated organizations), and the right of expression through various forms of what has been termed "symbolic speech" (such as peaceful picketing and the wearing of armbands or buttons that promote causes or political ideas).

In all, this one brief paragraph, Article I of the Bill of Rights, assures us of the most vital ingredients of personal and political freedom. They are rare and precious. Few people have them. No citizen of any nation ever had them guaranteed before our country was founded. Many men and women of our nation-family died to win them, and since then many more have died to protect them. This we must never forget.

Begin gearing this into your mind and heart by reviewing what the Constitution actually says. That's the first order of business: Read the Constitution. Know it. Don't be one of the many Americans who talk about the Constitution without knowing exactly what is in it.

Then, in reading this book, concerned as it is with freedom of the press, you will understand some of the ways in which the Constitution is applied in daily life. These ways are complex and sometimes controversial, but they prove that the Constitution remains a living document—as well as a powerful bulwark protecting the freedoms we all enjoy.

DAN RATHER
New York City
March 12, 1986

PART ONE

High Schools and History

1.
The Challenge
of Charlie Quarterman

It came as no great surprise when Charlie Quarterman was slapped with his second suspension. What had shocked many of his classmates at Pine Forest was that after being suspended for ten days in November, and while he remained on probation, Charlie had once again recklessly dared to pass out copies of the underground newspaper to which he was the main contributor. Hadn't he learned his lesson? Didn't he realize he was courting expulsion by concluding his lead article with this statement, printed entirely in capital letters?

WE HAVE TO BE PREPARED TO FIGHT IN THE HALLS AND IN THE CLASSROOMS, OUT IN THE STREETS BECAUSE THE SCHOOLS BELONG TO THE PEOPLE. IF WE HAVE TO—WE'LL BURN THE BUILDINGS OF OUR SCHOOLS DOWN TO SHOW THE PIGS THAT WE WANT AN EDUCATION THAT WON'T BRAIN-

WASH US INTO BEING RACIST. AND THAT WE WANT AN EDU-
CATION THAT WILL TEACH US THE REAL TRUTH ABOUT
THINGS WE NEED TO KNOW, SO WE CAN BETTER SERVE THE
PEOPLE! ! ! !

Charlie's battle cry was written and circulated in January 1971,
a time when fierce, widespread, and deeply entrenched opposition
to the Vietnam War had made young people far more fearless in
their challenge to authority than they ever had been before (or,
probably, have been since). Nevertheless, Charlie's courage in
passing out his paper on school grounds bordered on, or perhaps
even invaded, the foolhardy. Pine Forest wasn't, after all, Berkeley
or Columbia or Kent State, scenes of some of the most inflamed
and highly publicized campus uprisings of the recent past. While
they were universities, Pine Forest was just a small-town high
school in North Carolina. And Charlie Quarterman was no more
than a tenth grader.

So when the principal suspended him again, the response "in
the halls and in the classroom [and] out in the streets" was not
a great surge of sympathy and support for Charlie the victim but,
rather, a feeling that Charlie the rebel was lucky to have gotten
off so lightly. The suspension was no big deal; he'd be back in
school in ten days and wouldn't miss anything he couldn't easily
catch up on—if, in fact, he didn't know it all already.

But Charlie, with his mother's determined encouragement, saw
this latest punishment in a rather different way, and he was about
to give everyone another jolt. Faced with his second suspension,
Charlie Quarterman answered his own call to arms—this time he
decided to fight back, in the courts of the United States.

Fortunately for Charlie, fighting back did not mean having to
defend his threat to burn down the school or to justify his calling

school authorities "pigs." For the curious fact was that the *content* of his newspaper had not been made the ground for his suspension. No, Charlie was being disciplined simply for *distributing* the paper. In doing so, it was charged, he had violated one regulation of Pine Forest High School, namely General School Rule 7, and had thereby triggered another, Rule 8:

7. Each pupil is specifically prohibited from distributing, while under school jurisdiction, any advertisements, pamphlets, printed material, written material . . . without the express permission of the principal of the school.

8. All students shall be subject to suspension or dismissal . . . who willfully and persistently violate the rules of the school.

Think for a moment about Rules 7 and 8 and you realize that Charlie could have been suspended for passing out invitations to a Valentine's Day party or announcements of a garage sale had he done so in the corridors of the school without the prior approval of the principal. However potentially disruptive or inflammatory the articles in his paper may have been, they were ignored in the official notice of Charlie's suspension. No doubt the school authorities believed their case against him was so strong—who could possibly deny that Charlie had defied Rule 7?—that it seemed unnecessary, and perhaps too controversial, to attack him for the articles themselves.

But if Charlie's paper was not to be the battleground, Rule 7 was. Charlie's lawyer saw to that. In their clash with Pine Forest, Charlie and his mother were represented by attorney James E. Keenan. From the start, Keenan argued that Rule 7 violated Charlie's constitutional rights of freedom of speech and of the press, and therefore Rule 8 could not legally be enforced. *Quarter-*

man v. Byrd, as the case came to be known (Byrd was the superintendent of schools of Cumberland County, N.C.), was first heard in the United States district court, with disappointing results for Charlie. The chief judge denied Keenan's request that the school be prevented, at least temporarily, from taking any disciplinary action against his client. Keenan immediately carried his motion to the next highest level, and there a circuit judge granted Charlie a reprieve: He could not be suspended until the United States court of appeals had ruled on the merits of his case. Implicit in this decision was the judge's recognition that Keenan was raising important constitutional issues and that there was more at stake here than one schoolboy's missing ten days of classes.

For all practical purposes, the decision of the circuit judge meant that Charlie had won. The wheels of justice grind slowly. Both sides had to present their arguments to the court of appeals, and those judges take their time, first in calling up a case and then in reaching a decision. Winter turned into spring and spring brought the school year to a close, but there were no further developments in the case of *Quarterman v. Byrd*. Since all the while Charlie continued to attend classes, he had already achieved a semblance of victory.

But Charlie and his lawyer were after a bigger prize and, again to the surprise of many, they got it. Their case was argued for the last time in early October. Almost two months later, on the day after Thanksgiving, 1971, the court of appeals announced its decision: Rule 7 was blatantly unconstitutional and Charlie's suspension, although never enforced, was to be stricken from his school records.

It's essential that we understand the real meaning of Charlie Quarterman's victory. Did the court of appeals reaffirm his right to threaten to burn down the school? Does the Constitution, as interpreted by this court, permit students to publicly call their teachers "pigs"? Were the Pine Forest authorities in violation of the First Amendment in trying to control the newspapers distributed on school premises during school hours? Although the court's ruling voided Charlie's suspension, it answered none of these questions in the affirmative. On the contrary, if you were to read the full text of the court's decision, you would find that it quite deliberately refrains from passing judgment on the content of Charlie's newspaper and equally deliberately upholds a school's right to "exercise prior restraint"—that is, to ban—printed material that can reasonably be considered a potential cause of disruption of school activities. Furthermore, the court made a special point of noting the difference that exists between the First Amendment rights of adults and those of children and, indeed, between those of college and secondary-school students. Declaring, in effect, that the younger the citizen, the more limited were his rights, the court certainly gave no seal of approval to Charlie's paper. All that the judges did—and, in fact, all that Charlie's lawyer had asked them to do—was to strike down Rule 7.

This was declared "constitutionally defective" because it was seen as too broad, too vague, and too final. Rule 7 amounted to *improper* prior restraint in that it contained no guidelines for the principal to follow in determining whether to grant or deny permission to pass out written material on school grounds. Moreover, school regulations provided no "procedural safeguards" for reconsideration of a decision to ban once that decision had been made. If Rule 7 had spelled out in some detail the kinds of publications students would not be permitted to distribute, and if Pine Forest had set up a review board to which a student could appeal a ban that was handed down by the principal alone, then Charlie's case and its resolution could have been quite different.

As it was, Charlie Quarterman became a hero at Pine Forest and, at the very least, a long footnote in shelves of books on constitutional law. His is considered a landmark case in that the decision in *Quarterman v. Byrd* defines what schools can and cannot do in limiting the free press rights of students so as to maintain discipline and order in the conduct of school affairs. The freedom that Charlie enjoyed was *not* total, said the court—he could have been legitimately prevented from distributing his paper, but only if certain valuable safeguards had been set in place. The court of appeals thus recognized that both students and school authorities have rights and that such rights may on occasion come into head-on conflict. Its ruling attempts to strike a proper balance between those rights, to offer *some* protection to both sides, total protection to neither.

In this book we will be looking at other cases where the right of freedom of the press when exercised without any restraint seems to endanger or even deny another kind of right, one which may be considered equally precious or perhaps, by some, even more precious. To illustrate: Does freedom of the press give a newspaper the right to print lies about a television superstar? Does it give a magazine the right to shatter the privacy of an ordinary family that now wants only to forget a terrifying crisis it survived years ago? Does it give a reporter the right to withhold evidence that a man on trial for murder claims is crucial to his defense? Does it give anyone the right to jeopardize the security of our country? These are some of the questions we will be asking—and trying to answer—in the chapters that follow. They stem from legal contests that are, for the most part, much more famous than *Quarterman v. Byrd*, involving as they do celebrities, influential publications, even the Presidency of the United States. But though such controversies may have rated more and larger headlines, they in no way dim the importance of Charlie's accomplishment. They are all included here because they serve to illuminate the boundaries of freedom of the press. As we will see, some of these cases produced decisions that extended those boundaries, others did not. In none of them did a single individual challenge authority quite as boldly as Charlie Quarterman, the tenth grader who strengthened freedom not only for himself and his fellow students but also for generations of students to come.

2.
"The Best Cause...
the Cause of Liberty"

Rule 7 of Pine Forest High School, which the court of appeals judged "constitutionally defective," was like a crack in a wall that can be traced to the building's foundation. From the late Middle Ages to the late twentieth century, from supreme monarchs to school superintendents, there is a long, if not glorious, tradition of governmental efforts to restrict the flow of the printed word. In fact, it wasn't too long after the very invention of the printing press that men of power recognized its potential for mischief—that is, disruption, however mild or modest, of the existing order—and first began to assert their heavy-handed control.

Movable type came to England in 1476, and within a few years the Crown, like the Pine Forest school authorities, had decreed that nothing could be printed or distributed without prior approval, in the form of a license, from the king's officials. For about two hundred years, until 1695, the licensing requirement remained in effect, and while it was certainly ignored from time to time, the authors and printers who brought out unauthorized books and pamphlets risked their limbs and their lives by doing so. In 1579 a fiery critic of Queen Elizabeth I had his right hand chopped off at the wrist, and a quarter of a century later a printer was hanged, drawn, and quartered for publishing a book that questioned the right of James I to follow Elizabeth I on the English throne.

Press censorship is but one particularly malignant outgrowth of the thought control that absolute rulers have always tried to impose upon their subjects. In fifteenth-century Britain it was treasonable and punishable by execution just to poke fun at the king or even to think about his death. Talk or imagining of this kind smacked of sedition—incitement to rebellion against the Crown—and as such was of necessity outlawed. But press sedition posed an especially dangerous threat in that the printed word, unlike the spoken one, does not disappear in the air, perhaps to be remembered and passed on, perhaps not. A printed statement retains the power to influence people for as long as it may continue to be read, and once something has been published it is exceedingly difficult to confiscate and destroy all the copies that have been put in circulation. Thus, on the heels of the licensing laws came a royal proclamation decreeing that all those caught with seditious books in their possession "shall without delay be executed," as would those who found such books and failed to burn them at once, before others could be exposed to their ideas.

Even when fear of the printed word eased and prior censorship in the form of licensing was abandoned—which came with the decline of the monarchy and the rise of Parliament—the British press stood hostage to the laws of sedition. Authors and printers were subject to punishment, including execution, if after publication their work was found to be offensive to the government—that is, the political party in power.

The ways of the English became the ways of the first colonists in prerevolutionary America. Searching for tolerance themselves, they were not inclined to extend it to those whose views differed from their own. The first public book burning in the New World took place in Boston as early as 1650: Left in ashes was a religious work that challenged the prevailing orthodoxy. And the colonies' very first newspaper, *Publick Occurrences Both Foreign and Domestick,* was banned almost at birth. It was suppressed after only one issue, and its publisher, Benjamin Harris, was condemned for printing without a license. Although this act of censorship took place in 1690, Massachusetts had imposed the need for prior approval long before, in 1662, and by prosecuting Harris, it demonstrated the severity of the licensing act and succeeded in discouraging anyone else from starting a newspaper until a full decade later.

Clearly, then, while today we tend to think of a free press as an inherent and unassailable part of the American heritage, in truth it was a cause that people had to do battle for, which means that, as in any fight for the establishment of a principle, inevitably heroes emerged. Our first great champions of a free press were John Peter Zenger and Andrew Hamilton. Zenger, an immigrant from Germany, arrived in America in 1710, at the age of thirteen. For eight years he learned his trade as an apprentice to a printer and then eventually set up his own printing business in the city of New York in 1726. From his little shop seven years later, on November 5, 1733, came the first issue of the *New-York Weekly Journal.* While it may have called itself a newspaper, it was not one by today's standards, for it did not even pretend to provide its readers with news. The *Journal* was strictly an organ of opinion, offering to Zenger and his writers an ideal forum for attacking the policies of the royal governor of New York, one William Cosby. That gentleman—arrogant, obstinate, hated, and, of course, singularly powerful—endured Zenger's stinging assaults for just about one year. In issue after issue, the *Journal* accused him of being incompetent and discriminatory in his administration of the colony, lax in preparing defenses against the marauding French, and, perhaps most serious, neglectful of the rights and property of the people. It charged Cosby with endangering and ignoring the honored democratic tradition of trial by jury and it denounced him for his involvement in various fraudulent elections.

Early in November 1734, Cosby's patience and silence cracked. He issued a proclamation condemning the "scandalous, virulent, false, and seditious reflections" that had been printed in the *Journal* and demanding the immediate arrest of their author. John Peter Zenger was taken into custody on November 17, charged with seditious libel, and remanded to prison. He vowed to continue to edit his newspaper "thro' the Hole of the Door of the Prison," and for nine months, virtually without interruption— only one issue was skipped—the *Journal* made its defiant weekly appearance. That this was due more to the efforts of Zenger's wife and associates than to the labors of the prisoner in his cell was cold comfort to Governor Cosby. At the very least he had expected that the incarceration of Zenger would bring him some relief from the unremitting assault of the *Journal.* But, like others after him, Cosby learned that once the seeds of democracy have been planted and have put down roots, a newspaper, however brash and opinionated, takes on an insistent life of its own and cannot easily be stilled.

On a sweltering August day in 1735 the Zenger case finally came to trial. Appearing for the defense was one of the most brilliant, eloquent, and respected lawyers in the colonies, Andrew Hamilton of Philadelphia. Almost eighty years old, he made the trip up to

New York that hot, dusty summer because he saw in the Zenger case an issue that was truly crucial to the cause of liberty in the new land, indeed so crucial that, as eminent and acclaimed as he was, he would accept no fee for his services.

Weak and infirm, he hobbled into a courtroom where his client seemed doomed from the start. Today in the United States the most common defense against the charge of libel is the truth of the offending statement. No matter how severely a victim's reputation may be sullied by a derogatory or critical comment, if that comment is proved to be accurate, the person making it has committed no offense in the eyes of the law. But truth as a defense against libel did not exist in the colonies in 1735. Quite the contrary with regard to seditious libel. For if seditious libel was true, it was all the more likely to breed suspicion of government and to rouse the people to rebellion.

The attorney general who prosecuted the case argued quite correctly that he had only to prove to the jury that Zenger had printed the offending statements; the *court* would then decide whether they were actually seditious libel. Imagine his perplexity— and the surprise of everyone else in the courtroom—when Hamilton in his opening statement admitted that Zenger had indeed printed the newspapers in which the articles in question had appeared. But from this apparent confession of his client's guilt, Hamilton immediately pressed on to construct a new line of defense. The criminal act, he declared, could *not* be defined as the mere publication of a statement. "By no means," Hamilton continued. "It is not the bare printing and publishing of a paper that will make it a libel: the words themselves must be libelous, that is, false, scandalous, and seditious, else my client is not guilty."

Here was strategy that, then and now, astonishes in its audacity. Hamilton was claiming the law to be something that it clearly was

Andrew Hamilton, right, with arm upraised, speaks in defense of John Peter Zenger (nineteenth-century wood engraving).

not and it took the court no time to set the record straight. Presiding was Chief Justice James De Lancey, an appointee and supporter of the Cosby administration, and he interrupted Hamilton at once to remind him that he could not "give the truth of a libel in evidence."

Bowing to the chief justice, Hamilton thanked him and proceeded to disregard the judicial warning. If he was to be denied the opportunity to prove the truth of the offending articles, he would simply look to others for that proof. He found his witnesses in the box before him and, his voice and his courage rising, he dared to challenge them: "Then, gentlemen of the jury, it is to you we must now appeal. . . . You are citizens of New York [and the facts] are notoriously known to be truc. . . . Therefore, in your justice lies our safety."

Yet again De Lancey broke in. "No, Mr. Hamilton," he admonished. It was *not* for this jury to judge whether Zenger's articles were true or false. De Lancey and his judicial colleagues would decide that. The jury was to determine only whether the defendant had published the critical articles.

The running battle continued as Hamilton, once more with the utmost politeness, begged to disagree. The jury, he contended, did indeed have "the right, beyond all dispute," to judge both the fact—had Zenger published the articles?—and the law—were those articles truly seditious libel? While appearing to be irritatingly obtuse, or willfully unhearing, Hamilton was, of course, neither. In his stubborn refusal to accept and abide by the chief justice's repeated admonitions, Hamilton was attempting nothing less than the creation of a new law.

He was well aware of the existing statutes—he needed neither judge nor prosecutor to explain them to him—and he also knew that measured against those statutes his client had not even a prayer of acquittal. What the immigrant printer needed was a miracle, and it was to achieve that miracle that Hamilton journeyed to New York City that long-ago summer. His aim was to persuade the jury to see Zenger in a light that was then no more than a star on the horizon and, by doing so, to advance a principle that would not be formally recognized until more than half a century, and a great rebellion, had passed into history.

And so in his concluding statement to the jury, Hamilton persisted in the course he had undertaken—now not only deaf to De Lancey's words but also seemingly blind to his very presence and to the presence of the other justices and the prosecutor as well. "As you see," he began, "I labor under the weight of many years, and am borne down with great infirmities of body; yet old and weak as I am, I should think it my duty, if required, to go to the utmost part of the land where my service could be of any use in assisting to quench the flame of prosecutions by the Government to deprive a People of the remonstrating (and complaining too) [against] the arbitrary attempts of men in power. Men who injure and oppress the people under their administration; provoke them to cry out and complain; and then make that very complaint the foundation for new oppressions and prosecutions . . . The question before the court and you gentlemen of the jury is not of small nor private concern. It is not the cause of the poor printer, nor of New York alone, which you are now trying. No! It may in its consequence affect every free man that lives under a British government on the main of America. It is the best cause. It is the cause of Liberty."

Juries have long been known, under certain circumstances, to disregard the law they have been sworn to uphold. This is an action neither frequent nor lightly taken: Unable to escape the fact that a defendant is, in a narrow sense, guilty as charged, the jurors nevertheless vote to acquit. Called *jury nullification*, it happens when the law at issue is an unpopular one—Prohibition and minor antigambling statutes are examples—or, more important, when a person who has clearly violated the law is considered to have been acting in dedication to a higher principle—war protesters who deface or destroy government property, young men who refuse to register for the draft. It was to this inclination and this ability to see beyond the law to a nobler cause that Hamilton was appealing as he addressed the jury for the last time. The jurors heard and responded. Embracing those powers that only Andrew Hamilton had conferred upon them, they found John Peter Zenger not guilty.

What a jubilant outcry greeted the verdict! Spectators jumped to their feet in that small, hot, crowded courtroom and raised their voices in cheers so loud they shook the walls. A monumental legal precedent had just been established, but it was not this that prompted such a wild reaction. No, if the citizens of New York rejoiced in Zenger's acquittal it was because they saw in it a welcome and long overdue repudiation of the despised royal governor. And, in fact, elation was so intense and widespread that Chief Justice De Lancey did not dare set aside the verdict. Legally, he had full power to do so, but the Cosby administration could not—and would not—risk further inflaming public opinion.

Abroad, where the political situation in New York was of far less consequence, the Zenger trial nonetheless did not go unnoticed. Indeed, the implications of the verdict may have been more keenly appreciated in England than in the colonies. When a record of the trial eventually appeared in London, taken from Zenger's own account as published in his *Journal* the following year, the editor who chose to print it observed that the jury's decision had "made a great noise in the world."

Noise there was, but it took many decades for the clamor to produce hard results. The legal precepts that Hamilton had advanced—truth as a defense against seditious libel, the power of a jury to decide whether material is libelous—were soon recognized as basic goals throughout the colonies, but they remained no more than that until long after the Revolution had been fought and won. The commonwealth of Pennsylvania, Andrew Hamilton's home state, was the first to embody the precepts in the constitution it adopted in 1790. In New York, where Hamilton had championed these principles so eloquently and so effectively, it took seventy years for them to pass into law, in the state constitution of 1805.

But the larger meaning of the Zenger case had burst upon the New World long before. The verdict was a dramatic, fearless, and irresistible proclamation that the people demanded and would have the right to criticize their government. To Gouverneur Morris, one of the civilian leaders of the Revolution, Zenger's acquittal was the first blow struck in the cause of independence, "the morning star," he called it, "of that liberty which revolutionized America." Here was an event that fixed in the public mind, indelibly and forever, the idea that freedom of thought and expression is an inherent right. To achieve that right much had to be done—independence declared, a rebellion waged, a Constitution adopted, and, finally, a Bill of Rights ratified. In all, fifty-seven turbulent years stretched between the arrest of John Peter Zenger and the formal acceptance of the First Amendment, which guarantees that "Congress shall make no law . . . abridging the freedom of speech, or of the press." Fifty-seven years, more than half a century—today that's considerably less than the average lifetime, and in the context of history it's no more than an instant. But, of course, the struggle to achieve these freedoms began long, long before Zenger printed the first issue of his newspaper, and the vigilance needed to preserve them is, it has been said, eternal.

PART TWO

In Conflict
with Individuals

3.
The Right to Be Let Alone

There are some, former Supreme Court justices among them, who believe that the constitutional guarantee of a free press is complete and absolute, that, as Virginian George Hay once wrote, "If the words 'freedom of the press' have any meaning at all, they mean a total exemption from any law making any publication whatever criminal." Carried to its logical conclusion, such an interpretation of the First Amendment would allow newspapers and magazines to print *anything*—the most scurrilous gossip, smut, lies, errors; anything—even if it was malicious or destructive in intent, even if it was known to be false.

The absolutists who maintain that the press should enjoy freedom without exception or qualification have, of course, never been in a majority—neither on the Supreme Court, where if theirs were to be the commanding position it would profoundly expand the power of the press, nor among the overall population. Most

Americans would surely agree—in a kind of knee-jerk reflex action, perhaps—that, in general, freedom of the press is one of our most cherished and essential rights. But when questioned more specifically about the kinds of material that should be allowed to appear in newspapers and magazines, they immediately and quite overwhelmingly reveal a conviction that the press should operate under all sorts of restraints. As we shall see, the need for these restraints comes from a whole constellation of reasons, but one among them, which dates back for centuries, is close to being supreme.

In a recent poll a mighty 78 percent of the respondents were opposed to disclosure in the press of the details of a public official's romantic involvements, 71 percent felt the names of people on welfare should not be publicized, and 51 percent did not want the names of youthful lawbreakers (under sixteen) to be published. Clearly, in these instances a majority believed that the public's right to know is subordinate to an individual's right to privacy, that the harm certain information, were it to be aired, would inflict on the subject far outweighs whatever benefit it might offer to the rest of us.

We see, then, that high among the rights that are likely to be in conflict with the interests of a free press is the right to privacy or, "simply stated," to quote former Supreme Court Justice Abe Fortas, "the right to be let alone; to live one's life as one chooses, free from assault, intrusion, or invasion except as they may be justified by the clear needs of community living under a government of law." The right of privacy is nowhere mentioned in the Constitution, but it is recognized in the laws of at least thirty-five states. Such laws are distinct from laws dealing with defamation of character, which we will consider in the next chapter, but like them, laws acknowledging a right to privacy provide a legal remedy—that is, the right to sue—for people who feel that the publication of an article is irresponsible and injurious to them, usually serving no purpose except to help sell copies of the offending newspaper or magazine.

In September 1952, three convicts broke out of the penitentiary in Lewisburg, Pennsylvania, escaped to suburban Philadelphia, and there, in the town of Whitemarsh, took over the home of James Hill and his family. Here was invasion of privacy of the most horrifying kind. BANK ROBBERS HOLD FAMILY IN WHITE-MARSH PRISONERS proclaimed a newspaper headline of the time. And for nineteen fearful hours, Hill, his wife, and five children were held hostage as the armed convicts hid out from an ever-intensifying manhunt. After the three had departed, leaving the family unharmed, Hill stressed to reporters that the convicts had treated them all courteously, had not molested them in any way, and had not engaged in any acts of violence. Violence, however, was to be their destiny all the same; later the escapees were trapped by police and, in a storm of bullets, one was captured and the other two were shot dead.

For the Hill family the experience was a nightmare that, understandably, they wanted to put out of their minds. Soon afterward they sold their house in Whitemarsh and moved to Connecticut, and James Hill, once the initial interviews were behind him, resisted all the continuing efforts of magazine and television people to restore the family to the public eye. He had no intention of making them relive their ordeal, for readers and viewers everywhere, just one more time.

Imagine, then, the shock the Hill household received when, two and a half years later, they found themselves the subject of a major story in *Life* magazine. There it was, in a February 1955 issue:

DAILY NEWS 7 STAR

BANK ROBBERS HOLD FAMILY IN WHITEMARSH PRISONERS;

TRUE CRIME INSPIRES TENSE PLAY

The ordeal of a family trapped by convicts gives Broadway a new thriller, 'The Desperate Hours'

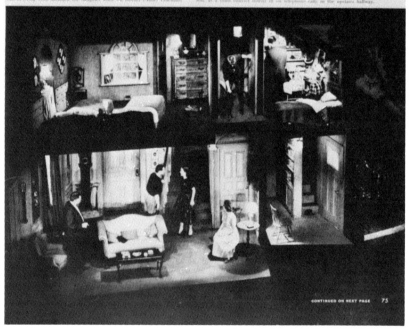

CONTINUED ON NEXT PAGE 75

The first page of the Life *photo story that led to James Hill's invasion-of-privacy suit.*

Under the title "True Crime Inspires Tense Play," ran the line: "The ordeal of a family trapped by convicts gives Broadway a new thriller, *The Desperate Hours*." The article itself began, "Three years ago Americans all over the country read about the desperate ordeal of the James Hill family, who were held prisoners in their home. . . ." It went on to describe the play, *The Desperate Hours*, which author Joseph Hayes had adapted from his own best-selling novel of the same name, and it concluded, "LIFE photographed the play during its Philadelphia tryout, transporting some of the actors to the actual house where the Hills were besieged. On the next page scenes from the play are re-enacted on the site of the crime." There followed seven photographs of crucial moments in the play—one of the young son being "roughed up" by a "brutish convict," another of the "daring daughter" biting the hand of a convict to make him drop his gun, and a third of the father tossing his gun through the door after a "brave try" to save his family has failed (quotations are from the captions under the photos).

James Hill sued. In a legal action officially known as *Time, Inc. v. Hill* (*Life* is owned by Time, Inc.) but later to be called more familiarly the *Desperate Hours* Case, Hill demanded damages on the basis that the *Life* article was intended to, and did, give the impression that the play mirrored his family's experience, "which, to the knowledge of the defendant . . . was false and untrue." Earlier we noted how Hill, in his press interviews, had emphasized that the convicts had been polite and nonviolent throughout their nineteen-hour siege. Determined then to disabuse anyone of the notion that his family's ordeal, however frightening, had been marked by brutality, false heroics, or daring deeds, Hill was equally determined now to gain satisfaction from those who had not only thrust him and his family back into an unwelcome spotlight but had also filtered that light through garish and disfiguring colors.

When Charlie Quarterman went to court, he lost the first battle but won the war. For James Hill just the reverse proved true. He brought suit in New York State, the corporate home of Time, Inc., citing the right of privacy section of the New York Civil Rights Law, which states that any person whose name is used "for advertising purposes or for the purpose of trade" without his written consent may sue and recover damages for any injuries sustained, provided that the defendant "knowingly used such person's name . . . in such manner."

At the trial, before the state supreme court, Hill's attorney argued that *Life* had printed the *Desperate Hours* story knowing that the play was not an accurate reflection of the Hill family's experience. The defense's position was that the article was "a subject of legitimate news interest," "a subject of general interest and of value to the public" at the time of publication, and that it was "published in good faith without any malice whatsoever. . . ." A strong legal argument, perhaps, but it left the jurors unmoved. Upon deliberation, they awarded James Hill a total of $75,000 in damages.

Time, Inc., appealed the decision and the award to the appellate division of the New York State Supreme Court, where it won a small victory and suffered a major defeat. For although the appellate division found the damages to be excessive and ordered a new trial for the purpose of reducing them, it affirmed the correctness of the jury's decision in words that were a complete vindication of the basis for James Hill's suit: "Although the play was fictionalized, *Life*'s article portrayed it as a reenactment of the Hills' experience. It is an inescapable conclusion that this was done to advertise and attract further attention to the play, and to increase present and future magazine circulation as well. It is evident that the article cannot be characterized as a mere dissemination of news, nor even an effort to supply legitimate newsworthy information in which the public had, or might have, a proper interest."

The case went back to court, and this time, in the absence of a jury, a judge cut the damage award by more than half, to $30,000. Meanwhile, Time, Inc.'s appeal of the original decision was slowly making its way up the judicial ladder. At the state's top rung, the Court of Appeals concurred in the opinion of the appellate division. For Time, Inc., there was now nowhere to go but to the Supreme Court of the United States.

That nine-member body agreed to hear the case (it could have refused) because it involved "important constitutional questions of freedom of speech and press." It is interesting to note that at this, the highest possible judicial level, Hill was represented by Richard M. Nixon, former Vice President of the United States, defeated candidate for the Presidency six years earlier, President-elect two years later. Nixon, who had his troubles with the press throughout his political career (see chapter 9), was here advocate in a losing cause. After hearing arguments in October 1966, more than a decade after James Hill had initiated his suit, the Supreme Court announced its decision early in 1967, ruling in favor of Time, Inc.

In what is known as a split decision—with five justices in agreement, three dissenting, and one dissenting in part—the majority upheld the constitutionality of the New York right of privacy statute but set aside the judgment of the Court of Appeals on the narrowest of grounds. The prevailing opinion concluded that the instructions given to the jury by the trial judge were defective in that they did not sufficiently emphasize that a verdict of liability had to be based on "a finding of *knowing* and *reckless falsity* in the publication of the *Life* article." Merely deciding that the article was inaccurate in linking the Hill family to the play, that *Life* had failed to investigate the situation properly, and that the magazine was published and sold for profit was not, in the view of the majority, an adequate basis for judgment against Time, Inc. Quoting James Madison, who said, "Some degree of abuse is inseparable from the proper use of everything, and in no instance is this more true than in that of the press," the majority opinion observed that we gravely risk impairing the service of a free press if we saddle it "with the impossible burden of verifying to a certainty the facts associated in news articles with a person's name . . . particularly as related to nondefamatory matter."

Very often with Supreme Court decisions, the dissents and concurrences that accompany a majority opinion are as significant as the official ruling itself. For not only is the law ever-changing but so is the makeup of the Court. As justices retire or die, they may well be succeeded by men and women whose views differ markedly from those of the remaining members, and thus today's dissent could become tomorrow's majority opinion. Beyond that, however, simply as statements of personal belief, dissents and concurrences are sometimes so powerfully argued, so deeply infused with a sense of principle, so eloquently phrased that they reach timeless consequence in the realm of thought even though they have no immediate impact on the annals of justice.

The case of *Time, Inc. v. Hill* is perhaps more notable for a dissent and a concurrence than it is for its majority opinion. The outcome surely merited no boom of triumph from the press— some muffled applause would have been more appropriate. Suppose, in the Court's view, the presiding judge at the original trial *had* made unmistakably clear to the jury that to award damages to James Hill they had to be convinced that *Life* had recklessly disregarded the truth in running their *Desperate Hours* article. Suppose, after hearing those instructions, the jury had made the same decision, a rather likely occurrence give or take a few thousand in the financial award. Presumably, then, the Court would have upheld the jury's verdict and the affirmations of that verdict by the various lower courts, and Time, Inc., would have lost.

As it was, three justices, including the chief justice, Earl Warren, believed the instructions the jury received were perfectly adequate to support the verdict. Warren and Justice Tom Clark joined in the dissent written by Justice Fortas. It is both a stinging attack on the Court's ruling and an impassioned defense of the right of privacy. Said Fortas: "Such drastic action—the reversal of a jury verdict by this remote Court—is justified by the Court on the ground that the standard of liability on which the jury was instructed [violates] the First Amendment. But a jury instruction is not abracadabra. It is not a magical incantation, the slightest deviation from which will break the spell. . . . At its best, it is simple, rugged communication from a trial judge to a jury of ordinary people. . . . Instructions are to be viewed in a common-sense perspective, and not through the remote and distorting knothole of a distant appellate fence." Fortas went on to argue that from such a perspective "the core of the instructions" was sufficient to meet the majority's test. After showing how, in his view, the trial judge's words were equivalent to the Court's insistence on "knowing and reckless falsity," Fortas concluded:

The English language is not so esoteric as to permit serious consequences to turn upon a supposed difference between the instructions to the jury and this Court's formulation. Nor is the First Amendment in such delicate health that it requires or permits this kind of surgery, the net effect of which is not only an individual injustice, but an encouragement to recklessness and careless readiness to ride roughshod over the interests of others.

The courts may not and must not permit either public or private action that censors or inhibits the press. But part of this responsibility is to preserve values and procedures which assure the ordinary citizen that the press is not above the reach of the law—that its special prerogatives, granted because of its special and vital functions, are reasonably equated with its needs in the performance of these functions. For this Court totally to immunize the press . . . in areas far beyond the need of news, comment on public persons and events . . . would be no service to freedom of the press, but an invitation to public hostility to that freedom. . . .

Earlier in his dissent, Fortas wrote:

I, too, believe that freedom of the press, of speech, assembly, and religion . . . are delicate and vulnerable, as well as supremely precious in our society. But I do not believe that whatever is in words, however much an aggression it may be upon individual rights, is beyond the reach of the law. I do not believe that the First Amendment precludes effective protection of the right of privacy. . . . I do not believe that we must or should . . . strike down all state action . . . which penalizes the use of words as instruments of aggression and personal assault. There are great and important values in our society, none of which is greater than those reflected in the First Amendment, but which are also fundamental and entitled to this Court's careful respect and protection. Among these is the right of privacy. . . . As Mr. Justice Brandeis said . . . "the most comprehensive of rights and the right most valued by civilized men."

But let the last words on the *Desperate Hours* Case belong to the winning side. Earlier we made reference to former Supreme Court justices who took an absolutist stand on the First Amendment. None was more eminent than Hugo Black. This giant among jurists wrote a concurrence to the majority opinion, to which he had reluctantly agreed and only to ensure the Time, Inc., victory. If Black's statement had been the majority opinion, rather than merely an accompaniment to it, then *Time, Inc. v. Hill* would now be regarded as truly a milestone in our constitutional history. Instead, his opinion is the testament of one man who stood at the outermost limits of press freedom, often alone. This time he chose to be part of the majority, but in his concurrence you hear a solo voice, though a brave one, with which a large chorus has yet to join.

The words "malicious" and particularly "reckless disregard of the truth" can never serve as effective substitutes for the First Amendment words: "make no law . . . abridging the freedom of speech, or of the press. . . ." The prohibitions of the Constitution were written to prohibit certain specific things, and one of the specific things prohibited is a law which abridges freedom of the press. That freedom was written into the Constitution and that Constitution is or should be binding on judges as well as other public officers. . . . The freedoms guaranteed by the First Amendment are essential freedoms in a government like ours. That Amendment was deliberately written in language designed to put its freedoms beyond the reach of government to change. . . . If judges have, however, by their own fiat today created a right of privacy equal to or superior to the right of a free press that the Constitution created, then tomorrow and the next day and the next, judges can create more rights that balance away other cherished Bill of Rights freedoms. . . . One does not have to be a prophet to foresee that judgments like the one we here reverse can frighten and punish the press so much that publishers will cease trying to report news in a lively and readable fashion as long as there is—and there always will be—doubt as to the complete accuracy of the newsworthy facts. Such a result hardly seems consistent with the clearly expressed purpose of the Founders to guarantee the press a favored spot in our free society.

4.
"These Are Bad Guys—
I'm Going to Sue"

In 1956, a tall, gawky young woman, whom hardly anyone had ever heard of, appeared on "The Tonight Show," singing a specialty number called "I Made a Fool of Myself over John Foster Dulles" (Dulles was the very proper-seeming secretary of state under then-President Dwight Eisenhower). The host of the show, Jack Paar, cracked up, the studio audience roared, and across the country millions of late-night television viewers laughed so hard that by morning a not-uncommon show business phenomenon had happened again: A star was born. Her name was Carol Burnett.

Twenty years later, the entertainer, now a supercelebrity, was linked, again in a less than sober way, with another secretary of state, Henry A. Kissinger. But this time no one was laughing, least of all Carol Burnett. She sued for $10 million.

The object of her disaffection, in what was to become one of the most highly publicized libel cases in the past decade, was a weekly publication called the *National Enquirer*. While some would refer to it as a "scandal sheet" and others would deny it even that much dignity, the *Enquirer* looks like a newspaper and feels like a newspaper, though it carries no news as that term would generally be defined. Its pages are filled with features on astrology, health and beauty tips (diets are particularly frequent), and—most notably—gossip. Here you will find in profusion stories of the stars—of television, movies, sports, and politics—their coming together and their breaking apart, their neglected children and their bitter ex-spouses, their daytime rages and their nighttime romps.

Falling under that last classification was an item that appeared in the March 2, 1976, *Enquirer* headlined "Carol Burnett and Henry K. in Row." Said the column: "At a Washington restaurant, a boisterous Carol Burnett had a loud argument with another diner, Henry Kissinger. She traipsed around the place offering everyone a bite of her dessert. But Carol really raised eyebrows when she accidentally knocked a glass of wine over one diner—and started giggling instead of apologizing. The guy wasn't amused and accidentally spilled a glass of water over Carol's dress."

As *Enquirer* morsels go, this was probably not among the most spicy, although it was apparently among the more cooked-up. Both Burnett and Kissinger denied the story, as did, more significantly, two employees of the restaurant where the "events" were said to have taken place. But its untruth aside, the article was distressing to Burnett for another reason: By implying that she was intoxicated, it cast a shadow over her well-known personal campaign against alcoholism. The daughter of parents who had both died of excessive drinking, Burnett is a virtual teetotaler herself, and to have millions read of her supposed drunken cavorting (the *Enquirer* then claimed a circulation of about five million) inevitably triggered her fury. Later she was to testify that when she first learned about the column, "I started to cry. I started to shake. . . . I started . . . and then I calmed down and called my lawyer, and said, 'These are bad guys—I'm going to sue.' "

The journey to the Los Angeles Superior Court was long and halting. Having received a protest from Burnett's attorney, the *Enquirer* printed a kind of retraction in its gossip column a month after the first item appeared. While it did not totally disavow the original story, the correction acknowledged that the "boisterous Carol Burnett" report had been inaccurate. The lady was not appeased. She found the second item neither explicit nor conspicuous enough to clear her reputation. She then initiated her libel suit, which the *Enquirer* tried several times to have dismissed. These attempts failed because by then the court had in its possession the sworn statements of the restaurant employees. There followed efforts by the *Enquirer* to settle out of court, all of which Burnett spurned. Afterward, though before the courtroom confrontation, she recalled, "Every time they tried to settle, I said, 'No, I want to go to trial.' . . . Thank God, I can afford it. I keep thinking of all the people who would have had to give up by now. I'm so fortunate to be able to do this. I just hope I live long enough to see it through."

She did, although five years passed before, in March 1981, the case finally went to trial. Whatever one may think of the justification for the Burnett suit and allowing for the deep affection in which the star was, and is, held, it was no small challenge that she and her lawyers faced in convincing the eleven-member jury that she had been libeled. By legal definition, libel is defamation of character in printing and writing (as opposed to *slander*, which is defamation in speech), defamation being "a false communication which injures an individual's reputation by lowering the community's regard for that person or by otherwise holding an individual up to hatred, contempt, or ridicule." However, a 1964 Supreme Court decision of historic importance, in the case of *The New York Times Company v. Sullivan*, had made it much more difficult for a public official to win a libel suit than it is for a private citizen, and later the Court extended the added protection it offered the press to cover actions by "public figures" as well. This added protection took the form of a new rule that severely tightened the application of all libel laws. A public official, wrote Justice William J. Brennan, Jr., cannot collect "damages for a defamatory falsehood relating to his official conduct unless he proves that the statement was made with 'actual malice'—that is, with knowledge that it was false or with reckless disregard of whether it was false or not." (If these words sound familiar, it is because they were also the standard the Court applied three years later in *Time, Inc. v. Hill,* Hill having been considered a "public figure" in that, as hostage for three escaped convicts, he had made the front page of many newspapers.) Carol Burnett was unquestionably a public figure; as such, she had to prove that the *Enquirer* printed its story knowing it was false or making no reasonable effort to determine whether it was true.

Given the sworn affidavits of the two restaurant employees, it was not hard to prove that the article was fabricated, and at the trial the *Enquirer*'s attorneys never even tried to defend its accuracy. Instead, they argued that information about the incident had come from someone the editors considered a reliable source, that staff members had conscientiously attempted to verify the report, and that after they had learned it was in error, they promptly published a statement acknowledging that fact. The defense further contended that the story had not implied that Burnett was intoxicated and had not affected her reputation or her earning power.

A succession of current and former editorial employees of the

Enquirer took the witness stand to testify that they had believed the article was accurate at the time it was published. When Burnett's lawyers presented their case, however, much of this testimony was undermined by other disclosures. For example:

The writer whose byline appeared over the disputed column implied that *he* had not trusted the so-called "reliable source" and that, in fact, he had not been responsible for the item.

A senior editor of the publication, it was revealed, had actually written the story, although it was in no way attributed to him.

A reporter who had been assigned to double-check the article's accuracy about an hour before it was to go to press testified that he had not been able to do so to his own satisfaction but, because of the impending deadline, had been pressured by the senior editor who had written the item into giving his approval of it.

Most damaging of all, the sworn affidavits of the two restaurant employees brought to light not only that the story was untrue but also that when questioned by *Enquirer* staff members, the employees had told the *Enquirer* staff that the account of Burnett's boisterous behavior was wrong.

The star witness for the plaintiff was, of course, Carol Burnett herself. Emotional but controlled, she testified as to the effect the *Enquirer* article had had upon her, both in the immediate, physical sense—she had started to cry and her body had begun to shake and "do flip-flops"—and in terms of her work—her antialcoholism activities had suffered a serious loss of credibility. Condemning the story as "disgusting" and "a pack of lies," she was indignant, contemptuous, but still vulnerable as she told the court, "I wouldn't believe that anyone could sit down and make that up and write it. It will never, ever, not be a part of me."

Can there be any doubt that, listening to the Burnett testimony, the jurors were swept up in a wave of sympathy for this wronged and gallant woman? Yes, she was famous, wealthy, talented, and beloved, but—like the rest of us—she could be hurt and she could feel pain, and she could seek satisfaction from those who had injured her.

Amid thoughts like these it was easy to forget that a constitutional issue had to be decided here. As the chief defense attorney reminded the jurors after Burnett had left the witness stand, "You can't say the First Amendment applies to everybody except the *National Enquirer.*" Throughout the trial he and his associates argued that the publication had acted responsibly within the standards set down in *Times v. Sullivan* and that a ruling in Burnett's favor would hamper the ability of the press generally to report on public figures. He repeated this point, the core of the defense position, in his closing argument to the jury: "I speak not only for a client but also for a principle, and that is the freedom of the press—your right to know."

Evidently the jurors (or at least nine of them, the number needed, under California law, to reach a verdict) did not see their right to know imperiled by the legal action of a determined Carol Burnett. Announcing their decision after more than two days of deliberation, they ordered the *National Enquirer* to pay her a total of $1.6 million. (This was actually $100,000 *more* than her attorneys had requested, since during the trial they had scaled down their original demand for $10 million to $1.5 million.)

Upon hearing the verdict, Burnett smiled and then burst into tears. Later she announced that she would donate the money to charity. "If they'd given me one dollar plus carfare, I'd have been happy, because it was the principle," she told reporters. "They didn't give a darn about my rights as a human being. I didn't do a thing to the *National Enquirer.* They did it to themselves." Added her husband, "I don't think it'll hurt good journalism. It will hurt bad journalism, yellow journalism."

Carol Burnett, after hearing the jury's verdict and award in her libel suit against the National Enquirer.

But doesn't the Constitution protect all colors of journalism? The chief attorney for the *Enquirer* thought so as he announced that he would appeal the decision. "The verdict is an affront to the First Amendment," he charged, "and on appeal it cannot stand."

He was to be disappointed. The verdict of libel was never over-turned, although the award for damages kept being sliced away until it less resembled a Pentagon expenditure. First, the trial judge reduced the amount to $800,000, but this was cut further, to $200,000, by an appellate court. At that point, in 1984, Burnett had the option of seeking a new trial or reaching a higher, out-of-court settlement. She chose the latter course, but the figure agreed upon has remained—and, presumably, will forever remain—un-disclosed. And news of the settlement itself, which finally laid the Burnett case to rest, went almost unnoticed by the media.

Even three years earlier, in the aftermath of the original award for damages, with its lofty seven digits, there was a surprising calm. No outcries thundered from the staunchest champions of a free press, the journalists and publishers themselves. Their reactions ranged from the mildly approving to the somewhat troubled. Declared an editorial in the august *New York Times*, "The lawyer for the *National Enquirer* overstated his case when he called the $1.6 million libel award to Carol Burnett 'an affront to the First Amendment.' The amount is indeed inflated when measured against any damage to the comedienne's estimable reputation. The trial judge or higher courts should reduce the award. But the verdict is no blow to a free press. It posts a warning for extra care where that warning is most needed, in the gossip sheets that thrive on tarnished images of celebrities. . . ." The *Times* was comfortable with the decision because within the rules set down by *Times v. Sullivan* Burnett had proved her case to the satisfaction of a jury. But other journalists were worried nevertheless. The editor of the *Minneapolis Tribune* sounded a note of caution in observing that "a decision by a single jury in a single case in a single court would not by itself change the libel laws, but the appeals process could." If in this instance his concern proved groundless—the Burnett case never became an instrument of change and, in fact, in February 1984 the Supreme Court refused to hear the *National Enquirer's* appeal—the possibility that another libel dispute will reach the Supreme Court looms for the press like a dormant volcano.

For the fact is that in the years since *Times v. Sullivan*, the trend in Supreme Court libel rulings has not favored the media. In two key cases of the 1970s a majority of the justices severely restricted the definition of a "public figure." The Court determined that the plaintiffs in those cases—both involved in public issues but neither really famous—did not have to prove "actual malice" in order to win a libel suit. After the second decision, *Time* magazine commented, "The media now knows that they must be more cautious, and readers and listeners will almost surely receive less detail about people they thought were in the news."

Even more disturbing to reporters was a 1979 High Court decision in a case brought against the CBS television program *60 Minutes.* Colonel Anthony Herbert had accused various fellow officers of having suppressed evidence of American war crimes in Vietnam. His charges had been publicized and, in his view, he had been regarded as an honorable soldier responding to the dictates of his conscience. But, his lawyers claimed, when Mike Wallace devoted a segment of *60 Minutes* to Colonel Herbert, "the broadcast was a deliberately selective presentation directed at creating but a single impression—that Herbert was a liar, an opportunist, and a brutal person." As a result, "Herbert's reputation and good name were destroyed and he sustained severe financial losses."

As of this writing, the Herbert libel suit has yet to come to trial,* but from the point of view of the guardians of a free press, *Herbert v. Lando* (Lando was the producer of the offending segment of *60 Minutes*) has already done a good deal of damage. During pretrial proceedings in which parties to a lawsuit can be questioned by opposing lawyers, Herbert demanded the right to probe the state of mind of the defendants (Lando and Wallace) as they went about preparing "The Selling of Colonel Herbert" for broadcast. Why, he wanted to know, was certain material included and other material left out? Why was one soldier interviewed three times and another not at all? Lando declined to answer such

---

*On January 15, 1986, in a unanimous decision, a three-judge panel of a federal appeals court dismissed the case summarily, ruling that the evidence CBS had presented proved its program to be essentially accurate. The opinion acknowledged that certain "subsidiary" statements remained in dispute, but, it held, to go to trial over these minor issues would be a "classic case of the tail wagging the dog." Colonel Herbert could of course appeal this decision to the Supreme Court.

questions, though his replies to other queries required twenty-six days of interrogation and 2,903 pages of transcript. His refusal was the issue that eventually landed in the Supreme Court.

The first ruling on it, by a federal district judge, was in Herbert's favor. The second, by the court of appeals, reversed the decision of the lower court, saying, among other things, "A reporter or editor, aware that his thoughts might have to be justified in a court of law, would often be discouraged from the creative verbal testing, probing, and discussion . . . which are the *sine qua non* of responsible journalism." To the consternation of the press, the Supreme Court disagreed. In April 1979, in a split decision (six to three), it upheld Herbert's right to explore Lando's state of mind. Writing for the majority, Justice Byron White held that to prove "actual malice," public figures must be able to get "direct evidence through inquiry into the thoughts, opinions, and conclusions" of the alleged defamer. "How else," White asked, "will the public figure be able to prove, if he can, that the journalist knew that what he printed or broadcast was false—or that he recklessly didn't care?"

In reply, Justice Potter Stewart, dissenting, wrote that "why" questions are irrelevant. It does not matter why some material was included and some omitted, because all that counts is "that which was in fact published. What was not published has nothing to do with the case." As for whether the defendant knew that what he was publishing was false or had doubts about its truth or recklessly disregarded the question altogether, attorney Floyd Abrams, who represented CBS, pointed out that it wasn't necessary to probe the defendant's state of mind to get an answer. "If a jury hears that ten people have told a journalist that something is not true, and yet he goes ahead and prints it, the jury quite properly may find that he published with serious doubts as to the truth of the story."

The *Herbert v. Lando* decision was greeted with a roar of outrage from the media. Months later, responding to the attacks of commentators and columnists, Justice William J. Brennan, Jr., who had dissented in part, said, "The injury done . . . was simply not of the magnitude to justify the resulting firestorm of acrimonious criticism." But the prospect that someday a reporter would have to publicly divulge his intentions in preparing a story remained a source of deep concern. That concern was not diminished when, a few years later, as Colonel Herbert's lawyers presumably continued their probe, their case was largely overshadowed by another libel action brought against CBS, this time by General William Childs Westmoreland.

All networks customarily promote important programs in advance. On the *CBS Morning News* of January 21, 1982, reporter Diane Sawyer began a plug by saying, "It is an axiom of war that, above all, one must know the enemy." She went on, "On Saturday night, the CBS News broadcast *CBS Reports* will show that the American government in Washington was deceived about the enemy in Vietnam. . . . The broadcast is called 'The Uncounted Enemy: A Vietnam Deception,' reported by Mike Wallace and producer-reporter George Crile, who found at the heart of the deception not the hand of the enemy but the American military command." Print ads for the upcoming documentary used the word "conspiracy" boldly, and with justification, for when the program aired, on January 23, it unquestionably conveyed the message that in Vietnam in 1967 and 1968 a deliberate effort was made to mislead President Johnson, Congress, and the public about the progress of our war against the Vietnamese insurgents. At the center of this effort, according to correspondent Mike Wallace, stood the commander of the United States forces, General William Westmoreland, the key figure in "a conspiracy at the highest levels of American military intelligence to suppress and alter critical intelligence on the enemy. . . ."

Specifically, the program charged that intelligence reports transmitted to Washington contained a calculated underestimate of the number of South Vietnamese who were sympathetic to the Viet Cong and the rate at which North Vietnamese reinforcements were infiltrating the south. The effect of this twin deception was seriously to understate the strength and size of the enemy forces we faced and to give a falsely optimistic picture of our progress in the war. These accusations found support in a series of interviews with an array of Central Intelligence Agency and military analysts, some of whom had served in Westmoreland's own intelligence department. Their testimony was devastating—and only feebly countered by Westmoreland himself and by a single subordinate whose on-screen defense of his boss lasted a total of twenty-one seconds.

Within two days Westmoreland came to his own defense, calling a press conference at which he was joined by his chief intelligence officer during 1967–68, the U.S. ambassador to Vietnam for that same period, and other members of his staff. How effectively they fielded the reporters' questions over the course of two hours remains a matter of opinion—for one thing, they disagreed among themselves—but certainly everyone present thought that the general performed impressively: a ramrod figure shooting off sparks of indignation as he compared the CBS documentary to a recent movie, *Absence of Malice*, in which the life of an innocent man is ruined by ruthless journalists. "Little did I know," said Westmoreland, "that . . . a real-life, notorious reporter, Mike Wallace, would try to prosecute me in a star-chamber procedure with distorted, false, and specious information. . . . It was all there: the arrogance, the color, the drama, the contrived plot, the close shots—everything but the truth."

Mike Wallace   General William C. Westmoreland

If Westmoreland's truth did not clearly emerge from the press conference, it was not long before facts severely damaging to CBS did burst into the open. At issue was not so much the substance of the program's charges but the way the show had been put together. Documents leaked from within the network—the complete transcripts of the interviews, for example, and internal memorandums regarding research and production—strongly suggested that the raw material of the program had been quite consciously cut and tailored to make its point.

Trust the media to bring this to light. Two reporters for *TV Guide* gained access to the CBS documents and in May the magazine treated its readers to an "Anatomy of a Smear—How CBS News Broke the Rules and 'Got' General Westmoreland." The article inside proved almost as sensational as the title so dramatically headlined on the cover. Here was evidence that CBS had coached some witnesses to make their answers more sharply critical of Westmoreland, had deliberately chosen not to interview people who would probably have been on the general's side, and had edited out statements that obscured, weakened, or contradicted the program's "conspiracy thesis." Most important, the article charged that CBS had embarked on the project "already convinced that a conspiracy had been perpetrated, and turned a deaf ear toward evidence that suggested otherwise." As proof *TV Guide* cited a sixteen-page, single-spaced memorandum that George Crile, producer of the program, had submitted to the CBS News Department for initial approval to proceed with "The Uncounted Enemy." In it, the word "conspiracy" appeared twenty-four times.

Stung, CBS reacted in governmental fashion: It asked Burton Benjamin, one of its own senior executive producers, to investigate the magazine's charges. But if those associated with the documentary expected from their highly regarded colleague a congratulatory embrace or an understanding pat on the head, they were crushingly disappointed. What they got was almost a knockout punch. The Benjamin Report, in some ways more harshly disapproving than the *TV Guide* article had been, accused the program of "imbalance" in its presentation, of "coddling" anti-Westmoreland witnesses, and of a "lack of journalistic enterprise" in its failure to locate and interview the general's chief intelligence officer. Benjamin concluded that the broadcast had violated the network's self-imposed news guidelines and, perhaps most damaging of all, that "a 'conspiracy,' given the accepted definition of the word, was not proved."

Benjamin's investigation did not emerge as wholly negative, however; in fact, it endorsed the program in two crucial ways: by pointing out, first, that none of the on-air witnesses had ever retracted the statements they had made or claimed their comments had been taken out of context, and second, that "to get a group of high-ranking military men and former Central Intelligence Agents to say that this is what happened was an achievement of no small dimension." On the basis of these findings, the president of CBS News, while conceding the program's faults, was firm—if not exactly defiant—in stating, when he released a summary of the report, "We support the substance of the broadcast."

The anger Westmoreland had been nursing for six months erupted all over again. His continued demand for an apology from CBS was countered with a network offer of fifteen minutes of free, unedited airtime. He insisted on forty-five minutes—and a retraction. CBS was willing to issue a statement softening its criticism of Westmoreland but upholding the basic integrity of the program. Time passed, discussions hobbled along, but, as one well-known columnist wrote, "In keeping with the history of the war itself, negotiations failed." On September 13, 1982, the general finally launched his attack, suing CBS for $120 million.

His specific targets included the *CBS Morning News* promotion, the print ads, the documentary itself, and the CBS statement about the Benjamin Report. All, he claimed, had been put forth with "knowledge that they were false, unfair, inaccurate and defamatory" or with "reckless disregard" as to whether they were. Westmoreland charged CBS with having put him "in a false light in the public eye, portraying him, among other things, as dishonest, unethical and ruthless." At a news conference called to explain his latest course of action, his wrath seemed uncontained: "I have been reviled, burned in effigy, spat upon. Neither I nor my wife nor my family want me to go to battle again. . . . [But] there is no way left for me to clear my name, my honor, and the honor of the military."

From the start, CBS's attorneys argued that the *Times v. Sullivan* decision protected their client against the Westmoreland suit. That decision, they held, not only required the general to prove that he had been defamed with "actual malice," but also went on to limit his very right to sue: The Court had ruled that because public figures cannot be sued for anything they may say while acting in their official capacity, which would have applied to Westmoreland, they consequently cannot themselves sue in response to criticism of their official conduct unless they can prove actual malice. The full implication of this argument comes very close to totally disarming a public figure in any possible fight against assaults on his reputation and character. In effect, it says, to paraphrase a famous sign in President Harry Truman's office, "If you can't stand the heat, however suspicious its nature and causes, stay out of the kitchen."

To the relief of the general and his backers, Judge Pierre Leval, presiding in *Westmoreland v. CBS*, was not ready to accept such a position. In the spring of 1984, in considering a CBS motion to dismiss the suit before it went to trial, he dismissed instead the notion that Westmoreland was "libelproof," ruling that public figures had to be given an opportunity to defend themselves against what they believed to be defamation. He made no judgment of the merits of either side's case, leaving that for a jury to decide.

The case went to trial in October 1984, and what had been dimly apparent during the preceding two years soon became dramatically clear. *Westmoreland v. CBS* was not so much a legal dispute as a political one, not so much a contest between one military man and a communications giant as a clash between two opposing interpretations of recent history. Repeatedly the courtroom turned into an arena where the Vietnam War was fought all over again.

While it was being waged the first time, particularly during the latter years of the conflict, the "hawks," those who, with unwavering enthusiasm, championed our war effort, had maintained that the press had generally and relentlessly distorted the military and political reality of Vietnam. The media, they said, had focused on American casualties, the constantly increasing "body count," on retreat and stalemate, ignoring or underplaying the progress our forces had been making, the reverses inflicted on the enemy, and the evil of North Vietnam's Communist regime. The hawks charged that ultimately all the negative reporting on the nightly news had caused much of the American public and Congress to lose their resolve—and, as a result, to withdraw support for the military and make our defeat inevitable.

Ten years after the war's end the hawks clung to their antipress views with little loss in intensity. The libel suit, which some in their ranks had forcefully urged on Westmoreland, gave them an opportunity at last to see their position vindicated. For them, the general was the forgotten hero, a symbol of the military betrayed, and CBS the all-powerful villain, emblematic of all the faint-hearted self-deceivers who had been known as "doves."

The only problem was that now, as then, the hawks' chief asset lay in their unshakable conviction that they were right. When it came to producing facts that would serve to buttress their beliefs, they fell conspicuously short. Thus, as the trial began and Westmoreland's friendly witnesses followed one another to the stand, the impact of their testimony was at best a defense of the general that left CBS, the supposed perpetrator of malicious libel, relatively unscathed. No, the reports to Washington from Westmoreland's headquarters back in 1967–68 did not deliberately falsify or deflate the figures from the battlefield, but since the battlefield was everywhere, it was difficult to come up with hard, accurate, and reliable numbers. Yes, there was disagreement between the military and the CIA about the strength of the enemy forces, but it was honest disagreement that centered on whether teenagers and old men, however sympathetic to the Viet Cong, could justifiably be considered combatants. No, General Westmoreland did not mislead the White House with "cooked" figures, because President Johnson understood the conflicting ways of evaluating the same complex situation. Yes, the discrepancy between the Westmoreland and CIA numbers may have been as great as a quarter of a million men, but if the CIA's higher estimate had been released, the American people would have judged the enemy to be stronger than it actually was.

And so it went, with the 1960s arguments in favor of and against the Vietnam War rephrased in that 1984 courtroom but, in essence, remaining the same: We were, or were not, acting in accord with the wishes of the South Vietnamese in trying to repel the Red invaders from the north. We were, or were not, doomed to failure in fighting a guerrilla war against an enemy we did not know. On cross-examination particularly, Westmoreland's military witnesses affirmed the hawks' positions on the war in answer to defense questions that reflected the premises of the doves.

The case against CBS did not gain significant shape or substance until Westmoreland's attorneys called to the stand George Crile, a hostile witness, producer of "The Uncounted Enemy," and one of the four named defendants (the others being Samuel Adams, a former CIA analyst who was a paid consultant in the preparation of the documentary, Mike Wallace, and Van Gordon Sauter, the president of CBS News). Armed with the Benjamin Report,* Dan M. Burt, the chief lawyer for the plaintiff, got Crile to acknowledge those flaws in the preparation of the program that had already been publicized: the interviews sympathetic to the general that had either not been attempted or left on the cutting room

---

*In a pretrial ruling, Judge Leval had ordered that Westmoreland be given access to the complete text of the investigation.

floor (some of the key officials involved had testified for Westmoreland earlier), the coaching of witnesses, and the rest. But the effect of Crile's testimony was probably not as harmful to CBS as Burt had hoped. For one thing, while being forced to admit that the program may have lacked balance, Crile remained adamant in his insistence that it did not lack truth. For another, the judge kept reminding the jury that "fairness" was not an issue—and that Burt had to prove his case by "clear and convincing" evidence that the broadcast was false and CBS knew it was false.

To that end, the plaintiff's most powerful witness was undoubtedly the general himself. An impressive figure as he took the stand, he commanded respect by his very presence—the military bearing, the firm, square jaw, the carefully cropped white hair, the penetrating gaze—and throughout his testimony he conveyed the idea that in an unpopular war he had tried to do the very best job he could. He had relied on subordinates, perhaps to some extent he had been misinformed, but in issuing his intelligence reports he had never conspired to mislead the president or the American people. Much later, the jurors generally agreed that as his own witness General Westmoreland had helped his cause immeasurably.

But if the tide was perhaps running in his direction as his lawyers concluded their case, it seemed to shift almost as soon as CBS began presenting theirs. Attorney David Boies called to the stand one CIA agent after another—some retired, others still on active duty—and to a man they testified that estimates of enemy troop strength had been colored by political considerations. George Crile, giving testimony again but under friendlier auspices, was able to pinpoint the evidence behind each assertion the documentary had made. Most dramatic of all was the appearance of retired Major General Joseph A. McChristian, Westmoreland's onetime intelligence chief and still supposedly his close friend. McChristian testified that his former boss had acted "improperly" on at least one occasion by suppressing a cable containing high troop estimates, explaining that it would cause a "political bombshell" in Washington.

In the face of the continuing pileup of such evidence, it seemed to most observers that the jurors would prove incapable of determining the "truth" in this controversy and highly unlikely to find CBS guilty of knowingly presenting a false program. (One juror was to comment later that what "came out in court was much more damaging than the documentary ever was.") Moreover, Westmoreland's legal expenses, which had already passed the $3 million mark and put him deeply in debt, were mounting steadily with every discouraging day. And so, soon after General McChristian's testimony, lawyers for both sides were meeting privately, as they had done many times in the preceding months and years, to try to reach an out-of-court settlement. While once CBS had offered to make a financial contribution to the general's legal expenses, now, confident of the strength of its case, it was no longer so generous. Therefore, the merciful end of the libel suit came—after eighteen weeks of testimony, untold millions in legal fees, and a profound toll in personal anguish—with the issuance of nothing more than a joint statement, accompanied by separate statements from each side. Released on February 18, 1985 (though agreed to the day before), the joint statement contained the following keys to the settlement:

. . . both General Westmoreland and CBS believe that their respective positions have been effectively placed before the public for its consideration and that continuing the legal process at this stage would serve no useful purpose.

CBS respects General Westmoreland's long and faithful service to his country and never intended to assert, and does not believe, that General Westmoreland was unpatriotic or disloyal in performing his duties as he saw them.

General Westmoreland respects the long and distinguished journalistic tradition of CBS and the rights of journalists to examine the complex issues of Vietnam and to present perspectives contrary to his own.

Thus, both sides saved face and went on to justify their positions in their individual statements. Said CBS, after conceding that the program had contained "minor procedural violations" of its news standards, "Nothing has surfaced . . . that in any way diminishes our conviction that the broadcast was fair and accurate, and that it was a valuable contribution to the ongoing study of the Vietnam era. We continue to stand by the broadcast and are pleased that General Westmoreland has withdrawn his legal challenge to it." Said the general, referring to the "CBS respects" sentence in the joint statement, "If that statement had been made after the CBS program was aired, it would have satisfied me. After my press conference in Washington three days after the broadcast, it would have satisfied me. . . . If made during the first days in Federal Court, it would have ended the episode. The court action has certainly exposed some of the problems and complexities of producing intelligence on an elusive enemy." He concluded his statement by observing that court proceedings had emphasized that "The scope of the enemy's offensive did exceed expectation [but that] the size of the enemy troops committed was in line with the estimates of my intelligence chief. . . ." And he hoped that the end of his suit would "allow historians and scholars to assess the facts of [the Vietnam] war in accurate and nonsensational terms."

The settlement produced its own minor controversy, Westmoreland asserting that the joint statement included "in essence" an apology from CBS, and CBS denying that it had apologized for anything. In any case, both sides claimed a victory, but only CBS celebrated one—with champagne and dancing at one of New York's most expensive discotheques. Indeed, many of the general's most steadfast supporters expressed disappointment at the outcome and questioned whether he should "have quit at that point." Asked one, "Is it really worth $8 million to get CBS to say you're not unpatriotic?" To that Westmoreland might have replied as he did to a *New York Times* reporter when asked to evaluate the settlement, "It was the best I could get."

He was probably right, because the very nature of *Westmoreland v. CBS* placed it beyond the purpose and scope of a court of law. The case was at last put in proper perspective by the judge in his remarks to the jury after the settlement had been announced. Explaining that he understood their "sense of letdown . . . of disappointment" at not being able to render a verdict after so long a trial, he went on "to suggest some thoughts on the other side."

> We have been participants in a most interesting and unusual proceeding, a trial seeking the judgment of history. There can be no such thing as the legal power to fix the judgment of history. . . .
>
> We have watched the creation in this courtroom of an extraordinary, unique and rich record for historians to study. I suggest that the value of this proceeding may have more to do with the record it has created than with the verdict it could have produced.
>
> Judgments of history are too subtle and too complex to be resolved satisfactorily with the simplicity of a jury's verdict, such as "we find for the plaintiff," or "we find for the defendant." Also, they are too subject to debate and disagreement to

be resolved by any legally constituted authority.

I think it safe to say that no verdict or judgment that either you or I would have been able to render in this case could have escaped widespread disagreement.

So I suggest to you that it may be for the best that the verdict will be left to history.

For about half its run, the Westmoreland case had to share the news spotlight and New York's federal district court building with another libel action involving another famous general and another media colossus: *Ariel Sharon v. Time, Inc.* In June 1983, the former Israeli defense minister had filed a suit charging that he had been defamed by a *Time* cover story of four months earlier. A substantial part of the article, which covered eight pages in all, concerned the 1982 massacre by Christian militiamen of hundreds of Palestinians who had been interned in refugee camps in Lebanon. One paragraph reported that prior to the attack Sharon had "expected the Christian forces to go into the . . . camps" and had "discussed" their need "to take revenge for the assassination of [the Lebanese President-elect]." The unavoidable implication was that Sharon had anticipated the slaughter and done little or nothing to prevent it. Claiming *Time* had lied, Sharon sued for $50 million.

Time, Inc., tried to get the case dismissed on the ground that a United States court was not "a proper place to debate the actions of a foreign government," but its motion was denied, and the suit went to trial in November 1984, before federal judge Abraham Sofaer. The keys to a successful "truth defense" lay in Israel, and *Time*'s attorneys attempted, for the most part in vain, to enlist the cooperation of the Israeli government in preparing their case. They requested and were denied opportunities to interview various high-level military and intelligence officials. Nor were they permitted to call these people as witnesses. Most crucial to their defense was the classified report of a special Israeli commission that had investigated the massacre. It was known as the Kahan Report, and its conclusions had been made public—among them, a finding that Sharon had "disregarded the danger of acts of vengeance" and thereby bore "indirect responsibility" for what had happened at the refugee camps—but it was the report's still-secret Appendix B that, *Time* claimed, contained details that would substantiate the offending paragraph of their story. Only after the trial had begun was Judge Sofaer able to arrange with the Israeli government an accommodation that permitted representatives of both sides to examine Appendix B and related documents. To *Time*'s dismay, its lawyer found nothing to corroborate the magazine's disputed statements about Sharon. As a result, it printed a retraction of those statements soon thereafter, and its truth defense was virtually shattered. What remained to it was to prove the absence of "actual malice"—that is, knowingly publishing a false report—and, with this in view, various reporters and editors testified to their trust in the integrity and reliability of *Time*'s Israeli correspondent and, therefore, their assumption that the story was completely factual. In retrospect, it is apparent that the magazine's entire case rested on the credibility of those witnesses.

Like a director intent on heightening the suspense of a play, Judge Sofaer had the jury follow an unusual procedure in delivering its verdict. It was to disclose its findings on each of the three elements of the case as it reached them, step by step. Not only did this method enhance the drama of the situation, it practically guaranteed to Sharon at least one moment of pure triumph. As it was, he achieved two. On the third day of deliberation, the jurors announced that they considered the disputed paragraph defamatory in meaning. Sharon beamed for the cameras and boasted that he was already satisfied. Two days later his smile broadened as the jury declared the contested passage to be false. But after winning two battles, General Sharon was about to lose the war. It took six more days for the jury to reach its final verdict, and then the foreman read each word precisely: "On actual malice . . . Has the plaintiff proved by clear and convincing evidence that a person or persons at Time, Inc., knew that the defamatory statement was false or had serious doubts to its truth? We find the answer is no." Sharon had not been libeled and, therefore, he could collect no damages. In this world where money talks, silence meant a victory for *Time.*

It was, however, a decidedly tainted victory, for the foreman, as if expressing regret for the verdict he had just delivered, went on to read a statement on behalf of the jury severely critical of the defendant: "Certain *Time* employees, particularly correspondent David Halevy [the magazine's Israeli reporter], acted negligently and carelessly in reporting and verifying the information which ultimately found its way into the published paragraph of interest in this case." An epilogue to the drama, the censure was clearly not designed to send the winners dancing into a discotheque. And this time no such celebration was reported.

Indeed, the media in general reacted with restraint to the resolution of the Sharon case, just as they did to the Westmoreland settlement a few weeks later. Certainly neither outcome offered the defendants, however successful, much reason for pride, just as neither trial provided evidence of how the press upholds the highest standards of journalism. What both libel actions did demonstrate, resoundingly and conclusively, was the formidable power of the "actual malice" test. By requiring a public figure plaintiff to prove not only that a defendant had published or broadcast a defamatory falsehood but had *knowingly* done so, *Times v. Sul-*

General Ariel Sharon, surrounded by his lawyers, supporters, and the press, on the steps of the courthouse before the jury announced its final verdict in his libel suit against Time, Inc.

livan had armed the press with a shield that seems all but impenetrable.

Do people who are in the public eye, sometimes forced there unwillingly, have no effective recourse, then, if they believe they have been libeled? Must they spend millions in legal fees trying, probably unsuccessfully, to prove malicious intent? A defender of the status quo would reply that they can write a letter to the editor or call a news conference to rebut the offending statements. But some consider this a powder-puff reaction to what is often a cannonball shot. Among them stands, not surprisingly, General Westmoreland, who, in a talk before the National Press Club a month after he had settled with CBS, proposed another alternative: "something like a National News Council . . . a committee of journalists and public citizens which handed down nonbinding decisions and let the public and news media draw its own conclusions." But this plan went largely ignored by the media and has met with no acceptance.

More significantly, perhaps, in June 1985, two Supreme Court justices indicated dissatisfaction with the current libel tests. In opinions accompanying a five to four decision that helped private individuals under certain circumstances recover damages for libel, both Chief Justice Warren Earl Burger and Associate Justice Byron R. White called for reconsideration of *Times v. Sullivan*, Justice White commenting that it made it too difficult for libeled public officials to clear their names.

Comments like these coming from our highest tribunal send tremors through newsrooms everywhere. Whether journalists believe, as many do, that reporting on the official acts of government figures should enjoy complete protection from libel suits (the officials, after all, have total immunity for whatever *they* may say), or whether they suspect, as many do, that such a shelter would become a license for media irresponsibility, newspeople are close to unanimous in their conviction that the current tests for libel should not be relaxed. For the fact is that, according to the Libel Defense Resource Center, libel suits have been mounting rapidly over the past several years, and damage awards of the Carol Burnett magnitude are increasingly common. The million-dollar verdicts may usually be reduced on appeal, but probably not the $10,000 judgment won by a high school cafeteria chef whose lunchtime fare the school paper had rated as "not fit for dogs." Actually, this plaintiff, who got his award during the week of the Westmoreland settlement, was unusual in winning anything, since surveys have shown that only a small percentage of the libel suits that go through trial and appeal procedures result in damages. But uncounted are the host of libel actions settled out of court—and unknown are the effects that the mere possibility of a libel suit may have on a particular reporter or editor. It is this, finally, that poses the greatest danger. Should the number of libel suits continue to increase, should the damage awards soar to record highs, and, most important, should the Supreme Court retreat from the liberating thrust of *Times v. Sullivan*, then change may indeed come to the way some of the press, particularly the smaller, less affluent newspapers, pursue and comment upon the news. If, rather than penetrating investigation and robust debate, we get timidity, caution, and what *Time* magazine has called "a dimmer light cast on critical issues," then the price we would be paying for libel suits would far exceed the largest award ever made.

PART THREE

In Conflict with
Law Enforcement
and the Courts

5.
The Right to Rummage

In 1971, when Charlie Quarterman was passing out copies of his underground newspaper in quite an aboveground spot, campus sit-ins were almost as common as pep rallies and panty raids had been in the fifties. Just about every respectable college and university suffered through one—or perhaps several—during the school year. They weren't big news, as they had been back in the sixties, when angry students first started invading the offices of college administrators and occasionally taking over entire buildings. In those days, demonstrators could count on full press coverage, not only from local newspapers and radio and television stations but also—if the school was prominent enough or the sit-in was violent enough or both—from the wire services, the national magazines, the major U.S. dailies, and all three networks. There were some people then who said that gaining publicity for a cause was what brought about the sit-ins in the first place. Whether that cause was opposition to the Vietnam War effort, a better deal for minority students or staff members, or reform of some academic policy, a lot of outsiders thought that if the reporters and cameramen took off, the students would be right behind them.

But by 1971 whatever truth there was in this notion had been dispelled: Sit-ins were continuing even though they were no longer attracting much attention. In April of that year, when student activists marched on Stanford University Hospital to protest the firing of a black janitor, the only newspaper that bothered to cover the event was the *Stanford Daily*, whose circulation of about 15,000 was made up almost exclusively of campus people. Student editors had *Daily* reporters and photographers on the scene from the moment the demonstrators moved into and took over a hospital office and corridor until long after the sit-in had turned ugly. When authorities summoned the police, violence erupted, and nine cops and numerous students suffered injuries. Like many such demonstrations, the hospital sit-in had begun with chants, slogans, and high spirits, but it ended in sirens, curses, and blood. Some arrests were made, Stanford University Hospital was cleared of all intruders, and the next morning the front page of the *Daily* told the whole story, complete with pictures.

Meanwhile the Palo Alto police had already begun a hunt for their assailants. During the melee, it had been almost impossible to tell which student had struck which blow or who had thrown the few well-aimed rocks. Those protestors taken into custody were, of course, questioned before they were released, but as could be expected, no one seemed to know anything. With few, if any, worthwhile leads, the police were stymied—but resolute, and in their determination to apprehend the culprits, they turned to one possible source of information that many would think out of bounds. Three days after the sit-in was over, they raided the offices of the *Stanford Daily*.

They were armed with a search warrant, obtained easily from a local magistrate, but they arrived unannounced. Perhaps they had the groundless fear that, given advance warning, the student editors would have hidden or even destroyed the evidence the lawmen were looking for: photographs that might help them identify the offenders. The pictures that had already appeared in the *Daily* were worthless in this regard, but, it was thought, there was a good chance that the newspaper's files contained others that would be of value. So the police barged in, flashing their warrant and startling the few *Daily* staff members around the office, and began their search. They combed through filing cabinets, desk drawers, and wastebaskets, and while they found rolls and rolls of unexposed film—and a *Daily* photographer took their pictures as they peered at every inch—they came away with nothing. Except a damage suit filed by the student editors.

A law officer studying file film in the office of the Stanford Daily.

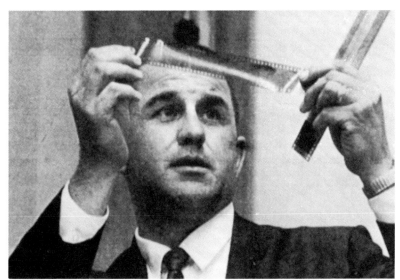

The *Daily*'s case against the Palo Alto police rested on the marriage of two constitutional rights: the protection against unreasonable search and seizure guaranteed by the Fourth Amendment plus the additional protection afforded to the press by the First. Lawyers for the campus newspaper argued that since the *Daily* was not suspected of having committed a crime, as a minimum safeguard law-enforcement officials should have been required to *subpoena* the evidence they wanted. For the press, the *Daily* maintained, a warrant was simply not sufficient; the police can almost always find a judge who will issue such a writ with the slightest justification. Then, warrant in hand, "the law" could descend upon a newsroom and proceed to pore over all sorts of documents that are unrelated to the crime they are investigating. Confidential news sources (which we will be discussing in the next chapter) would immediately be jeopardized. At least a subpoena, unlike a search warrant, can be contested at a court hearing: The police must explain exactly what evidence they are seeking and why they need it, while the newspaper can try to convince a judge that the police are, let's say, on "a fishing expedition."

The invasion of the *Stanford Daily* offices had drawn a ground swell of protest from press circles throughout the nation, and the paper's suit enjoyed solid journalistic support as it made its way through the judicial process. Eventually two lower courts ruled in the *Daily*'s favor, finding that the police had blatantly violated the newspaper's constitutional rights and ordering them to pay $47,000 in legal fees. The Palo Alto police appealed, and *Zurcher* [the Palo Alto police chief] *v. Stanford Daily* was accepted for review by the Supreme Court.

There, in May 1978, to the astonishment of many, a sharply divided Court reversed the earlier rulings. Split five to three (one justice abstained), the High Bench upheld the actions of the police, maintaining that law-enforcement authorities in search of evidence most assuredly do have the right to enter unannounced into a newsroom—or any other place—as long as a judge has issued a warrant and even if the occupant is not suspected of involvement in the crime that is under investigation. In effect, the Court was denying the press any unique privileges. In a decision issued just a few weeks earlier, Chief Justice Warren Burger, writing for the majority, had declared that journalists have no greater free speech rights than anyone else, and this view was echoed by Justice Byron White in the *Stanford Daily* opinion. Rejecting the newspaper's contention that the police should have sought a subpoena, White made the point that such a requirement might "seriously impede" criminal investigations, and he concluded, "Valid warrants may be issued to search *any* property . . . at which there is probable cause to believe that fruits, instrumentalities, or evidence of crime may be found."

A cartoon comment on the Supreme Court ruling in the Stanford Daily *case.*

"The Supreme Court media style book prefers a semi-colon to a comma after the use of the past pluperfect subjunctive."

Among the minority was Justice Potter Stewart, and in his dissent he held that the press, in performing its special role in our society, does have claim to the additional protection granted by the lower court decisions. Thus, a hearing should be required to afford journalists an opportunity to defend themselves against surprise searches. Justice John Paul Stevens, filing a separate dissent, went even further in disagreeing with the majority. Because of the possibility that in looking for one document the police might see others they were not entitled to, Stevens would have forbidden searches without notice for material in the hands of *any* third party not suspected of a crime. Newspapers, lawyers, psychiatrists, anyone should have this protection—unless there was serious risk of the destruction of evidence.

The press would have gladly settled for the Stewart opinion. What they got seemed intolerable. Their reaction to the police raid on the *Stanford Daily* was but a sun-shower compared to the storm of protest that greeted the *Zurcher* decision. An ABC News commentator called it the "most dangerous ruling the Court has made in memory." One Washington newspaper editor thought that the Court had removed an essential press safeguard, while another said that the police had been given the "right to rummage" in journalists' files. In Los Angeles, the editor of the *Times* thundered that the decision was "incredible and terrible."

While there is no appealing a ruling of the Supreme Court, the separation of powers within the American government assures that the unpopular decisions of one branch may be modified, if not nullified, by one or both of the others. Thus, from the executive branch, within a week after the *Zurcher* ruling, the deputy attorney general, under then-President Jimmy Carter, announced that the Justice Department would draw up procedures limiting federal searches of newsrooms and would in the future seek subpoenas before undertaking any such searches. Of course, this new policy applied only to law enforcement on the federal level. The deputy attorney general could hope but could not promise that judges and police on the state and local levels would follow his lead.

Only the third branch of government, the legislative, could guarantee that, and in the wake of *Zurcher v. Stanford Daily,* President Carter proposed to Congress a bill that would accomplish exactly what Justice Stewart had outlined in his dissent. It took a while, as most new laws do in Congress, but about two and a half years after the unexpected Supreme Court ruling, Congress passed the Privacy Protection Act of 1980. Previously approved in the Senate, it sailed through the House of Representatives on a vote of 357 to 2! President Carter signed the bill into law on October 14, saying that his goal in recommending the legislation had been to prevent searches that "could have a chilling effect on the ability of reporters to develop sources and pursue stories."

The Privacy Protection Act bars unannounced searches of newsrooms by federal, state, and local law-enforcement authorities except in certain narrowly defined circumstances. Subpoenas are required whenever police or investigators are looking for notes, film, tapes, or other documentary materials used by reporters and other authors writing for publication. Exceptions to the rule are limited to situations in which (1) there is reason to believe that the person holding the possible evidence himself committed the crime in question, (2) the immediate seizure of the materials is necessary to prevent death or serious injury, or (3) there is strong suspicion that the evidence would be concealed, altered, or destroyed if advance notice was given through a subpoena. An additional exception permits surprise searches when material has not been produced in response to a previously issued lawful subpoena. Reporters and others who believe their rights under the new law have been violated may file suit for damages against the governmental agency responsible for the search, with a minimum award of $1,000 assured should the violation be proved.

It's estimated that, across the country, state and local authorities carried out at least twenty-five unannounced searches of newsrooms in the decade between the Palo Alto police raid and the passage of the Privacy Protection Act. Presumably the new law has put a stop to all that. Earlier we made reference to cases whose decisions extended the boundaries of freedom of the press. Does the *Stanford Daily* case fall into that category? Given the ruling that resulted, it would certainly not appear so. The majority, said one champion of a free press at the time, "feels the press is arrogant and greedy and powerful enough to get what it wants without help from the court. But most of the press is not the big, rich, influential media that the Justices see in Washington, and all those local reporters do need support from the court to do their job." Fortunately, in our system of government there was another source for the support that our highest tribunal had failed to provide. But we cannot forget that it was the student editors of the *Stanford Daily* who led the way and, to be just, their case must rank high among those that have strengthened and brightened the First Amendment.

6.
Fishing for Panthers

The decade of the sixties, especially the years following the assassination of John F. Kennedy, witnessed a profound radicalization of the United States. It was as if the bullets that had felled the president had gone on to shatter a set of values, traditions, and myths that we had clung to for too long, hardly aware of how corroded they had become or how flawed they had always been. Women, blacks and other minorities, the young, the elderly, and the handicapped started to assert themselves as they never had before. In politics, music, and art, in homes, schools, and workplaces, new ideas and trends pushed aside the old ways—and out of this hectic ferment came pervasive and permanent changes in the fabric of our society.

But the activism of the sixties was as doomed as were many of its targets. It harbored the agents of its own demise—among them, excesses of violence and drug-taking, and the disillusionment that is inevitable when goals are reached too slowly or, perhaps, never attained at all. And so, by the middle of the following decade, the drive for social reform had degenerated into self-absorption that was characterized as the "me generation," to be replaced in turn by the conservative mood that swept Ronald Reagan into the White House. Nonetheless, for those who had been caught up in what the Germans call *Zeitgeist*, the spirit of the times, the sixties will always be remembered as a period of extraordinary discovery and accomplishment, when long-ignored injustices were finally recognized and long-delayed efforts were made to correct the wrongs of the past.

Supreme among these efforts, and a hallmark of the sixties, was surely the unrelenting crusade for civil rights. It began in the South, with bus boycotts, soda fountain sit-ins, and mass marches, but it eventually came to challenge and envelop the entire nation, producing landmark legislation and ending forever various centuries-old patterns of discrimination. Somewhere along the way, however, the civil rights movement lost a good deal of its original nonviolent character: If in the early sixties blacks found inspiration in the ideals of Dr. Martin Luther King, Jr., by the end of the decade many were responding with fervor to the slogans of the advocates of Black Power. King was gone by then, as were two other leaders to whom blacks had once turned in hope, Malcolm X and Robert F. Kennedy. All struck down by assassins, their deaths deepened the frustration and heightened the militancy of black communities everywhere. As emblems of the campaign for equal rights and opportunity, feet blistered from miles of walking had grown far less appropriate than fists upraised in defiant resolve.

Some of those fists belonged to members of the Black Panthers, an association founded late in 1966 in Oakland, California, by

Huey P. Newton and Bobby Seale. Intent on "doing something for the black revolution in America and . . . moving some grains of sand," as Seale was to write much later, these angry young militants drew up a ten-point platform and program for their new organization, which they named the Black Panther Party for Self-Defense. To the white majority those last words had the frightening sound of the crack of a whip, for the fact was that, unlike most other groups spawned by the civil rights movement, the Black Panthers were armed. Their name implied that they carried guns; their unconcealed holsters proved it.

They needed weapons, they said, to protect themselves against the police, "those racist swine who brutalize and harass our black community to death." The fiercely aggressive stance of the Panthers—their determination not to avoid confrontation with the police but to seek it out—was bound to gain them notoriety. Within months they were, to quote Seale, "a household word in the Bay area," and not much later—after a particularly daring armed demonstration on the steps of the state capitol in Sacramento—they were known around the world and boasted that they "had hit the front page of the London *Times.*"

In 1967 and 1968 Black Panther offices were opened in just about every major city in the United States. At no time was the extent of its fast-increasing membership ever divulged, but the party proudly acknowledged some of the circulation figures achieved by its newspaper—as many as 30,000 copies sold in Chicago and 35,000 in New York—with a readership that spanned the globe, from San Francisco to Boston, from Paris to Tokyo, from Copenhagen to Nairobi. The newspaper itself was merciless to the white establishment and contemptuous of moderate black leadership. (In the months before his death, Dr. King was referred to as "bootlicker" and worse.) By offering its readers a steady diet of venom, the Panther newspaper, like the Panther street-corner rallies, had one overriding purpose: to advance the cause of a black armed revolution.

In this the party was destined to fail, but not before the conflict sparked had claimed a number of victims. The Panthers' scorching attacks on white authority in all its forms, but particularly in law enforcement, made violence as inevitable as the flame that bursts from a struck match. As provocations intensified in both number and kind, the police found it increasingly difficult to react with restraint, control, and caution. Thus, a raid on a Panther stronghold in Chicago became a bloodbath in which two party members were killed, and another in Los Angeles yielded a body count that was even—three Panthers and three officers were wounded.

Shoot-outs like these, as well as other raids that almost invariably uncovered caches of high-powered weapons, brought the Panthers wave upon wave of public attention. Headline-making stories triggered invitations to those new celebrities, Huey Newton, Bobby Seale, and other party leaders, to appear on radio and television talk shows. The Panthers were hungry for publicity, and the media, equally insatiable in their need for "guests," were delighted to oblige.

Ironically, however, while their manifestos and their confrontations with the law had become fodder for the nightly news, the Black Panthers remained in many ways a secret society. Since they regarded establishment journalists with the same distrust they felt toward all other members of "the ruling class," press credentials were meaningless to them. They spurned all requests for newspaper interviews and publicly revealed only such information as they believed would further their mission. It went without saying that if a journalist were even to hope to gain their confidence, at the very least he had to be black. No doubt with this in mind, *The New York Times* assigned coverage of the Black Panther Party to a reporter named Earl Caldwell.

Caldwell was not only black, he was also thoroughly experienced in working with black community organizations. He had demonstrated his effectiveness with such groups by regularly filing his stories without ever having to betray a trust. In spite of this, the Panthers were not easily persuaded, and it took Caldwell a good long while to gain their acceptance. Later, in a court affidavit, he said, "I began covering and writing articles about the Black Panthers almost from the time of their inception, but I myself found that in those first months . . . they were very brief and reluctant to discuss any substantive matter with me. However, as they realized I could be trusted and that my sole purpose was to collect information and present it objectively in the newspaper and I had no other motive, I found that not only were the party leaders available for in-depth interviews but also the rank and file members were cooperative in aiding me in the newspaper stories that I wanted to do. During the time that I have been covering the party, I have noticed other newspapermen representing legitimate organizations in the news media being turned away because they were not known and trusted by the party leadership."

Once Caldwell had opened lines of communication to the Panthers, he was able to gather information for lengthy articles that appeared throughout 1968 and 1969 in *The Times* and syndicated in fifty to sixty other newspapers around the country. The nature of these stories was such that writers who did not know the party intimately could not possibly have written them. They included, for example, an interview with Black Panther Chief of Staff David Hilliard, who told Caldwell, "We are special. We advocate the very direct overthrow of the Government by way of force and violence. By picking up guns and moving against it because we recognize it as being oppressive and in recognizing that we know that the only solution to it is armed struggle [sic]." What made this interview, part of a Caldwell article in *The Times* of December 14, 1969, particularly significant was that at the time Dave Hilliard was under indictment by a federal grand jury for uttering threats against the life of the President of the United States.

A month before the interview appeared, Hilliard had delivered a publicly televised speech in which he declared that "we [the Panthers] will kill Richard Nixon." It was this threat, which had then been repeated in three subsequent issues of the Panther newspaper, that had led to Hilliard's indictment. Earlier, the federal grand jury had been impaneled to investigate various possible Black Panther violations of the U.S. Criminal Code: conspiracy to assassinate the President, interstate travel to incite a riot, mail fraud and swindles, and other crimes not specified. Hilliard's indictment was, however, the only one the grand jury ever handed up—though this was certainly not from any lack of trying on the part of the government. Two months after Hilliard was indicted, a subpoena was issued to Earl Caldwell, ordering him to testify before the grand jury and "to bring with him notes and tape recordings of interviews given him for publication by officers and spokesmen of the Black Panther Party concerning the aims, purposes, and activities of that organization." Earl Caldwell, with the backing of *The New York Times*, refused to comply; jointly they tried to have the subpoena set aside.

Its enforcement was postponed three times over the course of a month while government attorneys negotiated with counsel for Caldwell and *The Times.* Eventually, the grand jury issued a modified warrant, omitting the documentary requirement and simply ordering Caldwell "to appear . . . to testify." Again Caldwell

Earl Caldwell

and *The Times* moved to quash the subpoena. They argued that its unlimited scope and its essential demand that the reporter testify in secret (grand jury proceedings are always closed to the press and public) were certain to destroy Caldwell's working relationship with the Black Panther Party and, further, would "suppress vital First Amendment freedoms . . . by driving a wedge of distrust and silence between the news media and the militants." Their motion concluded by stating that "so drastic an incursion upon First Amendment freedoms" should not be permitted unless there were "a compelling governmental interest—not shown here—in requiring Mr. Caldwell's appearance before the grand jury."

Like a Gospel according to Caldwell, these arguments were to be repeated many times during the next two years. At the lowest judicial level they were received with a good deal of sympathy, but they did not prevail. In April 1970, the district court in northern California denied the Caldwell-*Times* motion to quash the subpoena on the ground that *"every person* within the jurisdiction of the government" is obligated to testify before a grand jury when properly summoned. While affirming this view, which was the very heart of the United States government's position, the court proceeded to qualify it in a most crucial way. Yes, Caldwell must indeed appear before the grand jury but, the judge declared, he cannot be forced to reveal confidential information unless the government can show "a compelling overriding national interest in requiring . . . testimony" and no "alternative means" of obtaining the same information. The decision, then, was a kind of balancing act, with the First Amendment rights of the press delicately poised against the law enforcement needs of the government. The ever-so-slight tilt appeared to be in the latter's favor, but because in his ruling the judge had said he was prepared to issue a court order, if necessary, to restrict the questioning of Caldwell, he had every reason to expect the *government* to appeal his decision. He even implied that he would welcome such a move when he wrote, "The issues involved in the subpoena controversy go to the very core of the First Amendment . . . sensitive areas of freedom of the press . . . not heretofore fully explored and decided by the Supreme Court of the United States."

No doubt to the surprise of some, including the judge, the U.S. Justice Department, clearly reluctant to force a High Court showdown on media rights, swallowed hard and chose to live with the district court ruling. So, too, to the surprise of others, did *The New York Times.* Said its executive vice president: "A reporter's appearance before a grand jury can have a chilling effect on press freedom, but we believe that reporters, like other citizens, have a duty to testify when they are subpoenaed." Nevertheless, the decision *was* appealed—by Earl Caldwell, now acting alone.

He was afraid, he explained, that if he testified, the government would ignore the judge's qualification and question him about confidential material, arguing that it was not truly privileged information at all. Furthermore, Caldwell contended, "I don't have any non-confidential information. Everything I could print has been printed. If I go before the grand jury, my credibility with the black community is gone." At this point the reporter's concerns found no sympathetic judicial ears. His appeal was dismissed without opinion.

Meanwhile, the term of the original grand jury had expired; a new grand jury was convened to investigate the Panthers and another subpoena was issued. Caldwell once again moved to quash, and once again his motion was denied. Repeating the special-protection guarantee of the first ruling, the court directed Caldwell to appear before the grand jury. When Caldwell once more refused, he was found to be in contempt of court and was thereby sentenced to jail until he complied with the court order or until the expiration of the term of the grand jury.

Facing the prospect of incarceration, Caldwell appealed the contempt-of-court finding. As before, he was represented by Anthony G. Amsterdam, a Stanford University law professor; as before, he was supported by "friends of the court" briefs filed by such organizations as the Columbia Broadcasting System, the Associated Press, and the American Civil Liberties Union; as before, he argued that his professional standing would be destroyed if his sources could not trust him to protect their confidence. This time Caldwell won an unqualified victory as the court of appeals reversed the previous rulings. Addressing the question of whether Caldwell was required to appear before the grand jury at all, rather than the issue of what kind of interrogation he could be subjected to, the court declared that he was free to ignore the subpoena.

The champions of a free press exulted. *Time* magazine's report of the decision began: "Earl Caldwell's challenge came at a time when the U.S. press community felt that Government investigators were using subpoenas far too liberally as a means of fishing through reporters' notes on the off chance of finding evidence of crime." Finally, *Time* said, somebody was blowing the whistle on such fishing expeditions, for the court of appeals had held that they would turn a reporter "into an investigative agent of the Government." But, more fundamentally, the decision reflected the court's view that the First Amendment, under certain circumstances, did offer newsmen special privileges: Forcing a reporter like Caldwell to testify would discourage his informants from communicating with him in the future and would cause him to censor his writings in order to avoid being subpoenaed. Since the government had demonstrated no compelling need for his testimony, Caldwell was not only privileged to withhold it, he was also privileged to refuse to attend a secret meeting of the grand jury. At last a judicial body had expressed agreement with the basic premise of Caldwell's argument—that simply to go before the grand jury would impair his ability to do the job of gathering news and presenting it to the public. *Time* hailed the decision as a "triumph for Caldwell, for Constitutional Lawyer Tony Amsterdam . . . and for press freedom." And a jubilant Earl Caldwell was quoted as saying, "We got 100% of what we asked. I could not have continued as a journalist if I knew I'd have to submit to what the Government has been demanding."

"Show me a good loser," said Notre Dame's legendary Knute Rockne, "and I'll show you a loser." In its contest with Earl Caldwell, the Justice Department was determined to be neither. Although the court of appeals had specifically emphasized that its decision applied only to the one case at hand and was not to be interpreted as affording the press generally protection against grand jury subpoenas, the government saw it differently. This Caldwell ruling was one it could not live with. Its petition to the U.S. Supreme Court for review consisted of a single question: "Whether a newspaper reporter who has published articles about an organization can, under the First Amendment, properly refuse to appear before a grand jury investigating possible crimes by members of that organization who have been quoted in the published articles."

Six months after the court of appeals gave Caldwell his victory, the Supreme Court agreed to review the case in conjunction with two others in which reporters had refused to reveal their news sources. Arguments were heard in late February 1972, more than two years after Caldwell had been served with his first subpoena. The historic ruling was handed down four months later, on June 29, 1972. Familiarly known as the *Branzburg* decision, it takes its name from the first of the three cases considered *(Branzburg v. Hayes),* though *United States v. Earl Caldwell,* which was the last, had by far commanded the most widespread attention. Thus, it was Earl Caldwell who seemed to be the biggest loser—aside from the press itself—when the Supreme Court ruled that reporters do not have a constitutional right to withhold confidential information from a grand jury.

In a bitterly split decision, five to four, the majority consisted of all four of President Nixon's appointees to the court, plus Justice Byron R. White, who had been appointed by President Kennedy and who wrote the prevailing opinion. To him the "heart of the [press] claim is that the burden on news gathering resulting from compelling reporters to disclose confidential information outweighs any public interest in obtaining the information." This claim White rejected, noting that the only constitutional restriction on testifying is the Fifth Amendment's guarantee against compelled self-incrimination. "We are asked to create another by interpreting the First Amendment to grant newsmen a testimonial privilege that other citizens do not enjoy. This we decline to do." If news sources had to remain confidential and unidentified because they themselves were implicated in a crime, White found it absurd to provide a constitutional shield for them: "We cannot seriously entertain the notion that the First Amendment protects a newsman's agreement to conceal the criminal conduct of his source . . . on the theory that it is better to write about crime than to do something about it." White acknowledged that there may be news sources not engaged in criminal activity who desire anonymity for other reasons, but estimates of the inhibiting effect subpoenas would have on such sources he found to be "widely divergent and to a great extent speculative." And in an obvious reference to the Black Panthers, although he did not name them, White noted that many confidential sources need the press as much as the press needs them: "Quite often, such informants are members of a minority political or cultural group that relies heavily on the media to propagate its views, publicize its aims, and magnify its exposure to the public." In any case, White conceded that some noncriminal informants might, for whatever reason, refuse to talk to newsmen if they risked being later identified in an official investigation. But, he went on, "we cannot accept the argument that the public interest in possible future news about crime from undisclosed, unverified sources must take precedence over the public interest in pursuing and prosecuting those crimes reported to the press by informants and in thus deterring the commission of such crimes in the future." In conclusion, turning to the Caldwell case specifically, White declared, "[The court of appeals] decision must be reversed. If there is no First Amendment privilege to refuse to answer the relevant and material questions asked during a good-faith grand jury investigation, then it is [all the more] true that there is no privilege to refuse to appear before such a grand jury until the Government demonstrates some 'compelling need' for a newsman's testimony."

White's opinion provoked two stinging dissents—one written by Justice Potter Stewart, in which two other justices joined, the other by Justice William O. Douglas. Stewart's statement, the more temperate of the two, began: "The Court's crabbed view of the First Amendment reflects a disturbing insensitivity to the critical role of an independent press in our society." Repeating an observation made by the court of appeals, Stewart charged that the majority was inviting "state and federal authorities . . . to annex the journalistic profession as an investigative arm of government. Not only will this decision impair performance of the press's constitutionally protected functions, but it will, I am convinced, in the long run, harm rather than help the administration of justice." Stewart based his conclusion on a trio of factors: first, reporters need informants to gather news; second, informants may demand a promise of confidentiality; third, "an unbridled subpoena power . . . will either deter sources from divulging information or deter reporters from gathering and publishing information." Elaborating upon the last point, Stewart observed, "A public-spirited person inside government, who is not implicated in any crime, will now be fearful of revealing corruption or other government wrongdoing, because he will know he can subsequently be identified by use of [a subpoena]. The potential source must, therefore, choose between risking exposure by giving information or avoiding risk by remaining silent." Similarly, a reporter, "in the event of a subpoena, under today's decision . . . will know that he must choose between being punished for contempt if he refuses to testify, or violating his profession's ethics and impairing his resourcefulness as a reporter if he discloses his confidential information." To bolster his argument that the Court's decision would hinder the flow of news to the public, Stewart cited a Justice Department memorandum that recognized that "compulsory process [i.e., a subpoena] in some circumstances may have a limiting effect on the exercise of First Amendment rights." And Stewart went on to note, "*No* evidence contradicting the existence of such deterrent effects was offered at the trials or in the briefs here. . . ."

Acknowledging "society's interest in the use of the grand jury to administer justice fairly and effectively," Stewart quite explicitly denied the press privilege "to ignore any subpoena that was issued." A reporter would have to move to quash the subpoena and the government would then have to "(1) show that there is probable cause to believe [he] has information that is clearly relevant to a specific probable violation of law; (2) demonstrate that the information sought cannot be obtained by alternative means less destructive of First Amendment rights; and (3) demonstrate a compelling and overriding interest in the information." There are echoes here of the decision the California district court had rendered two years earlier, but at the conclusion of his dissent Stewart took a giant step beyond that decision, embracing fully Caldwell's argument that his very appearance before the grand jury "would jeopardize his relationship with his sources." Wrote Stewart, "Obviously, only in very rare circumstances would a confidential relationship between a reporter and his source be so sensitive that mere appearance before the grand jury by the newsman would substantially impair his news-gathering function." But Stewart found such circumstances in the Caldwell case, and since the government had not even attempted to dispute the reporter's assertion that there was nothing to which he could testify that had not already been printed, Stewart firmly decided that Caldwell's appearance "would . . . indeed be a barren performance."

Like the judges of the court of appeals, Stewart stressed that his pro-Caldwell opinion was a very narrow one. Justice William O. Douglas, however, did his very best to widen it. A borderline absolutist on First Amendment issues, Douglas, in his dissent (which no other justice joined), was blunt and unequivocal: "A newsman has an absolute right not to appear before a grand jury." For Douglas, the Constitution conferred upon Caldwell all the immunity he needed, and no "compelling need" could ever cancel or even restrict that privilege. As for the balancing acts performed by all the other judges involved in Caldwell rulings, carefully weighing the First Amendment rights of the press against the law-enforcement needs of the government, Douglas had no patience with any of them. To the lower courts, to the members of the White majority, and to Stewart and his fellow dissenters, Douglas's message could not have been simpler: "My belief is that all of the 'balancing' was done by those who wrote the Bill of Rights. By casting the First Amendment in absolute terms, they repudiated the timid, watered-down, emasculated version of the First Amendment" that the government had advanced in the Caldwell case.

Douglas's dissent was filled to bursting with the most dire predictions about the effect of the High Court ruling.

> Today's decision will impede the wide-open and robust dissemination of ideas and counterthought which a free press both fosters and protects and which is essential to the success of intelligent self-government. Forcing a reporter before a grand jury will have two retarding effects upon the ear and the pen of the press. Fear of exposure will cause dissidents to communi-

cate less openly to trusted reporters. And, fear of accountability will cause editors and critics to write with more restrained pens. . . . Unless [a reporter] has a privilege to withhold the identity of his source, he will be the victim of governmental intrigue or aggression. If he can be summoned to testify in secret . . . his sources will dry up and the attempted exposure, the effort to enlighten the public, will be ended. If what the Court sanctions today becomes settled law, then the reporter's main function in American society will be to pass on to the public the press releases which the various departments of government issue.

Douglas summed up his reaction to the Caldwell decision in a final paragraph that strikes a note of intense sadness as well as scathing condemnation:

The intrusion of government into this domain is symptomatic of the disease of this society. As the years pass the power of government becomes more and more pervasive. It is a power to suffocate both people and causes. Those in power, whatever their politics, want only to perpetuate it. Now that the fences of the law and the tradition that has protected the press are broken down, the people are the victims. The First Amendment, as I read it, was designed precisely to prevent that tragedy.

In these words we can sense the breadth and depth of Douglas's commitment to the First Amendment. One of the most admired, and controversial, jurists of his time, Douglas served on the Supreme Court for thirty-six years, from 1939 to 1975, and while those years were marked by crisis, turbulence, and change, he remained steadfast in his battle for the rights of the individual against the power of government. But as a prophet he was not always right. It should detract from neither his courage nor his conviction to point out that about nine months after the Caldwell decision that Douglas found so insidious, two reporters from *The Washington Post* broke the Watergate story, thereby setting in motion a series of events that was to culminate in the collapse of the Nixon administration and the first resignation of a president in United States history. So much for the charge that a reporter's main function would become passing on government press releases!

But, of course, Douglas's was not a lonely voice crying in the wilderness. In response to the majority ruling, out pealed a chorus of catcalls. Journalists denounced the decision as a threat to nearly all their behind-the-scenes investigations of current events. Said the president of the National Press Club: "It's not only going to inhibit sources in crime reporting but in the reporting of foreign policy and domestic politics as well." Beloved reporters like Walter Cronkite joined aggressive ones like Mike Wallace in voicing their belief that "the public would be the loser in the long run." The American Society of Newspaper Editors called on Congress to enact legislation that would protect the confidentiality of press sources, so-called shield laws, which will be discussed in the next chapter.

Congress failed to do so but newspapers have continued to publish and, as Watergate so dramatically proved, reporters have continued to use confidential sources to uncover all sorts of crime, corruption, and chicanery. Earl Caldwell, meanwhile, fought to stay out of jail. So did Huey Newton and Bobby Seale, both of whom had been indicted on a variety of charges, including murder, in the late sixties and early seventies. Between them they spent years behind bars, waiting for their cases to be tried, but neither was ever convicted of a serious crime. By 1972, all felony charges against them had been dropped, the Black Panther Party had split between violent and antiviolent factions, the former had gone underground, and the latter was preparing to run Bobby Seale as its candidate for mayor of Oakland. In the elections the following year, Seale came in second in a field of four, thus making the runoff, which he then lost with only 36 percent of the vote. But that close to 44,000 Oakland citizens thought enough of Bobby Seale to give him their electoral support was striking evidence of how times had changed. The sixties were over, but the new perceptions they had brought remained. There seemed no question that people were looking at the world and at each other in a markedly different way.

In the world of journalism, Earl Caldwell was a pioneer in setting forth the idea that the Constitution gives reporters a privilege not to testify about their sources. The claim had been made initially in 1958, but it was the Caldwell case that first presented it in a powerful and insistent manner. It is, of course, a privilege that has yet to be recognized by the Supreme Court, and the fact is that it may never be, although in the past decade many states have acknowledged and, to a varying extent, protected the press's need for confidentiality. And, indeed, there are champions of the First Amendment who believe these limited steps are the only ones that should be taken. Columnist Anthony Lewis has written that "the press has continued to talk about a 'First Amendment privilege' as if it existed. It does not, and in my strong opinion it should not. The press has always used confidential sources, and it must. But necessity is a long way from exalting the practice into a constitutional right. . . . Reporters who promise confidentiality to get a vital story must keep that promise. Not many judges will push them to disclose, in the end. But if a few brave journalists go to prison for their promise, it is no disrespect to them to say that the battle is better fought that way—in the balance of courtroom interests and public opinion—than under the distorting guise of constitutional privilege for journalists."

Earl Caldwell never did go to jail, but in recent years several other reporters who refused to testify about their sources have served time behind bars. Insistence upon a privilege that courts do not recognize has become, then, a not-uncommon act of civil disobedience. Such acts have an honorable and productive history in our Republic, one that goes back to earliest colonial days, but it was in the sixties that civil disobedience suddenly seemed to have been rediscovered—and enthusiastically practiced. War protesters and demonstrators on behalf of other causes were carted off to jail, often by the dozens and sometimes by the hundreds, singing their songs, chanting their slogans, and generally setting an example of determined resistance to governmental laws, policies, and demands that they considered unjust and destructive. They were heroes of a kind, these citizens who responded to their own conscience rather than to the word from Washington, and they were heroes regardless of whether the causes they fought for won out in the end. In very much the same way, Earl Caldwell was a hero, too, and very much of his time. In his clash with authority he may have gained no legal victory but, for himself, he preserved his integrity and, for the rest of us, he demonstrated how precious a reporter's freedom and responsibility can be.

7.
Keeping Secrets

For a long time it was thought that the trouble at Riverdell Hospital began with the unexplained death of young Nancy Savino. Having undergone emergency abdominal surgery, she seemed well on the way to a full recovery when, two days after her operation, at about eight A.M. on March 21, 1966, a laboratory technician came into her room to take a blood sample and found Nancy lying very, very still. "Wake up," the technician commanded, but the little girl wouldn't move. The technician cried out for help, and two nurses rushed into the room, followed by an intern and, moments later, the hospital's chief surgeon. But all their efforts to revive the patient failed, and at eight-fifteen A.M. Nancy Savino, four years old, was pronounced dead.

Although an autopsy was performed, it provided not even a clue, let alone an explanation, as to the cause of the child's sudden and totally unexpected death. Officially, it was—and would long remain—"undetermined."

The passing of Nancy Savino, mysterious and tragic as it was, aroused no suspicions. Neither did the death of Margaret Henderson, age twenty-six, another Riverdell postoperative patient, on April 22. Nor the deaths later that spring and summer of several elderly patients who had undergone extensive surgery. Nor the death of Frank Biggs, fifty-nine, on August 28. Nor the death of Emma Arzt, seventy, on September 23. No, it wasn't until Eileen Shaw, thirty-six, died on October 23, two days after a successful caesarean delivery of her baby, that two staff surgeons, alarmed by the hospital's soaring postsurgical mortality rate, began to suspect that there was "something very seriously wrong with these cases." Reviewing them in detail, from Nancy Savino on, the doctors soon came to the realization that some common elements linked many of the deaths. And then, like a figure stepping out of the shadows, there suddenly appeared to them the very real and fearsome possibility that the patients had all been injected with a fatal poison.

Although nobody could be—or ever would be—sure, the apparent death toll stood at thirteen when, on November 2, the board of directors of Riverdell Hospital presented themselves at the office of Bergen County (New Jersey) Prosecutor Guy Calissi. They had a tale to tell that strained belief, starting with all those unexpected and unexplained mortalities—postoperative patients who had been making satisfactory progress toward recovery but who then, unaccountably, stopped breathing. For months, the doctors admitted, their concern had grown, but they had done nothing because they had suspected no one. Finally, however, they had been made aware of certain facts, horrifying in their implications, that demanded immediate action: First, there was the uncanny circumstance that the hospital's chief surgeon seemed always to have been present at or shortly before each patient's death, usually for no discernible reason. And then, there was the startling discovery, a day earlier, in that same doctor's dressing-room locker, of several vials of a potentially lethal drug called curare.

Calissi wasted no time. By four-thirty that afternoon he had a judge issue a search warrant, on the basis of suspicion of "murder . . . by means of poison," and two prosecutors and two detectives descended on Riverdell Hospital, there to appropriate the contents of the chief surgeon's locker. Among other items they found hypodermic needles, syringes, and eighteen vials of curare, most of them just about empty.

The raid was the opening move in a halting, scattershot investigation that was said to cost $40,000—and that produced virtually no results. A chemical analysis of the tissues of Eileen Shaw proved inconclusive—curare could have been present but was impossible to detect because of the formalin solution in which the body had been soaked when embalmed. Many—but not all—of the hospital's staff members were questioned at length about the events and findings that had prompted the directors' suspicions. Investigators were able to substantiate the chief surgeon's purchase of curare from a local medical supply company: Twenty-four bottles had been bought between September 1965 and September 1966. And, not surprisingly, the chief surgeon himself, accompanied by his attorney, gave a voluntary deposition that would eventually fill a 209-page transcript: He categorically denied any wrongdoing; he offered explanations for his presence in the rooms of the various patients around the time of death; and he described in great detail experiments he had been conducting, unobserved, on live dogs, all of which, he said, required the use of curare.

Viewed in retrospect, the seizure of the contents of the chief surgeon's locker and the extended deposition the doctor made nine days later form a kind of frame around the investigation. For although the inquiry was not officially closed for another three months, once the doctor had given his testimony, little more was accomplished or even tried. Certainly clouds of suspicion still hung in the air, but Prosecutor Calissi seemed unable to dispel them. And when, early in 1967, the "suspect" resigned his position as chief of surgery at Riverdell Hospital, the investigation, like the thirteen patients, simply expired. Some incriminating facts had been uncovered—facts that could not be explained away—but, in the opinion of the prosecutor, he had turned up no motive and nothing solid enough to build a case on. There was "something here," but, he was quoted as saying, "it sure beats me."

Normalcy returned to Riverdell Hospital. With the investigation abandoned, a new chief surgeon in office, and no mysterious postoperative deaths since October, almost everyone involved in the case forgot about Nancy Savino and Margaret Henderson and Eileen Shaw and the other ten patients who had quite possibly been poisoned. Of course, their survivors remembered, and no doubt others did as well. And because one person among them was determined, after nearly ten years, to share the memory with the world, on the morning of January 7, 1976, readers of *The New York Times* learned in a front-page story of the shocking events at Riverdell Hospital so long before, and of an apparently demoniacal Doctor X.

The man who wrote that story was a reporter named Myron A. Farber, and he was destined to become every bit as famous as the surgeon he thrust into the limelight. For Farber, it all began one day in late June 1975, when a *Times* editor received a three-page typewritten letter that contained a number of scandalous charges. He immediately turned it over to Farber, who specialized in stories requiring intensive investigation. Years later, in his book about the Doctor X case, *Somebody Is Lying*, Farber wrote: "I scanned the letter on the way back to my desk, where, filling my pipe, I read it again. A hospital was cited, but not identified. Doctors were referred to, but not by name. A prosecutor was mentioned, but not which one. . . . But the charge animating the letter was clear and chilling: the chief surgeon of a hospital had, a decade earlier, murdered thirty to forty patients. Not simple malpractice . . . not some errors in medical judgment, not some unfortunate slips of the knife. But murder."

The letter could have come from a crank, but the tone suggested otherwise, as did the fact that the writer of the letter had met the editor to whom it was addressed. In any case, the accusations were too sensational to be ignored, and within moments Farber had placed a call to a recently retired director of New York City's medical examiner's office. From his farm upstate, this gentleman, prodded by Farber's insistent questioning, managed to recall "a case over in New Jersey. Maybe ten or twelve years ago . . . a whole series of deaths in a small hospital. All under very peculiar circumstances . . . over in Bergen County. . . . The case was dropped. . . . Thirteen is the number that comes back to me. And the hospital . . . was it Riverhead? Or Riverdale? No, that's not it. But it was something like that. *Riverdell*—that's it . . . Riverdell Hospital."

A letter and a remarkably productive telephone call thus set in motion an investigation that was to continue for six months. Farber first had to finish an assignment he had already been working on, but by mid-October he was able to pursue the Riverdell matter full-time. In the offices of the Bergen County prosecutor and the Narcotics Task Force, he found voluminous files pertaining to the 1966 investigation, and as Farber combed through them, the charges contained in the letter to the *Times* editor gradually took coherent shape and became reality. Here were the names of the thirteen patients and of the doctors and the nurses who had been responsible for caring for them. Here were the dates of their operations and the deaths that followed. Here were the incidents and the findings that had eventually aroused suspicion and led to the most serious of accusations. And here were countless leads that Farber was to follow up in a long progression of interviews.

As he tracked down and spoke with various members of the Riverdell staff and of the county prosecutor's office, it became increasingly clear to him that the earlier investigation had been deeply flawed and strangely incomplete. He learned, for example, that no attempt had been made to question the nurses who had been present at the deaths of Nancy Savino and Margaret Henderson or the relatives of any of the thirteen presumed victims— indeed, Farber discovered, none of the survivors even knew that an investigation had once taken place.

He was troubled by other, more serious faults of omission. Upon reading the transcript of the chief surgeon's deposition, located only after a good deal of detective work, since it was missing from the prosecutor's files, he came upon a number of responses that seemed to him dubious, inconsistent, or otherwise suspect; yet there was no indication in the files that Calissi—who, incidentally, had since become a judge—had tried to check out any of these statements. It was almost as if the prosecutor had accepted the doctor's allegation that he was being framed, and thus had left largely unexplored the paths that might have led to a different conclusion.

By far the most promising of these would have been disinterment of the bodies of at least some of the putative victims to test them for the presence of curare. Calissi was not necessarily to be faulted for his failure to have this done. Since the tests on Eileen

Shaw had proved of no value, he had decided that further efforts along such lines would have been equally useless, and, given the technology of the time, his judgment may well have been the correct one. But now, ten years later, it occurred to Farber that the means of tracing a drug like curare might be much improved, and this notion was confirmed by a member of the New York City medical examiner's office.

In conducting his investigation, Farber obviously needed the co-operation of the current Bergen County prosecutor, a man named Joe Woodcock. When Farber first met him, Woodcock, who had been in office for two years, had learned of the Riverdell case only a week before. The county chief of detectives had shown him a news-paper article about some suspicious deaths at a Veterans Adminis-tration hospital in Michigan and had wondered whether any Riverdell doctors might have moved west. At that point Woodcock had no thought of reviving a decade-old case that he knew almost nothing about. But in the months that followed, with Farber openly pursuing his own investigation—poring over the files that Wood-cock himself had provided, interviewing Judge Calissi and other former members of the county prosecutor's staff—Woodcock's in-terest, predictably, became aroused. Soon he had detectives study-ing the Riverdell files, including the deposition that Farber had ferreted out, and when they found substantial "inconsistencies" in the latter, Woodcock decided to submit the patients' medical rec-ords to an independent expert for review. The specialist chosen turned out to be the same member of the New York City medical examiner's office that Farber had consulted.

Suddenly a new sense of urgency pervaded the reporter's office at *The Times*. After months of digging and probing and speculat-ing, Farber stared at the grim possibility that his "exclusive" story would be wrenched right out from under him. Woodcock, who had once been so helpful, had now "clammed up." Was he perhaps planning to reveal the results of his investigation to a local New Jersey newspaper? It was time for Farber to pull the strands of his research together and start writing his article. Day and night for a week he pounded away at his typewriter. Some nights, too tired to go home, he slept on the carpeted floor of his office. Finally, he produced a first draft and then, responding to suggestions and criticisms from his editors, a second. Sixty-seven hundred words long, enough to fill nine columns of *Times* newsprint, clearly it would have to run in two installments. And, with the completion and approval of the second draft, another key decision was made: The chief surgeon, never having been charged with any crime, could not be named. He became "Doctor X."

It was late December. Farber was putting the finishing touches on his story when he called Woodcock to ask about the progress of his investigation. The prosecutor would say only that his office was drawing up some "papers," but that was enough to prompt a delay in publication of Farber's article. If the "papers" were to be made public, they had to be part of the story.

Farber did not have to wait long. On January 6, 1976, Sybil Moses, a Bergen County assistant prosecutor, filed two affidavits with a county judge. In the first, the expert from the New York City medical examiner's office swore that in his professional opinion deaths in "the majority of the cases reviewed are not explainable on the basis of natural causes and are consistent with having been caused by a respiratory depressant . . . that recent technological advances now permit the detection of very minute amounts of [curare] in tissues from dead bodies . . . that exhumation, autopsy, and reexamination is warranted. . . ." In the second affidavit, the assistant prosecutor stated that her office had reopened its investigation into the Riverdell deaths "as a result of (a) . . . a series of similar deaths at a veterans' hospital in Michigan . . . and (b) questioning and investigation by a reporter for *The New York Times*. . . ." The second affidavit concluded with a request that the court authorize the disinterment of five Riverdell patients who had died suspicious deaths. Among them was one Carl Rohrbeck. Having passed away in December 1965, three months before Nancy Savino, Rohrbeck was now presumed to have been the first of the victims. He was late in gaining this distinction, however, because his had not been a postoperative death. He had stopped breathing about fifteen minutes *prior to* scheduled surgery, which was to have been performed by Doctor X himself.

The county judge signed the authorization to exhume the bodies of Rohrbeck, Nancy Savino, Frank Biggs, Margaret Henderson, and Emma Arzt. And in a few hours the giant presses of *The New York Times* started to roll, spewing out the early edition of the next day's paper. There on the front page was a story that opened with a report of the court order and went on to do some exhuming of its own, bringing to light at last all those sinister happenings that had been buried deep in the uncaring past.

When Myron Farber, in the course of his investigation, had tried to interview Doctor X, the former chief surgeon had adamantly refused to talk about the Riverdell affair. After the *Times* story broke, other reporters managed to learn his identity and locate him, and again the doctor, now in successful private practice, chose to hold out behind a wall of silence. But other walls around him were beginning to crack. On January 11, Prosecutor Woodcock announced that he had asked the New Jersey Board of Medical Examiners to suspend the surgeon's license—Woodcock, too, referred to him as Doctor X—pending the outcome of the county's investigation. The board agreed to take the matter under consideration. On January 13, with a television camera recording

Evidence of Curare
Sought in 9 Deaths

By M. A. FARBER

Testimony by Dr. X in 1966 About Curare
A Key Factor of New Inquiry Into Deaths

By M.A. FARBER

The headlines of the two New York Times *articles in which Farber first broke the story of Doctor X.*

the event, the body of Nancy Savino was exhumed from a snow-covered grave. In measured succession, over the course of a month, came the disinterment of Margaret Henderson, Emma Arzt, Carl Rohrbeck, and Frank Biggs. On February 4, the day after Emma Arzt was exhumed, Doctor X, in a proceeding hidden from the press, began a new deposition to the county prosecutor. By March 3, when he returned to Woodcock's office to continue with his statement, the results of the first autopsy were in: Curare was present in the corpse of Nancy Savino.

Four days later, these findings were made public, Woodcock disclosed that he was convening a grand jury to probe the River-dell affair—and Doctor X's attorney set the date for a press conference. His client was nowhere to be seen as about fifty reporters jammed into a motel meeting room on March 16 to hear the lawyer declare that the doctor "was not the only man" to have had access to curare at Riverdell Hospital and that if "any of the patients expired of curare poisoning, anyone could have done it." And in response to a question posed by Myron Farber, he said, "You have shown an amazing amount of knowledge about what happened ten years ago, and I don't think really there's anything I can do to enlighten you. You, perhaps, have more knowledge of this case than I do." The next day, in its account of the press conference, *The Times* finally revealed a critical piece of that knowledge: it identified Doctor X as Mario Jascalevich.

The Times found justification for its action—which was, of course, immediately copied by most of the other news media—in the fact that the doctor's real name had already appeared in the grand jury proceedings and in various legal documents that were publicly available. One such document was a subpoena served by the prosecutor on Christ Hospital in Jersey City, where Dr. Jascalevich now performed 90 percent of his surgery. On March 23 the hospital suspended the doctor's right to operate, explaining that it did so "in the best interest of patient care." Doctor Jascalevich fought back—and won. Declining to appear in court himself, he was represented by a new attorney, Ray Brown, considered by many to be the best criminal defense lawyer in the state. And before a superior court judge, Brown thundered that the suspension was "so broad and vague as to be incredible." The judge agreed, ruling in the doctor's favor, and hardly more than a week after the suspension was announced, Christ Hospital reinstated Dr. Jascalevich's clinical privileges.

It was a victory that was quickly followed by two severe setbacks. In May the grand jury investigating the Riverdell affair heard testimony that curare had been detected in the bodies of Frank Biggs, Emma Arzt, and Nancy Savino, and that while tests were continuing on Margaret Henderson and Carl Rohrbeck, the "most reasonable" cause of their deaths was also curare poisoning. On May 18, having sat for two months and heard thirty-three witnesses, the grand jury handed up a five-count indictment, charging that Mario Jascalevich "did willfully, feloniously, and of his malice aforethought, kill and murder" each of the five people whose bodies had been exhumed. The next day the doctor was arrested, then released on $150,000 bail. On May 21, he resumed his practice, performing three operations that morning. But in the afternoon the State Board of Medical Examiners charged him with several counts of malpractice, relating not to the deaths for which he stood indicted but to a much more recent Jersey City case, in which he was accused of negligence. Although Ray Brown announced that he would contest the suspension of his client's license, Dr. Jascalevich voluntarily agreed to give up his surgical practice until the hearing on the charges was completed. That was to take three years—and Dr. Jascalevich was never to perform an operation in New Jersey again.

Almost two years passed before he went on trial for murder. During that time a variety of legal skirmishes was fought, and, incidentally, Riverdell Hospital declared bankruptcy. At last, on February 27, 1978, in a fourth-floor courtroom of the Bergen County Courthouse, the trial began. And almost at once a First Amendment issue arose: On the third day of jury selection, in a corridor outside the courtroom, Myron Farber was served with a subpoena to testify for the defense.

Here was the first indication that *The New York Times* and Ray Brown were embarked on a collision course. The immediate problem was not Farber's admitted reluctance to appear as a witness for Dr. Jascalevich—though it was clear from the start that *The Times* would fight the subpoena if it required their reporter to give totally unrestricted testimony. No, the issue at this early point in the trial was whether *The Times*'s coverage of it could be provided by the man who probably knew more about the case than just about anyone else. For under the court's "sequestration" rule, a witness could not be present in the courtroom until after he or she had testified; if Farber was to be a witness and this rule were not waived, *The Times* would have to assign someone else to the trial.

At a hearing before trial judge William J. Arnold, *The Times*, represented by attorney Floyd Abrams, argued that any other reporter "will know less, have less background, and the public will be less served." In Abrams's view, press freedom ensured Farber access to the courtroom unless Brown could show that the reporter's presence "would pose a substantial and immediate and direct threat to a fair trial." In reply, Brown asked simply whether "Mr. Myron Farber will . . . be subject to the same rule of law as . . . is applied to literally well over 150 citizens who are being kept out of this courtroom." The discussion that followed was marked by the following prophetic exchange:

> ARNOLD: Let me ask you, Mr. Abrams. . . . Let us assume for the moment no doubt the press has certain rights, but can the rights of the press ever exceed the rights of a defendant to a fair trial?
>
> ABRAMS: Your Honor, as so phrased, I can tell you that that is a question the Supreme Court of the United States and the Supreme Court of your own state have said they hope they never have to reach. . . .

It is the Sixth Amendment that guarantees a defendant the right to a fair trial. Once Myron Farber was propelled beyond a newsman's traditional role as observer and became a participant in the matter at hand, the clash between the Sixth Amendment and the First in the trial of Doctor X became as inexorable as combat between two armies blindly advancing upon each other.

In the first outbreak of hostilities, the First Amendment lost. Judge Arnold, in a fifteen-page opinion, found Farber to be "a first-rate investigative reporter," and as such he assumed "the duties . . . [and] the responsibility of an investigator and must be treated equally under the law, unless he comes under some exception." Rejecting Abrams's contention that the First Amendment privilege provides that exception, Judge Arnold concluded, "It is this Court's opinion that the rights of the press under the First Amendment can never exceed the rights of a defendant to a fair and impartial trial." So Myron Farber was to be a witness first, a reporter second, which meant, of course, that at the trial of Doctor X he would not be a reporter at all.

The Times chose not to appeal, and while its lawyers focused their attention on Farber's upcoming testimony, it sent another reporter to Courtroom 407 in the Bergen County Courthouse. There a jury had finally been selected for what was to become the longest criminal trial for a single defendant in the history of the United States.

The opening statement of Prosecutor Sybil Moses promised the jury that "the sum total of all the evidence" would prove that Dr. Jascalevich had "wilfully" murdered the five patients. She spoke of the defendant's presence before and after the mysterious deaths, of the discovery of curare in his locker, of the potentially lethal qualities of that drug if not properly administered. Legally, she did not have to offer a motive, but on the question of "why" that had bothered Calissi ten years before, she noted that Dr. Jascalevich had lost both status and income after two new surgeons were added to the Riverdell staff in 1965 and 1966—and, aside from Carl Rohrbeck, it was the patients of those surgeons who had furnished the ghastly death toll.

Speaking for the defense, Ray Brown attacked every aspect of the state's case. Dr. Jascalevich was "always around Riverdell Hospital" because that was where he earned his living. Curare was "no more dangerous than aspirin." All those chemical tests on the exhumed bodies were based on "speculation and concepts" that had no grounding in reality. His client was, in short, the victim of two conspiracies: framed first by doctors who had been stung by his well-justified criticism of their surgical competence; and then, ten years later, by the same doctors joined by "prosecutors, the newspapers, and politicians . . . for the sake of their careers, whether medicine, politics, or legal." Toward the end of his opening statement, Brown singled out Farber as an "enterprising reporter" who "brought certain items to the prosecutor that apparently had never been in the hands of the prosecutor. . . ." Brown's clear implication was that Farber had sparked this new plot against Dr. Jascalevich. And so, at least in spirit—and an evil spirit at that—Myron Farber quickly became a presence in the courtroom from which he had been barred.

Not *The New York Times* but the *Miami Herald* described the trial as "a debating society gone beserk." From the first it was apparent that the proceedings would be marked by constant, acerbic exchanges between defense and prosecution. Brown usually referred to his opponent as "she" or "that lady" or "that schoolteacher," rarely by her name or as prosecutor. He was equally disdainful of most of the state's key witnesses, particularly the Riverdell staff surgeons who had broken into Dr. Jascalevich's locker twelve years before and the various toxicologists who confirmed the presence of curare in the bodies of the exhumed victims. The defense attorney objected to the introduction of just about every item of evidence that the prosecution considered crucial to its case: the contents of Dr. Jascalevich's locker, the records of his curare purchases, the depositions he gave to Calissi in 1966 and to Woodcock ten years later. Of course, as Brown raised objection after objection, the prosecutor fought back strenuously, every step of the way, but too often, she thought, the judge was ruling in the defense's favor. At one point, denied equal time to respond to Brown's accusation that evidence may have been tampered with, Moses refused to obey a judicial command to sit down and be quiet and was, consequently, held in contempt of court. The prosecution countered by formally asking Judge Arnold to remove himself from the case because of his "inability to conduct . . . a fair and unbiased" trial. The judge, after pondering this accusation over a weekend, announced the following Monday that he would continue to preside. And the debating contest resumed.

High in the prosecution's loss column was Judge Arnold's decision to disallow the introduction as evidence of Dr. Jascalevich's second 1976 deposition unless the defendant himself took the stand. His ruling followed a special hearing on the question, conducted during the trial but, needless to say, out of the presence of the jury. The last witness at this proceeding, known as a target hearing, was Myron Farber, called by Ray Brown in an obvious and determined effort to uncover some sort of conspiracy between the reporter and Joe Woodcock. Wrote Farber in his book: "Brown threw about 100 questions at me in court that day, and I answered some 85 of them. Citing the First Amendment and the New Jersey shield law, I declined to answer a dozen questions that involved confidential information or sources, or information that I had gathered as a reporter but had not printed. . . . I exercised my rights, but I exercised them sparingly. Under questioning by Brown, I acknowledged that I had given Woodcock a copy of Dr. Jascalevich's 1966 deposition, and I said that was all I had given him. . . ."

Many of the questions that Farber did not answer the prosecutor objected to as being irrelevant, a view with which Judge Arnold agreed, at least for the moment. Said the judge, ominously for Farber, "I am not ruling that he may not have to answer these questions at a subsequent time." Such a warning emphasized the unusual nature of the target hearing as a kind of dry run, offering Brown and Farber a chance to size each other up for the confrontation that lay ahead.

Meanwhile, the character of that confrontation had grown immeasurably more hostile. A day before the target hearing, Farber and *The Times* had been informed that Judge Arnold, acting under an interstate agreement, had asked the New York State Supreme Court to subpoena various materials from them. Included were "all notes of interviews, memoranda, pictures, recordings, and other writings relating to a list of 193 potential witnesses for the Jascalevich trial." Judge Arnold's request stemmed from an affidavit by Ray Brown stating that everything listed was "critical" to the defense of his client. "I was stunned by the scope of the subpoena," Farber wrote later, ". . . in effect, he was asking for my desk. The request made no distinction between published and unpublished material, or between confidential and nonconfidential material. Just give me everything, Judge Arnold was saying, and . . . he would decide what to turn over to Brown."

In his book, Farber conjectures that Brown knew *The Times* would resist such a sweeping subpoena and was perhaps "counting on our opposition to further delay the trial and to suggest that *The Times* and I were hiding something." If this had been Brown's intention when he filed his affidavit, he had every reason to be encouraged by Judge Arnold's earlier opinion that the First Amendment could never take precedence over the Sixth. And now, in his request to the New York court, the judge went even further, for he found in the New Jersey shield law "no privilege . . .

that can prevent the withholding of these documents." The fact is that statute holds that a reporter "has a privilege to refuse to disclose . . . to any court . . . any news or information obtained in the course of pursuing his professional activities, whether or not it is disseminated." The privilege extends also to the source of such information. While there are exceptions to the privilege—if a reporter waives his rights or is an eyewitness to physical violence, for example—none of them applied to Farber.

To get around the shield law, the defense was arguing that Farber was not a reporter but an investigator, collaborating with the Bergen County prosecutor; this was the position taken by Ray Brown's assistant at the New York hearing on Judge Arnold's subpoena request. For his part, the *Times* attorney sought additional protection for Farber in New York's shield law (actually less strong than New Jersey's), contending that the substance of the dispute should be heard and ruled on by a New York court before the reporter was directed to turn anything over to another state. The acting state supreme court justice disagreed. Expressing certainty that the New Jersey courts would give Farber a hearing on "all issues of privilege" and would preserve all the rights the reporter enjoyed in New York, Justice Harold Rothwax ordered Farber and *The Times* to deliver to Judge Arnold all the documents he had requested. They had four days to comply.

Justice Rothwax signed the subpoena on June 2, two days after the United States Supreme Court had rendered its decision in the *Stanford Daily* case. For the group that gathered that afternoon in an office at *The Times*, the Stanford majority opinion—that a search warrant provided sufficient legal basis for a surprise police raid on a newsroom—struck an added note of gloom in proceedings that at best were grim and anxious. The assembled newsmen saw the ruling as another shot in the recent volley of judicial attacks on the independence of the press. The Farber subpoena was, then, part of a dangerous trend. It was also believed to be the most sweeping subpoena "ever served on an American reporter." It would have to be appealed immediately. Said one *Times* editor, "We're not going to become part of the very judicial process that we're expected to cover."

Several courts were soon to rule otherwise, insisting, just as Myron Farber feared they would, that reporters testify. Farber was only too well aware of the *Branzburg* decision of four years before, when the Supreme Court had found against his former colleague on *The Times*, Earl Caldwell. What little encouragement Farber could glean from that case sprouted from the words of Justice Lewis F. Powell, Jr., in his brief opinion concurring with the majority. He had written of the need to strike "a proper balance between freedom of the press and the obligation of all citizens to give relevant testimony with respect to criminal conduct," and he had held that such a balance could be determined only on a case-by-case basis. Thus, *Branzburg* did not necessarily apply to all subpoenas served on newsmen. Each reporter deserved his own day in court.

Those days were becoming more frequent than ever before. In the sixties about a dozen reporters had been served with subpoenas. From 1970 to 1976 more than 500 had been. But a surprisingly high number had fought off their subpoenas successfully. This was true especially in civil cases and in criminal cases where the defense demanded evidence from the press. In affirming a reporter's privilege to withhold confidential sources and information, courts had cited both the Stewart dissent and the Powell concurrence in *Branzburg*, as well as the growing number of state shield laws that had been passed or strengthened (as New Jersey's had been) in the years since Earl Caldwell had struggled and lost.

For the principals in what was now known as the Myron Farber case, that defeat was a matter of steadily increasing weight. Each court appearance seemed to bring the reporter and his paper a new reversal. The New York State Appellate Division ruled that Justice Rothwax's order could not be appealed in that state and that the subpoena could be fought only in New Jersey. So in late June the contest returned to its original arena, Judge Arnold's chambers, where Ray Brown now objected to Prosecutor Moses's presence and refused to sit on the same couch with her. The *Times* attorney argued, as he had before, that the "wholesale disclosure" demanded by the subpoena violated Farber's constitutional rights, that Brown hadn't demonstrated the need and relevance of the documents he sought, and that he hadn't shown that whatever pertinent information Farber might have wasn't available elsewhere. Brown responded by wrapping himself in the *Branzburg* decision to ward off Farber's right to withhold evidence, by characterizing the reporter as "a central figure in the process that led to Dr. Jascalevich's indictment," and by charging that it was absurd to suggest that notes on interviews with many of the trial witnesses might be immaterial. And as for New Jersey's shield law, it was overshadowed by the Sixth Amendment's guarantee of a fair trial for his client.

It was probably inevitable that at this point Judge Arnold would deny *The Times*'s motion to quash the subpoena. In any case, deny it he did, and he went on to insist that all the materials demanded be turned over to him, so that he could examine them in private. Only then would he call a hearing to consider the issues raised by Farber and *The Times.* He could not "make a decision in a vacuum," he said; after he had read the notes, he would "decide if the items are barred by the shield law" or for any other reason. Judge Arnold announced his ruling on June 30. He was to be given the files by July 3; otherwise, he threatened, Farber and *The Times* would be in contempt of court.

Forced to move with lightning speed, the *Times* attorney immediately turned to the appellate division of the New Jersey Superior Court. There he argued that Judge Arnold had all the authority he needed to kill such a sweeping subpoena without seeing the material and that forcing Farber to hand over his files to *anyone* would deprive him of the constitutional rights he was fighting to preserve. The appellate division, unimpressed, refused to hear the appeal. So did the New Jersey Supreme Court when presented with the same arguments. The only place left to go now was Washington, and on July 11—Judge Arnold's deadline had been extended to allow *The Times* an opportunity to carry its case up the judicial ladder—the matter was given over to Justice Byron White of the United States Supreme Court. Although he did not reject *The Times*'s position outright, he refused to delay Judge Arnold's order, suggesting that the Court might "address the issue . . . at a later stage in these proceedings." The next day *The Times* tried again, with Justice Thurgood Marshall, to the same result. Acutely sensitive to the potential danger in forcing the press to divulge confidential materials, Justice Marshall nevertheless agreed with his colleague that with the criminal trial continuing and with no contempt citations having yet been issued, the Court could wait for another day before deciding to intervene.

But for Farber there were very few days left. In all likelihood he would be imprisoned if he were found in contempt of court, and *The Times* was not going to pressure him into becoming a martyr. Said an editor, "*The Times* will support you, whatever you want to do, but you have to make your own decision now. Nobody here is going to tell you that you have to go to jail." Farber was, however, no more inclined to back down than Earl Caldwell had been, and unlike Caldwell, who had been left by *The Times* to "go it alone," Farber was assured of his employer's continuing financial and legal backing.

Legal advice from *The Times* made Farber a wanted man two days later. A *Times* lawyer, believing that Farber had been improperly served with the subpoena, counseled him not to attend the contempt hearing of June 14. The presiding judge had a rather different view of the matter. "With a man's life and liberty at stake," he found legal technicalities no justification for Farber's absence, and before adjourning the hearing he angrily issued a warrant for the reporter's arrest. Back in New York, Justice Rothwax ordered Farber to appear at the Bergen County Courthouse, and there bail was set at $10,000 to ensure that Farber would not stay away from the next session of the contempt hearing. *The Times* posted bail immediately, but Farber still had to spend an hour "in a locked, yellow-wire cage" and had to be photographed and fingerprinted before he was released.

Six days later the hearing was over and the locked cage proved to be a deadly accurate omen. *The Times* and Myron Farber were found guilty of contempt of court for refusing to hand over the subpoenaed files. Permitted to make a statement before being sentenced, Farber said:

> I would like to explain to the Court, and to the public, why I am refusing to surrender my reporter's file on the case of Dr. Mario E. Jascalevich. . . . What is at issue here is not Dr. Jascalevich's right to a fair trial; he has access to the same people that I interviewed, and more. Nor is the issue my "right" to place myself above or outside the law. I have no such right, and I seek none. The issue, I believe, is the right of the public to be informed through its press, in accordance with the First Amendment of the United States Constitution.

Farber went on to review his involvement in the Jascalevich case from 1975 until his recent appearance as a witness at the target hearing. He continued:

Some weeks ago . . . the trial court ordered me to turn over to it all my notes, documents, and other materials relating to the case. In effect, the order commands me to violate confidences that I received in my effort to learn, and report, the truth about this case. And this I cannot do. I gave my word that I would respect these confidences, and I gave it in what I believe to be the public interest. I am the custodian of that word today as yesterday.

. . . I did not join my profession to cloak myself in the First Amendment or to flaunt it. Few journalists do. But I cannot cast aside my obligations as a reporter simply because they are being contested. The inevitable result of my compliance with this order would be my conversion into an investigative agent for the parties to this case. This is not what Madison and his contemporaries had in mind for the press, nor is it what the legislatures of New Jersey, New York, and other states intended when they passed statutes protecting newsmen's confidential materials. If I give up my file, I will have undermined my professional integrity and diminished the credibility of my colleagues. And, most important, I will have given notice that [*The New York Times*] is no longer available to those men and women who would seek it out—or would respond to it—to talk freely without fear.

. . . [S]ometimes, people who have done no wrong yet who have information that is useful to a rounded understanding of an issue are reluctant to speak out. . . . They may agree to provide information only on a confidential basis. And if I . . . accept information on those terms, I cannot disavow that agreement later. . . . If I was willing to permit devaluation of my ethical currency, I would soon find that my worth had eroded completely. And I could not work that way.

Your Honor, Dr. Jascalevich says that the material in my possession is "critical" to his defense. But he is mistaken. The deaths for which he is charged occurred in 1965 and 1966, and, as the Court well knows, I have no first-hand knowledge of them. Nor have I seen the bodies that were exhumed. . . . There is nothing in my notes that would establish the defendant's guilt or innocence for the trial court, and there is certainly nothing that would lend credence to his theory that he is being framed. For more than 21 weeks, Your Honor, witnesses have trooped across the courtroom to tell, under oath, what they know about the lives and deaths of Nancy Savino and the others. No one is in hiding. And I respectfully submit that it is to their testimony, and to the testimony of others to come, that the Court must look to find the truth.

Thank you, Your Honor.

Responding to this statement, the judge had "only one comment to make": "It seems to me that somewhere within the whole fabric of constitutional protection and statutory newsmen's privilege, there has to be some person or body or tribunal that can say, 'Mr. Farber, we don't suspect your integrity at all, but let's take a little peek . . . to see whether or not what you say is the truth.' . . . If Mr. Brown isn't entitled to [the notes] so be it, let's get it over with. If he is, it seems to me it would be a grave injustice to go on with this trial depriving the defense of something they think they need."

Having refused to give anyone that "little peek," *The Times* was fined $100,000 and an additional $5,000 each day until it complied with the subpoena, and Myron Farber was fined $2,000 and sentenced to jail for as long as he held back his files, with an extra six-month term tacked on as a criminal penalty. With his attorney first protesting this surprisingly harsh sentence, and then pleading that its enforcement be delayed pending appeal, all to no avail, Farber was led away.

Not to a wire cage this time but to a fully furnished apartment that was part of the jail complex. It was Farber's home for only a few hours; around nine o'clock that night, he was released

Myron Farber, leaving the courthouse...

by order of a justice of the New Jersey Supreme Court. The next morning that same justice offered a lonely dissent to the full court's ruling that Farber be returned to jail. It did agree, however, to postpone the rejailing until the case could again be heard by the United States Supreme Court. During the week of freedom that followed, Farber was repeatedly interviewed by the press, appeared on network television, and received bushelsful of mail encouraging him to "hang in there" because he was "dead right."

No such letters would have come from Justice Byron R. White. After hearing the *Times* attorney argue that "to this day we have not been afforded a hearing by any court" on the First Amendment issue and Ray Brown reply that the crux of the matter was "whether Myron Farber and *The New York Times* can nullify the power of the courts to decide the validity of a subpoena and substitute their private conception of . . . privilege for the judgment of a court of law," and after thinking about these matters

and behind bars.

for three days, Justice White, on August 1, declined to delay imposition of the penalties against the defendants. He was not certain that the required four justices would vote to accept the Farber case for Supreme Court review "at this time," and he personally had no qualms about requiring Farber to give the subpoenaed materials to Judge Arnold for his private inspection. Although Justice Marshall was again far more concerned with and sympathetic to *The Times*'s legal position than Justice White, he, too, refused to delay enforcement of the sentences, on the ground that four justices were unlikely to agree to consider the case "in its present posture." There was some consolation in the rest of Justice Marshall's opinion—that were he "deciding this issue on the merits," he would not allow Farber to be sent to jail and *The Times* to be fined before the New Jersey Appellate Division had ruled on the constitutional questions being raised. But if Myron Farber enjoyed this consolation, he did so behind the bars of the jail cell to which he was confined less than two hours after Justice Marshall announced his decision. Farber began serving his sentence on August 4, 1978, the 243rd anniversary of the acquittal of John Peter Zenger.

For a week Farber was treated as much as a celebrity as he was as a prisoner. Later he was to write, "I had a steady stream of visitors. Reporters and television correspondents poured into the jail for interviews, and the sheriff, standing ramrod at my side, basked in the publicity." Of the hundreds of letters he received, some were violently hostile: "I hope you remain in jail for some time. You have wrong ideas of what is a free press. . . ." "Who died and appointed you God?" "If you can live with the thought that possibly you had a part in sending an innocent man to jail for life, you can live with it. *The Times* couldn't care less." But most of the mail was sympathetic, encouraging, and supportive. It offered legal advice and contributions toward the $5,000 daily fines *The Times* was paying (the newspaper returned all the money). From a Pennsylvania woman came a petition for Farber's release that had been signed by 190 of her neighbors: "I am afraid for my children and grandchildren if we lose freedom of the press," she wrote. "We are going to lose many more freedoms with it. . . ." And many letters echoed Farber's credo with gratifying precision: "You are not only standing up for your profession but also for me and all the public. I am 20 years old and hopefully have many years to live in this country. I am aware that when the time comes that reporters are no longer able to assure confidentiality to their sources, the public will no longer be informed on important matters." "You read the First Amendment much more accurately than the judge. . . ."

But the judge was still the judge, and when, at the end of that first week, "Meet the Press" asked if Farber could appear on the program, "live from the jail," Judge Arnold emphatically denied the request and ordered an end to all the reporter's "special privileges." Contact with the press was barred and visitors were limited to his attorneys and, briefly twice a week, members of his family. Bleak and dreary, the weeks of imprisonment seemed to stretch ahead as far as Myron Farber could imagine, for no one had any idea of exactly when he might be released.

Certainly his chances for freedom were not enhanced by two judicial hearings that were held in mid-August. The first, in a federal district court, was to consider a petition Farber's lawyer had filed arguing that his client was confined without due process of law. The judge, however, chose to focus on Farber's having signed a contract to write a book about the Doctor X case, and, with Ray Brown cheering him on, he accused the reporter of "standing on the altar of greed" and charged that he had "rendered evil," "misled judge after judge," become an "investigative arm of the state," and "joined forces against a defendant." At the root of this verbal abuse was the false assumption that Farber had already turned over to his publisher the notes and documents that had been subpoenaed. Ordered to disclose the location of his far-from-completed manuscript, Farber refused and, rather than face a federal contempt-of-court citation, he withdrew his petition.

The second August hearing followed *The Times*'s decision to give Judge Arnold its own rather scanty file on the Riverdell affair. By doing so, the paper hoped to purge itself of contempt and end the daily fine. Its efforts proved futile, as the hearing became mired in a dispute over whether *The Times* could or should force Farber to surrender his notes. *The Times*'s file the judge considered "worthless," and he went so far as to accuse the paper of "sanitizing" the material. In reply, *Times* president Arthur O. Sulzberger indignantly denied the accusation, declaring, "The unfounded attack on the integrity of *The Times* is a graphic example of the appalling state of justice with which *The Times* has been confronted since the Dr. Jascalevich trial began."

It was, however, from the halls of justice that a temporary reprieve came. In late August, John J. Degnan, the New Jersey attorney general, in an attempt to de-escalate the conflict, managed to persuade the state supreme court to reverse itself and agree to review the case immediately. Until a decision was announced, *The Times*'s fines were suspended—and Myron Farber was free.

At the New Jersey Supreme Court hearing, Farber and *The Times* were represented by Floyd Abrams, who argued that their challenges to the subpoena—on the grounds of its excessive scope, its violation of First Amendment rights, and its disregard of the state's shield law—had all been answered in the same way: *First* show the court all the confidential material that has been requested and *then* you will have your hearing on "whether such material need be disclosed at all! . . . But such a price for a hearing is totally destructive of First Amendment values . . . without being necessary to protect Dr. Jascalevich's Sixth Amendment rights."

Of course, Ray Brown saw nothing wrong in having Farber turn over all his notes to Judge Arnold. Although he would have preferred to gain immediate access to them himself, it was, he said, "a sensible accommodation to the competing interests in this case." He went on to accuse *The Times* and Farber of not really wanting a hearing at all, of indeed trying to avoid a hearing because it would lay bare their "true relationships and motivations." What *The Times* really sought, according to Brown, was "total immunity" from being subpoenaed: "It's a question of a great newspaper saying we're not going to conform; we're going to make the law. . . ."

Abrams tried to discredit these charges by offering to surrender particular items from Farber's files if only Brown would be specific about what he wanted. And in this position *The Times* was supported by the New Jersey attorney general. To the question of whether Dr. Jascalevich had "a Sixth Amendment right to rummage through a reporter's file," Degnan replied, "I suggest to you, Your Honors, that that is not so in New Jersey . . . a trial court subpoena must be specific with reasonable certainty . . ." and must show that the items sought "are relevant and material" to the defense. One of the justices wondered what would happen if a defendant didn't know for sure, or was unable to demonstrate, that a reporter's file contained material relevant to his defense— when, in fact, it did. Was it the price of the First Amendment that such evidence be concealed by permission of the court? Answered Degnan, "If the alternative to that is the granting of every subpoena for every reporter's file in every criminal case, which I suggest to you will happen, then the answer to that is yes."

At the conclusion of the state supreme court hearing, Farber remained free at least until the seven justices announced their decision. Thus, he did not have to be brought from a jail cell to testify for Dr. Jascalevich's defense.

The "other trial" was proceeding with all the speed of a glacier. Over a period of twenty-two weeks, the prosecution had called a total of fifty-eight witnesses, of whom perhaps the star was the acting medical examiner of New York City. He testified twice, first to explain the findings of his work on the exhumed bodies and then to offer his opinion as to the causes of the patients' deaths. Blisteringly cross-examined by Brown for more than three days, he admitted no doubts as to the presence of curare in the tissues he analyzed, and he stood equally firm in his certainty that Nancy Savino, Frank Biggs, and Carl Rohrbeck had each died of curare

Two cartoon comments on the Myron Farber case. The lower one is remarkably prophetic in that it anticipates the Supreme Court decision in Herbert v. Lando, which was not handed down until the following year.

poisoning. But because the medical examiner could only presume about the other patients' deaths, Judge Arnold ruled, after Sybil Moses had rested her case, that the prosecution had not proved that Margaret Henderson and Emma Arzt had also died of curare poisoning, and on that basis he threw out two of the five counts of murder.

Ray Brown began his defense by calling a number of Riverdell staff people to the stand, but his "big guns" were the expert medical witnesses who later testified that Nancy Savino, Frank Biggs, and Carol Rohrbeck had all died of natural causes and that curare could no longer be identified in a body that had been dead for ten years. On the key issues of the trial, then, it was one panel of experts pitted against another, with the jury left to decide between them.

Toward the end, Brown summoned two former prosecutors— Guy Calissi, who testified that he had not found sufficient evidence against Dr. Jascalevich to go to the grand jury, and Joe Woodcock, who said he had. But Brown was looking for some sign of collusion between Woodcock and Farber, and in this he was unsuccessful. Neither of these hostile defense witnesses could be made to suggest even the barest hint of conspiracy to "get" Dr. Jascalevich. In fact, in his interrogation of Farber, Brown was able to show very little. In a courtroom in which there was not a seat to be had, the eagerly awaited duel between two now-famous antagonists proved something of an anticlimax. Brown dug into various molehills—certainly there was not a mountain among them—and came up empty-handed every time. In his first three days on the witness stand, Farber furnished the defense with nothing of value except, insofar as it may have influenced the jury, his continuing refusal to turn over the notes that Brown, in questioning him, once again demanded.

The morning after Farber's third day of testimony, the state supreme court announced its decision to uphold the contempt convictions. The five-to-two majority based its opinion on the *Branzburg* decision, saying, "we do no weighing or balancing of societal interests in reaching our determination. . . . The weighing and balancing has been done by a higher court." In *Branzburg*, the U.S. Supreme Court was, of course, dealing with a grand jury subpoena, and the New Jersey ruling took note of that fact, observing "that the obligation to appear at a criminal trial on behalf of a defendant who is enforcing his Sixth Amendment rights is at least as compelling." And while it affirmed the constitutionality of the state's shield law, the majority held that the statute "must yield" when it collides with a defendant's Sixth Amendment rights.

In the face of *The Times*'s insistence on a judicial hearing to determine the "relevance, materiality, and overbreadth of the subpoena," the majority decision took a rather surprising turn. *The Times* was right, it said, and in the future the lower courts would have to make a "preliminary determination" as to whether the defense subpoena was justified before a reporter had to surrender his notes to anyone, including the judge. But if this was a victory for *The Times*, only others would enjoy it, since in the opinion of the majority, Judge Arnold knew the Jascalevich case and Farber's role in it so thoroughly that "nothing was to be gained by requiring the judge to start all over again." Furthermore, it was "perfectly clear" that Ray Brown's subpoena met the test: The information sought was "relevant to the defense . . . it could not be secured from any less intrusive source, and . . . the defendant had a legitimate need to see it. . . ."

To one of the two dissenting justices, this conclusion seemed "a flight of fancy," for to him the Brown subpoena did not meet the test at all. The other dissent was broader and even more emphatic: "Farber has . . . never received the hearing to which he is constitutionally entitled. . . . Mr. Farber probably assumed, as I did, that hearings were supposed to be held and findings made *before* a person went to jail and not *afterwards*."

But the majority had decreed otherwise: Farber was to return to jail unless he surrendered the subpoenaed materials to Judge Arnold within five days. Floyd Abrams immediately announced that he would seek a "definitive ruling" from the U.S. Supreme Court, whereupon Ray Brown requested and received an adjournment of the trial. Intending to recall Farber to the stand, Brown thought that perhaps a decision in Washington would finally get him that file without which, he said, he was left "dangling in the wind."

In *The Times*'s third petition to the Supreme Court, Abrams argued that, among other things, the New Jersey ruling was unconstitutional in holding that the state's shield law "must yield" to the Sixth Amendment and was erroneous in its interpretation of *Branzburg* because it ignored the "pivotal" opinion of Justice Powell. The petition was filed on September 26, the day Farber was to turn over the subpoenaed materials or return to jail, but forty-five minutes before the deadline Justice Potter Stewart delayed imposition of all penalties against Farber and *The Times* "pending further order of this Court." Ten days later the Court still had not announced whether it would review the Farber case but, acting on a motion by an impatient Ray Brown, it ordered an end to Justice Stewart's ban on enforcement of penalties.

On October 10, contempt-of-court citations were everywhere. The judge who had originally found Farber and *The Times* guilty now gave them another two days to turn over the file. Back in Judge Arnold's courtroom, the Jascalevich trial resumed; Farber was recalled to testify, refused to reveal any confidential sources or surrender his notes, and again and again declined to answer on the ground of his First Amendment rights. In response, Judge Arnold cited him for contempt nineteen times. And two days later he was back in jail.

There Farber languished while the U.S. Supreme Court remained silent on whether it would hear his appeal and while the Jascalevich trial lumbered to a close. On Friday the thirteenth Ray Brown rested his case, and five days later he delivered his summation to the jury. It went on for seven and a half hours, and for much of this time Brown blasted Farber for his greed for money and Woodcock for his "political ambition" and the Riverdell doctors for their ruthless determination to protect "their precious profit-making operation, the hospital." He mocked the prosecution's curare evidence, cited the opposing testimony of his own scientific team, insisted on the absence of a convincing motive for murder, discounted any discrepancies in the surgeon's depositions, and concluded: "This man is already destroyed. Let him live out the rest of his life knowing that no nation and . . . no citizen will stand for combinations of greed and gain and ambition . . . that justice says it won't happen here."

In beginning her summation, Prosecutor Moses recalled an event that had recently shared the front pages with Mario Jascalevich and Myron Farber: the 1978 World Series. The New York Yankees had beaten the Los Angeles Dodgers, four games to two, and in the reaction of the losers Moses found a striking parallel to the defense that Ray Brown had mounted. "You know . . . " she said, "the Dodgers were beaten very badly, and instead of blaming themselves, they blamed the press. They blamed the press, and they blamed the field, and they blamed the reporters. But it wasn't the bystanders who lost the games, and it wasn't the reporters who wrote the news who lost the games, and it wasn't the setting that lost the games. It's just so in this instance, ladies and gentlemen. It isn't the hospital that killed these people. It isn't the people who wrote about it that killed these people. It isn't the prosecutor . . . who is . . . sworn to investigate charges; he didn't kill anybody. Everybody is being attacked, ladies and gentlemen. Everybody is being attacked, but they didn't kill anyone. And I think it is crucial for you to remember that. . . ."

Moses went on to focus her attention on the patients, all of whom, she reminded the jury, had died "a silent death . . . unexpectedly, unexplainedly. They died when they shouldn't have . . . and one man and only one man was always there. . . . That's what this trial is all about, ladies and gentlemen. I wasn't there. Prosecutor Woodcock wasn't there . . . even Myron Farber wasn't there. But only one man, Mario E. Jascalevich, was there every time. . . ." Reviewing the victims' medical records, Moses found the only "logical" cause of death in every case to be curare poisoning, and there on the evidence table were the vials and syringes that Calissi had taken from Dr. Jascalevich's locker almost twelve years earlier. The prosecutor was losing her voice as she reached the end of her summation: "Ladies and gentlemen, I can go on and on telling you about all the implausible and incredible concocted lies this man made up to cover for the curare in his locker, to cover up for the murders by poisoning . . . when you find the liar . . . you will know that you will serve justice by . . . finding . . . the defendant guilty of the murders of Nancy Savino, Carl Rohrbeck, and Frank Biggs."

It was late in the day when the jurors retired to deliberate, and after only forty-five minutes they adjourned for the night. Surrounded by security guards, they were led from the courthouse to a waiting bus, their departure filmed by television cameras and watched from a cell window by Myron Farber. The next morning, as the jurors resumed their deliberations, Farber was once again a free man. Judge Arnold, who had found him in contempt, suspended his six-month sentence and dropped the fines against *The Times*, saying, "Where compliance becomes meaningless, continued confinement becomes meaningless." Farber was back home by the time the jury returned its verdict.

Unlike everyone else associated with the Jascalevich trial, the jurors worked fast. They took a mere two hours to reach a decision and did not ask to examine any evidence or rehear any of the

Dr. Mario E. Jascalevich (Doctor X)

voluminous testimony. Clearly Ray Brown had done his job well. To each of the three counts of murder the forewoman of the jury softly repeated the same verdict: "We find the defendant not guilty." As the courtroom rang with the cheers and applause of spectators, Dr. Jascalevich plucked a handkerchief from his breast pocket and waved it at the jurors, saying, "Thank God, justice was done."

Like a fire that has died but left embers that continue to smolder, the Jascalevich-Farber controversy, though legally settled, still contains secrets that will in all probability never be revealed. But the reason for the jury's verdict is not among them. The defense's expert witnesses had obviously convinced those twelve weary people that the victims could have died of natural causes. Uncertain, then, that murders had even been committed, the jurors had no way to find the defendant guilty.

If, in retrospect, the verdict is easy to explain, the passage of time has done little to throw light on various other areas of mystery, doubt, and disagreement. Consider, for example, the following:

Was Dr. Jascalevich truly innocent of the crimes of which he was accused? There are many who think not. When, in the longest license-review procedure in the state's history, the New Jersey Board of Medical Examiners finally reached a conclusion in the year following the murder trial, it found Dr. Jascalevich guilty of "gross malpractice or gross neglect and lack of good moral character." This decision, which was based on the doctor's conduct in two cases unrelated to the Riverdell deaths, led to the formal revocation of his license in New Jersey. At the hearing Dr. Jascalevich did not testify in his own defense. After his trial he had returned to his native Argentina, where he died in September 1984. It would seem that those who doubt the correctness of the verdict as well as those who support it must all resign themselves to uncertainty.

What was contained in the notes that Myron Farber refused to surrender to the court and the defense? Again, we are likely never to know. When it was revealed that Farber had signed a contract to write a book about the Jascalevich affair, the reporter was immediately and widely accused of having guarded his secrets solely for reasons of personal gain. Sheer greed, his opponents charged—that is, the desire to increase the sales of his forthcoming book—had kept Farber from turning over the subpoenaed documents. That argument was demolished four years later with the publication of *Somebody Is Lying.* Fascinating though the book is, it contains nothing in the way of disclosures that could possibly have influenced the course of the trial. The identity of the person who wrote to the *Times* editor in June 1975 remains a mystery, locked away with whatever other sources and information Farber feels, now as then, that he must conceal.

Why was Ray Brown so insistent on obtaining Farber's notes, anyway? There are two possible answers to this question, and one can choose either or, for that matter, both. Perhaps Brown genuinely believed that the files contained data that would be uniquely valuable to the defense. Or perhaps, suspecting from the start that Farber would never surrender his notes, Brown was planning to use his failure to gain access to the material as the basis for an appeal, should his client eventually be found guilty.

All things considered, was Farber's stubborn defiance of the courts justified? This question, which, of course, brings us to the core of the freedom of the press issue, remains a matter of severely divided opinion. In November 1978, with Dr. Jascalevich acquitted and Myron Farber's sentence suspended, the United States Supreme Court declined to hear Farber's appeal. While it may someday be forced to rule on this conflict between a reporter's rights under the First Amendment and a defendant's rights under the Sixth, the Court obviously saw no need to make Farber the test case. Many champions of a free press were grimly disappointed that the Court chose to forgo this opportunity to make a definitive ruling on a vital question. They argued that Farber and *The Times* had never been permitted to present their case for concealment— or, at least, never in the appropriate forum. (They certainly defended their position—repeatedly—on the editorial page of *The New York Times*.) In January 1982, they did receive a vindication of sorts when Governor Brendan Byrne of New Jersey pardoned Farber and *The Times* for criminal contempt and returned $101,-000 of the $286,000 that the newspaper had paid in fines. The Governor explained his action, taken on his next-to-last day in office, by saying, "Mr. Farber and the Times Company were attempting to uphold a principle they believed in. They should not be burdened by a record of criminal contempt any longer. . . . [Their] purpose was not to insult or frustrate the judicial process, but to stand on a noble, if sometimes imperfect, principle."

The question remains just how imperfect that principle is. Throughout the Farber controversy, some powerful and traditional advocates of civil liberties—most notably, the American Civil Liberties Union—were silent. Those who are usually quick to storm the barricades when they see a constitutional right invaded or imperiled held back while Myron Farber was first subpoenaed, then found in contempt of court, and finally jailed for a total of forty days. The truth is that a good many experts on constitutional law sided with Ray Brown and the courts. To them, nothing is more precious than a defendant's right to a fair trial, and in the Jascalevich case the only way that right could be preserved was to allow a learned, objective observer like the court to determine whether a reporter's notes held potentially useful evidence. No argument that Farber's attorneys might have offered to the Supreme Court, had they been given the chance, could have *proved* that the subpoenaed material was worthless to the defense. And when nothing less than a person's reputation and perhaps his entire life is at stake, the judicial system may not deny him *any* means of establishing his innocence of the crime with which he is charged. A promise of confidentiality that a reporter may make to a news source is of little moment when measured against the destiny of an embattled defendant.

So goes the anti-Farber position. Finding the greatest good in the protection of a single individual, it does not hesitate to place on the press the burden of proving it cannot help this individual when there is reason to suspect that it can. For those who regard Myron Farber as a hero—a twentieth-century John Peter Zenger or a grown-up Charlie Quarterman—that burden seems much too great. Indeed, so great that it could break the back of the press and cripple its ability to enlighten—and thereby protect—not just one individual but a community, a city, and a nation.

8.
Closing the Doors of Justice

More than 20 million Americans watched *60 Minutes* on Sunday, January 16, 1983. They saw exactly the program CBS News wanted them to see, and it reached homes in all the towns and cities where *60 Minutes* was normally shown. There was, then, nothing remarkable about the broadcast that evening—even the enormous size of the viewing audience was customary for a show that then enjoyed the greatest popularity of any show on television, leading in the weekly ratings with a predictability and consistency that remained the despair of the other networks. No, nothing remarkable—except that the broadcast was made possible not only by its sponsors and by CBS but also by a ruling of the United States court of appeals for the Fifth Circuit.

The chain of events that led to this historic decision began more than two years earlier, when, in November 1980, a white police officer was shot to death in the predominantly black Algiers section of New Orleans. The manhunt that followed, intensive and highly publicized, was, of course, targeted on the Algiers district, and before it was over, four more people, all blacks, had been slain. No one was ever arrested for any of those killings, but later five Algiers residents—three blacks and two whites—charged that they had been beaten, kicked, and threatened with death by police investigating the fatal shooting of their fellow officer. These accusations eventually led to the indictment by a federal grand jury of seven New Orleans policemen, all on charges of having deprived various individuals of their constitutional rights.

Inevitably, the case unleashed a storm of controversy in the New Orleans area. Reports of police brutality brought swift and indignant denials. A black detective who admitted his complicity in the beating of one purported victim was branded an incompetent with questionable motives for making a confession that seriously implicated several other officers. But in the aftermath of the Algiers incidents, the accusations could not be stilled and their reverberations shook the police force from the top down: Not only were the seven officers forced to stand trial, but, coming under severe attack, the police superintendent and his chief lieutenant felt compelled to hand in their resignations.

Like the menacing activities of the Black Panthers and the suspicious doings of Doctor X, police conduct in New Orleans soon became a major media event. Some notice was taken nationally, but obviously it was in the local press that the charges, denials, and countercharges commanded almost unceasing attention. As the date of the trial approached, the defense attorneys concluded that it would be difficult if not impossible to find twelve citizens of New Orleans who did not already have strong views about the defendants' guilt or innocence. And since the right to trial by jury has always been taken to mean trial by an unbiased jury, lawyers asked that the court proceedings be moved to a city where press coverage of the case had been much less inflammatory and where, presumably, hordes of people could be found who thought Algiers was only a city in North Africa. Early in January 1983, a federal judge agreed to a change of venue, and the trial, scheduled to start on February 7, was relocated to Dallas.

Less than a week later this key victory for the defense must have seemed like a mere handful of ashes, as CBS announced that the following Sunday *60 Minutes*, the most popular television program in America, would feature a segment on police brutality in New Orleans! The blank pages of all those Dallas minds were destined not to be blank after all, for many of them were sure to absorb the words and images provided by a skilled news team and a respected television correspondent. So, too, would the minds of all those other millions and millions of *60 Minutes* addicts across the country. To whom, then, could the beleaguered defendants turn in their search for the impartiality that promises justice?

They turned to the same man who had granted the change of venue, Judge Adrian Duplantier, of the federal district court in New Orleans. There, on Friday, January 14, two days before the *60 Minutes* program was to air, lawyers for the seven officers asked for a "silence order" to block the broadcast of the segment that, they argued, would make a fair trial impossible. It was only the Dallas area that they wanted blacked out, but they came close to getting far more than they had requested.

Judge Duplantier responded to the defense motion by demanding that CBS provide him with a copy of the script for the report on the New Orleans police controversy. CBS refused, and before the day was over the judge had enjoined them from broadcasting the segment anywhere in the United States.

Charging that the injunction was "unprecedented in the history of our nation" and "a blatant violation" of the First Amendment guarantee of freedom of the press, CBS appealed the ruling the next morning to the federal appeals court. Network lawyers argued that the ban "raises issues of national importance and seriously imperils freedom of expression which . . . had been secured to all citizens for more than 200 years." Unless it was overturned, they added, the decision would grant to the judiciary "the right of unbridled censorship over the content and timing of news programs."

The appeals panel was composed of three judges—one in New Orleans, another in Houston, and the third in Austin, Texas. Recognizing the urgency of the matter—airtime for the program was little more than twenty-four hours away—the judges arranged to have copies of the court papers flown to each of them, and they then conferred by telephone. Their deliberations produced a four-page decision rescinding Judge Duplantier's ban and permitting the *60 Minutes* segment to be shown as scheduled. While acknowledging the right of defendants to a fair trial before an impartial jury, the court of appeals cited a 1971 Supreme Court ruling against "prior restraint" (see chapter 9, on the Pentagon Papers case) and found "a heavy presumption against [the] constitutional validity" of the lower court's order. It noted further that the order was "not supported by any findings whatsoever" and was "unlimited geographically and temporally." In other words, the Duplantier ruling had offered no evidence of the potentially harmful effect of the program and no justification for banning it everywhere and forever. Finally, the three-judge panel observed that the lower court had apparently given no thought to less drastic alternatives like postponement of the trial.

Immediately after the court of appeals announced its decision, the executive producer of *60 Minutes* commented, "I somehow never doubted that we would not be prohibited from running this story." But in spite of his confidence, the opinion itself, which the Supreme Court later refused to review, carries an unsettling hint that had Judge Duplantier's ban been less sweeping—had it applied only to the Dallas area, for example—the appeal might have had a different result. Thus, the panel did not *necessarily* subscribe to the ancient backstage tradition that the show must go on. Under certain circumstances, perhaps . . .

But, of course, the show did go on and, three weeks later, so did the trial. A jury was chosen; it heard testimony for more than a month, deliberated for two and a half days, finally acquitted four of the defendants of all charges, and convicted the others of conspiracy and of violating the civil rights of a black witness who had been beaten while undergoing interrogation. Since this man was only one of five Algiers residents who claimed to be victims of police brutality, it would seem that the all-white jury had sifted through and weighed a mass of conflicting testimony before reaching its verdict, and had not been improperly influenced by any criticism of the police contained in the *60 Minutes* report. On the contrary, the judge who later ordered the three convicted defendants to serve five years in prison without parole based his sentence on a belief that they had been guilty of more than one beating. So, whether one agrees with the federal prosecutor who, after the trial, said, "Justice has been served," or with the defense attorney who found the jury's decision "unbelievable," certainly CBS emerges as guiltless—and as respectable—as a judge.

The attempt to ban the *60 Minutes* segment throughout the country because of the pending New Orleans police trial seems rather like trying to use surgery to cure a cold. But to ensure an uncontaminated pool of jurors, many courts have resorted in recent years to a comparable if less drastic measure: They have closed their doors to the press. Indeed, a survey showed that in the nine-month period between July 1979 and April 1980, in more than two hundred criminal cases throughout the country motions were filed to bar press and public from pretrial hearings. The survey period began when it did for good reason: On July 2, 1979, a majority of the U.S. Supreme Court agreed that in pretrial hearings closed courtroom doors did not have to be opened.

In journalistic quarters this decision was greeted with all the dismay we have come to expect whenever the High Court limits the power of the First Amendment. The cliché of the "chilling effect" was once again removed from cold storage and put to use by editorial writers everywhere. But while they all responded with, at the very least, displeasure, it is interesting to note that some found the ruling predictable, others surprising. It all depended on one's perspective. To those who took a short view, 1979 was the year of the "state of mind" decision in *Herbert v. Lando* and the year that followed *Zurcher*'s stamp of approval on the police's right to rummage. Permitting closed pretrial hearings was just another gust of the prevailing winds that emanated from the anti-press Burger Court. But those with longer memories recalled a 1976 decision, *Nebraska Press Association v. Stuart,* in which the Court denied a "gag order" that would have prohibited a newspaper from publishing facts already in its possession that had emerged from a pretrial hearing. Was that opinion simply a one-time-only reversal of the judicial trend toward ever-greater restrictions on the press?

Perhaps. The case whose ruling prompted the speculation itself began three years before, just outside of Rochester, New York. On the morning of July 16, 1976, Wayne Clapp, a forty-two-year-old former policeman, was observed going out in his boat with two companions to fish in Seneca Lake. Later that day the two companions returned in the boat, got into Clapp's pickup truck, and drove away. But Wayne Clapp was never to be seen again.

His family waited three days before reporting his disappearance to the police, who then soon found his boat—riddled with bullet holes. Theorizing that he had been shot with his own gun, robbed, and dumped overboard, the police dragged the lake in a lengthy but futile effort to locate his body. (They eventually concluded that it had been weighted with anchors before being submerged.) They also began an intensive search for the two companions, sending out an interstate bulletin describing the men and the missing pickup truck. Two days later Michigan police in Jackson County spotted the truck parked at a local motel adjacent to a park. Within a short time they had arrested one of the fugitives in the park and, using a helicopter and attack dogs, had tracked down the other man and his wife in some woods nearby. The younger of the two suspects then led Michigan police to the spot where he had buried Clapp's revolver. Five days after the manhunt began, the three fugitives were back in New York State—the men arraigned on charges of murder and grand larceny and held without bail in the Seneca County jail.

All these events the local press—consisting of Rochester's morning and evening newspapers, both owned by Gannett Co., Inc.—reported swiftly and in considerable detail, at the same time giving readers frequent reminders that Clapp's body had yet to be recovered. However, with the capture of the suspects came a nine-day pause in press coverage of the case. It ended on August 6, when the Gannett papers reported that the suspects had been indicted by a grand jury on multiple counts of murder, robbery, and grand larceny and had pleaded not guilty to all charges.

Then, again, for three months, all was quiet, until, in November, the silence was broken by a development that led directly to the confrontation between the judiciary and the press. Represented by new legal counsel, the defendants filed a motion to suppress statements they had made to the police, claiming that their confessions had been involuntary, and to suppress also any physical evidence seized as a result of their statements—that is, the revolver. The hearing to consider this motion took place on November 4, in the courtroom of trial judge Daniel A. DePasquale; but before the substance of the matter could be argued, defense attorneys asked that the press and public be barred from the proceeding. This was necessary, they said, because "the unabated buildup of adverse publicity had jeopardized the ability of the defendants to receive a fair trial." The district attorney did not oppose the request and, curiously enough, neither did Carol Ritter, the one reporter present. Judge DePasquale thereupon granted the motion, and the courtroom was cleared of everyone not directly involved in the hearing.

Although not immediate, press reaction was not long in coming. The very next day Carol Ritter wrote a letter to the trial judge contending that she had a "right to cover the hearing" and asking that she "be given access to the transcript." Within hours she had Judge DePasquale's reply: The suppression hearing was already over and he would reserve decision on the timing of the release of the transcript. Thus challenged, the Gannett Co., Ritter's employer, sailed into court with a motion of its own—that the exclusionary order be set aside. And so was born the landmark case of *Gannett Co., Inc., v. DePasquale.*

At a mid-November hearing on the Gannett motion, the trial judge acknowledged that the press had a constitutional "right of access" and deemed it "unfortunate" that Ritter had not objected to the closure motion when it had first been made. In any case,

*Reporter Carol Ritter, whose
exclusion from a pretrial hearing
resulted in* Gannett Co., Inc., v.
DePasquale.

the judge went on, the right of the press had to be balanced against
the right of the defendants to a fair trial. And since he believed
that opening the suppression hearing would have created a "reasonable probability of prejudice to these defendants," he reaf-
firmed his original decision. The defendants' right outweighed the
interests of the press and the public, and therefore he would
neither vacate his exclusionary order nor allow Gannett immediate access to a transcript of the pretrial hearing.

For Gannett, the ruling was a brief, temporary, and no doubt
fully expected setback. The following day their lawyers appealed
the decision in the appellate division of the Supreme Court of the
State of New York, and a month later that court emphatically
upheld Gannett's position. It found that the exclusionary order
violated the public's vital interest in open judicial proceedings and,
further, as an act of prior restraint infringed on the rights of the
press under the First and Fourteenth amendments.

But at best, Gannett's victory here, which was to prove short-lived anyway, had the hollow ring of an anticlimax. Shortly before the appellate division rendered its judgment, Wayne Clapp's fishing companions had pleaded guilty to lesser offenses than those they had originally been charged with, thus effectively closing their case. With no need for a trial, there was no need for a jury— and in a flash Gannett received a transcript of the now inconsequential suppression hearing.

The story, however, was far from over. The lights may have gone out for the confessed killers, now behind prison walls, but in the halls of justice the constitutional issue their case had ignited continued to burn brightly. By turning over to Gannett the contested transcript, Judge DePasquale had in no way surrendered his belief in the correctness of his earlier decisions. Rebuffed by the appellate division, he appealed to the New York State Court of Appeals, which, recognizing "the critical importance of the issues involved," agreed to consider the case. Its ruling solidly supported the judge, holding that the right of the public, including the press, to attend criminal trials was outweighed in this case by the "reasonable probability" that such access posed a danger to the defendants' ability to receive a fair trial.

Now it was Gannett's turn to fight for principle. They had their transcript. What they wanted was the overturn of a decision that might well keep them and their press colleagues out of countless courtrooms in the years to come.

Their quest took them to the United States Supreme Court, where the case was argued in November 1978 and where, as we have noted, their appeal was denied in July 1979. The vote was close, five to four in favor of DePasquale, and while three of the four Nixon appointees to the Court sided with the majority (one dissented in part), the opinion was written by Justice Potter Stewart, a twenty-one-year veteran of the Court, an appointee of President Eisenhower, and in *Zurcher* (the *Stanford Daily* Case) and *Branzburg* a vigorous dissenter on the side of the press. In the key passage of the *Gannett* decision, Stewart wrote, "Among the guarantees that the [Sixth] Amendment provides to a person charged with the commission of a criminal offense, and to him alone, is the 'right to a speedy and public trial, by an impartial jury.' The Constitution nowhere mentions any right of access to a criminal trial on the part of the public. . . ." So the right to a public trial belongs only to the accused—not to "strangers [who want] to attend a pretrial proceeding. . . ." Stewart acknowledged "the general desirability of open judicial proceedings," but, citing an earlier Court ruling, he saw the right to a public trial mainly "as a safeguard against any attempt to employ the courts as instruments of persecution." Stewart's opinion made no mention of the First Amendment. Clearly he found nothing in it that would force open a pretrial proceeding when all those directly involved agree "that it should be closed to protect the fair trial rights of the defendants."

Each of the three Nixon appointees in the majority wrote concurrences, but each sounded quite a different note of caution in interpreting the prevailing opinion. Justice Lewis F. Powell, Jr., allowed that Gannett's interest in attending the pretrial hearing *was* protected by the First Amendment but, he went on, that right "is not absolute. It is limited both by the constitutional right of defendants to a fair trial . . . and by the needs of government to obtain just convictions and to preserve the confidentiality of sensitive information and the identity of informants." Who is to weigh these conflicting factors and determine whether courtroom doors should be open or closed? The presiding judge, said Justice Powell, who found that in this case Judge DePasquale had properly discharged his responsibility before closing the hearing.

In *his* concurrence, Justice William H. Rehnquist in effect dissented from the view of his colleague in the majority, Justice Powell. If the Sixth Amendment reserves the right to a public trial to the defendant alone, said Justice Rehnquist, then "it necessarily follows that if the parties agree on a closed proceeding, the trial court is not required . . . to advance any reason whatsoever for declining to open a pretrial hearing or trial to the public." As for the balancing act recommended by Justice Powell, the presiding judge must decide for himself or herself whether it is necessary: "The lower courts are under no constitutional restraints either to accept or reject those procedures."

The third concurrence was filed by Chief Justice Warren Burger, whose intent was to stress a distinction that was later to become the basis for a profoundly different ruling. "By definition," wrote Burger, "a hearing on a motion before trial to suppress evidence is not a trial; it is a pretrial hearing." And while for centuries common-law tradition held that *trials* generally be public, among the "lawyers who drafted the Sixth Amendment . . . no one ever suggested that there was any 'right' of the public to be present at . . . pretrial proceedings. . . ."

All the Nixon appointees, it seemed, wanted to say something about *Gannett*: It was the fourth, Justice Harry A. Blackmun, who wrote the dissent. He, alone among those who filed opinions, cast a sharp eye on the way the press had covered the Clapp murder case. Characterizing the news articles as "placid, routine, and innocuous," he tallied the number that had appeared (fourteen in the eighteen days after Clapp's disappearance), the number of different days on which they had run (seven), and the number of photographs used (only one, of the murder victim). He described the stories as "straightforward reporting of the facts . . . nothing that a fairminded person could describe as sensational journalism." In short, "they gave no indication of being published to sustain popular interest in the case."

Thus, according to Blackmun, there was no justification for the defense attorneys' argument, to quote the majority opinion, "that the unabated buildup of adverse publicity had jeopardized the ability of the defendants to receive a fair trial." And without that justification, the need for closure disappeared, as did the basis for the majority opinion upholding DePasquale: "in order to assure a fair trial."

But in his dissent Blackmun traveled far beyond what he considered the flawed premise underlying the Court's ruling. Most of his forty-four-page opinion is devoted to determined advocacy of open courtroom hearings. They "enable the public to scrutinize the performance of police and prosecutors in the conduct of public judicial business," he contended. And of the reverse, he wrote: "Secret hearings—though they be scrupulously fair—are suspect by nature." He went on to note that about 90 percent of all criminal cases in New York, and in most other states, are settled before trial, leaving pretrial proceedings as "the only opportunity the public has to learn about police and prosecutorial conduct, and about allegations that those responsible . . . for the enforcement of law themselves are breaking it." Blackmun concluded: "It has been said that publicity 'is the soul of justice.' . . . [It] is essential to the preservation of public confidence in the rule of law and in the operation of courts. Only in rare circumstances does this principle clash with the rights of the criminal defendant to a fair trial so as to justify exclusion. . . . Those circumstances did not exist in this case."

Earlier in his opinion, Blackmun quoted a dissent from a 1965 Supreme Court ruling that overturned the conviction of Billie Sol Estes, a onetime friend of President Lyndon Johnson. In that decision the majority concluded that the presence of television cameras in the court had deprived Estes of a fair trial. The dissent contained these words: "The suggestion that there are limits upon the public's right to know what goes on in courts causes me deep concern." The dissenter was Justice Potter Stewart.

The author of the majority opinion in *Gannett* was probably not embarrassed to be reminded of this apparent inconsistency. No one has ever accused the Court of consistency. In truth, however, the constantly recurring conflict between the rights of the press and the right of a defendant to a fair trial has found the Court— though not necessarily any one justice—rather regularly on the side of the defendant. As early as 1961 the murder conviction of one Leslie Irvin, known variously in the press as "the mad dog killer" and "mad dog Irvin," was unanimously overturned be- cause of pretrial publicity. The first such opinion in Supreme Court history, it was written by Associate Justice Tom C. Clark, who noted that two-thirds of the jury members had admitted, "before hearing any testimony, to possessing a belief in the defen- dant's guilt." It was not asking too much, Clark wrote, that the defendant, "with his life at stake . . . be tried in an atmosphere undisturbed by so huge a wave of public passion. . . ."

In the twenty years that followed the decision in the Irvin case, the Court had shown little inclination to defend or uphold the rights of the press in their coverage of criminal cases. And, as we have seen, such key decisions of the seventies as *Branzburg*, *Zurcher*, and *Herbert*—though not directly involving criminal cases—did nothing to dispel the suspicion and despair with which much of the journalistic community had come to view the High Court. As the decade of the eighties began, another landmark case was approaching. It went one step beyond *Gannett* in that it challenged the right of the judiciary to exclude the press from a criminal *trial*, not a pretrial hearing, but many a gloomy prophet expected that one step to be in an all-too-familiar direction.

Very few murder suspects have to stand trial four times for the same offense but such was the fate of a man named Stevenson in Hanover County, Virginia, over the course of two summers two years apart. Indicted for the stabbing death of a hotel manager, Stevenson was first tried, and convicted, in July 1976, only to have the state supreme court reverse the verdict the following year. A retrial was ordered on the basis of the court's finding that a blood-stained shirt had been improperly admitted into evidence. Stevenson's second trial, in May 1978, ended soon after it began when a juror asked to be excused and no alternate was available. Reporting this development, a local newspaper made incidental reference to the bloodstained shirt. The third trial began a week later but it, too, ended in a mistrial, supposedly because one prospective juror had told other prospective jurors what he had read about the case in the press. Stevenson was retried for the last time early in September, but before the trial began, defense counsel moved that the public be excluded. At a closed hearing to consider this motion, to which the prosecutor did not object, Stevenson's attorney said that he "didn't want information to leak out," appear in the press perhaps inaccurately, and then be seen by the yet unchosen jurors. The trial judge responded, "[Since] it doesn't completely override all rights of everyone else . . . I'm inclined to go along with the defendant's motion."

With the press and the public thus barred from the courtroom, the trial resumed—and ended—the following day. After the prosecution had presented its case, defense counsel moved to strike the state's evidence; the judge sustained the motion, excused the jury, and declared Stevenson not guilty as charged. The trial was over—but, of course, few were there to enjoy the unexpectedly early conclusion.

If a stunted, scraggly tree can somehow sprout a gorgeous flower, so may a bizarre, almost laughable case ultimately produce a landmark in constitutional law. About two weeks after Stevenson had so abruptly regained his freedom, the local press, Richmond Newspapers, Inc., filed an appeal from the trial court's closure order. Ten months later, the Virginia Supreme Court denied the petition, "finding no reversible error." As this was the state's highest tribunal, there was now nowhere for the press to go but to the U.S. Supreme Court, which heard the case in February 1980 and announced its decision in July, on the first anniversary of *Gannett v. DePasquale. Richmond Newspapers, Inc., v. Commonwealth of Virginia* delivered quite a different message.

Different but, seen in retrospect, not altogether surprising. Few, however, would have anticipated the size of the lopsided majority: seven to one in favor of Richmond Newspapers. (One justice chose not to participate in the decision.) The opinion was written by Chief Justice Burger, who began by making a distinction between *Gannett* and the case at hand. In the former, he noted, "the Court was not required to decide whether a right of access to *trials*, as distinguished from hearings on *pre*trial motions, was constitutionally guaranteed. . . . [H]ere for the first time the Court is asked to decide whether a criminal trial itself may be closed to the public upon the unopposed request of a defendant, without any demonstration that closure is required to protect the defendant's superior right to a fair trial, or that some other overriding consideration requires closure." The chief justice then took a historical approach, going as far back as the period before the Norman Conquest to show that throughout the evolution of Anglo-American justice, "the trial has been open to all who care to observe." From this he concluded "that a presumption of openness inheres in the very nature of a criminal trial under our system of justice." In reply to the contention of the state of Virginia "that neither the Constitution nor the Bill of Rights contains any provision which . . . guarantees to the public the right to attend criminal trials," the chief justice conceded that there was no "explicit provision," but claimed that right to be "implicit in the . . . First Amendment; without the freedom to attend such trials, which people have exercised for centuries, important aspects of freedom of speech and the press could be eviscerated." On the specific role of the news media as representatives of the public, he wrote, "Instead of acquiring information about trials by firsthand observation or by the word of mouth from those who attended, people now acquire it through the print and electronic media. In a sense, this validates the media claim of functioning as surrogates for the public." In conclusion, the Burger opinion found in the Stevenson case neither circumstances that required closure nor consideration of the alternatives to closure (sequestering the jury being the most obvious), and in the absence of these factors, "the trial of a criminal case must be open to the public."

A burst of concurrences amplified the chief justice's decision. Justice White observed that the Court would not have had to bother with this case if the majority in *Gannett* had gone along with the four dissenters. Justice Stevens exulted, perhaps prematurely, that "never before has [the Court] squarely held that the acquisition of newsworthy matter is entitled to any constitutional protection whatsoever. . . . Today, for the first time, the Court unequivocally holds that an arbitrary interference with access to important information is an abridgement of the freedoms of speech and of the press protected by the First Amendment." Justice Brennan dwelt at length upon how essential was "our ingrained tradition of public trials," and declared that "public access is an indispensable element of the trial process itself." Justice Stewart, author of the *Gannett* opinion, hinted that he hadn't changed his mind about pretrial hearings and warned that the First Amendment right of the press and public to attend trials is not absolute. Justice Blackmun, alluding to the year-old decision, hailed "the Court's return to history [as] a welcome change in direction" and was gratified "to see the Court wash away at least some of the graffiti that marred the prevailing opinions in *Gannett*." Justice Rehnquist, in singular dissent, objected to having "nine persons, however gifted," impose their judgment on any of the fifty state judicial systems unless "the state decision violates some provision of the United States Constitution"—and in this case it clearly did not.

That last lonely voice singing its states' rights tune was all but drowned out by the chorus of praise that greeted the Burger opinion and all those many concurrences. The Supreme Court had given the press precious little to crow about in the last decade or so, but here—particularly in the statement of Justice Stevens— was a ringing reaffirmation of the rights of the news media. The Gannett Co. placed ads in various publications (not necessarily their own) lauding the seven-to-one landmark decision and quoting from it at length. It even ventured to hope "that the remaining obstructions to the public's right to know what happens in pretrial hearings will soon be washed away."

But little of that "washing away" (to quote Gannett quoting Blackmun) has occurred. As we have noted, in the wake of *Gannett*, closed pretrial hearings have become increasingly common. And when they have been challenged in lower federal courts and state appellate courts, a discordant variety of decisions has been rendered, with many upholding closure. The fact that in the seventies and early eighties thirty-six states reinstated capital punishment has had a marked impact on this issue. With their clients facing the death penalty, defense lawyers argue that the courts have a special responsibility to guard against prospective jurors' being exposed to the gory reports of violence and the involuntary confessions that so often emerge in pretrial hearings. The counterargument of the press is that potential jurors whose minds have been "poisoned" by the media can be identified by careful questioning and excused from service; if necessary, a trial can be moved to some distant city. But nothing should prevent journalists from discharging their basic news-gathering function.

Drawing featured in a Gannett Company advertisement praising the Supreme Court decision in Richmond Newspapers, Inc. v. Virginia.

The debate goes on, and it will continue at least until the Supreme Court modifies its decision in *Gannett*—and that is not likely to happen soon. Two years after *Richmond Newspapers*, however, it did reaffirm the public's right of access to criminal trials, holding unconstitutional a Massachusetts law that required courtrooms to be closed during the testimony of rape victims under the age of eighteen. Writing for the majority in a six-to-three decision, Justice Brennan agreed that the state had a "compelling" interest in protecting young victims of sex crimes from "the trauma of public testimony," but he held that the First Amendment's guarantee of freedom of the press does not allow the courtroom closing to be mandatory. Trial courts, he said, should "determine on a case-by-case basis whether the state's legitimate concern for the well-being of the minor victim necessitates closure." Moreover, he added, the press and public must not be excluded from the hearing at which the need for closure is argued and decided. The Massachusetts Supreme Court had upheld the law in question, contending that trials for sex crimes have been the "one notable exception" to the tradition of openness in criminal proceedings, and therefore the *Richmond Newspapers* decision did not apply. Indeed it did, countered Justice Brennan: The important point was not whether a particular type of trial was traditionally open or closed but that the First Amendment itself unequivocally guarantees public examination of the judicial process.

Among those dissenting in this case was Justice Rehnquist—no surprise there—but rather than file an opinion of his own, he joined the dissent of none other than the author of the *Richmond Newspapers* decision, Chief Justice Burger. In writing his opinion two years earlier, the chief justice had stressed that there could be circumstances dictating a closed criminal trial, but now the majority, he wrote, "seems to read our decision in *Richmond Newspapers* as spelling out a First Amendment right of access to all aspects of all criminal trials under all circumstances. . . . That is plainly incorrect." Certainly the protection of "children who [have] suffered the trauma of rape or other sexual abuse" is a legitimate reason for closure. The majority opinion, declared the chief justice, was a "gross invasion of state authority and a state's duty to protect its citizens."

There was another dissent in this case. It was based on a legal technicality that need not concern us here. But it is instructive to note that it was filed by Justice Stevens, one of the strongest supporters of the majority opinion in *Richmond Newspapers.* He had in no way changed his mind about the earlier case. He had simply found that another principle—namely, that Supreme Court review of a state law should be timely and appropriate—was being violated here, for the Court's action was, "at best, premature."

The Stevens dissent, whatever one may think of its substance, serves as a reminder of how complex the legal issues that confront the Court may often be. We have already remarked that the justices are not necessarily consistent. Similarly, the Court is not necessarily infallible: Its decisions may be substantially modified or even overturned in time. But for any age—and particularly our own—one thing is certain: Partisans on one side or another may argue that it's easy to be right, but those who administer justice know well that it is a painstaking struggle.

PART FOUR

In Conflict
with the
Federal Government

9.
In the Interests
of National Security

The Vietnam War was a nightmare from which the United States only gradually roused itself. Often referred to as the most unpopular war in American history, it began, in 1961, with President John F. Kennedy's decision to commit a few thousand military advisers to South Vietnam, a small, embattled Asian country halfway round the world. It ended, in 1975, with the evacuation of the last American troops from the war-shattered capital of Saigon. But as early as 1965, after President Lyndon B. Johnson had steeply escalated our involvement in the conflict and our soldiers faced enemy forces that seemed ever stronger in numbers and determination, at home opposition to the war—present in some measure almost from the start—had become vocal and widespread. We have already alluded to the campus protests of the late sixties, and while young people then probably climbed the highest barricades, staged the noisiest demonstrations, and shouted the crudest antiwar slogans, more and more older Americans were growing increasingly disillusioned with a military effort that constantly saw our casualties mount and our hopes for victory fade.

Thus, as the turbulent decade of the sixties came to an end, the questions that reflected the prevailing American mood centered not on how to fight the Vietnam War most effectively but on how to extricate ourselves from it honorably and expeditiously—and on how we had gotten into it in the first place. It took several years to find the right answer to the first question, much less time to find an encyclopedic answer to the second. When it came, we were at last bestirring ourselves, and the nightmare was soon to be over.

It was on Sunday, June 13, 1971, that *The New York Times* ran the first of a series of articles on the roots of the Vietnam War. Its three-column headline was typically cool and understated— *Vietnam Archive: Pentagon Study Traces 3 Decades of Growing U.S. Involvement*—but the reaction of the federal government was intense and unprecedented. The second installment of what was to become known as the Pentagon Papers appeared in *The Times* the next day, and on that evening of June 14, the attorney general of the United States sent the newspaper the following telex message:

I HAVE BEEN ADVISED BY THE SECRETARY OF DEFENSE THAT THE MATERIAL PUBLISHED IN THE NEW YORK TIMES ON JUNE 13, 14, 1971 . . . CONTAINS INFORMATION RELATING TO THE NATIONAL DEFENSE OF THE UNITED STATES AND BEARS A TOP SECRET CLASSIFICATION.

AS SUCH, PUBLICATION OF THIS INFORMATION IS DIRECTLY PROHIBITED BY THE PROVISIONS OF THE ESPIONAGE LAW, TITLE 18, UNITED STATES CODE, SECTION 793.

MOREOVER, FURTHER PUBLICATION OF INFORMATION OF

THIS CHARACTER WILL CAUSE IRREPARABLE INJURY TO THE DEFENSE INTERESTS OF THE UNITED STATES.

ACCORDINGLY, I RESPECTFULLY REQUEST THAT YOU PUBLISH NO FURTHER INFORMATION OF THIS CHARACTER AND ADVISE ME THAT YOU HAVE MADE ARRANGEMENTS FOR THE RETURN OF THESE DOCUMENTS TO THE DEPARTMENT OF DEFENSE.

JOHN N. MITCHELL

Following the dispatch of the telegram, a Justice Department deputy telephoned a *Times* executive to advise him that the government was prepared to seek an injunction should publication of the articles not be halted immediately.

Later that night, a high-level meeting at the newspaper's offices led to a decision to challenge the power of the administration. In reply to Attorney General Mitchell, *The Times* said:

> We have received the telegram from the Attorney General asking *The Times* to cease further publication of the Pentagon's Vietnam study. *The Times* must respectfully decline the request of the Attorney General, believing that it is in the interest of the people of this country to be informed of the material contained in this series of articles. We have also been informed of the Attorney General's intention to seek an injunction to restrict further publication. We believe that it is properly a matter for the courts to decide. *The Times* will oppose any request for an injunction for the same reason that led us to publish the articles in the first place. We will of course abide by the final decision of the court.

As Harrison Salisbury, an editor of the newspaper, was to write years later, "The message that *The Times* carried to its readers on the morning of June 15 was clear and bold. It was *The New York Times* versus the President and his government. The arena was the courts."

Vietnam Archive: Pentagon Study Traces 3 Decades of Growing U. S. Involvement

By NEIL SHEEHAN

The headline on the first installment in The New York Times *of what was to become known as the Pentagon Papers.*

Ahead, then, lay a historic confrontation, and the decision to enter into it had been a calculated one. Like the initial decision to publish the Vietnam Archive, it hinged on *The Times*'s belief that the demands of responsible journalism left them no alternative. The American people had a right to know the contents of these documents, which were entirely concerned with the past, no matter that the administration would be displeased, no matter that the papers could, in fact, be considered stolen property.

What were the Pentagon Papers? In 1967, while Lyndon Johnson was president and the Vietnam fighting raged on, fierce and seemingly endless, the then secretary of defense, Robert S. McNamara, ordered that the Pentagon make an objective study of the causes and nature of the conflict. A task that was expected to be finished in about three months required a year and a half and the final results weighed in at 60 pounds. The complete report consisted of 3,000 pages of text, 4,000 pages of documentation, and a total of 2.5 million words.

All those words told a tangled saga—some of it never before publicly revealed—of American interests in Indochina over a period of more than two decades. As far back as the Truman administration, the study proved, we had given military aid to France in her war against the Vietminh, the rebel forces that eventually gained power as the Communist state of North Vietnam. A creation of the Geneva Accords of 1954, which brought an end to the French presence in Indochina, North Vietnam was an immediate threat to the non-Communist state to the south, and, these documents showed, by the late fifties the Eisenhower administration was already trying to protect the independence of South Vietnam. Under President Kennedy what had been a minor involvement became a "broad commitment," and under President Johnson the broad commitment led to clandestine military action against the North Vietnamese that had been concealed from Congress and the American people.

Studded with evidence of evasion, pretense, and deceit, the final report was classified "top secret" and, in January 1969, delivered to a new Pentagon chief, Clark M. Clifford, who had succeeded Robert McNamara as secretary of defense while the study was being made. Clifford had not asked for it and, now that he had it, he chose to ignore it. Thus, the Vietnam Archive languished in the Pentagon files for two years, years of continuing warfare and ever-increasing casualties, until one of its authors decided, in every sense, to take the matter in his own hands. Daniel Ellsberg, a consultant at a defense research organization that had helped compile the study, had once been a supporter of American policy in Vietnam but two years spent in that war-battered country had convinced him that our military engagement there was nothing short of criminal folly. Failing in his efforts to persuade congressional committees to subpoena the study, Ellsberg, who had access to one of the fifteen copies, simply appropriated it and handed it over to a reporter for *The New York Times*.

The internal debate that followed involved the newspaper's executives, editors, reporters, and lawyers; after a vehement exchange of views, it was settled in favor of those who maintained that, in this case, both patriotism and journalistic ethics required publication of the top-secret documents. Although they had secretly been removed from government files and concerned a war that was still being fought, there was nothing in them, *The Times* concluded, that would endanger any lives or hamper the current military effort. And there was much in them that had been hidden for too long and that was crucial to an understanding of the Vietnam ordeal.

The morning after the exchange of messages with the attorney general, *The Times* was arguing its position before federal judge Murray Gurfein in the United States Courthouse in New York City. The government had wasted no time in seeking a temporary order restraining the newspaper from further publication of the Pentagon Papers. Without this censorship, the U.S. attorney contended, national security would be severely compromised, for additional articles would "result in irreparable injury to the national defense." *The Times*'s attorneys countered that the government's charges were couched in the most general terms. Where were the specifics that might justify an action unprecedented in American history? On what basis was Judge Gurfein, appointed to the federal bench only a few days earlier, to impose prior restraint—that is, banning something before publication—on a newspaper for the first time in the two-hundred-year history of a free press?

Clearly reluctant to occupy a dubious niche in our annals of justice, Judge Gurfein tried to get *The Times* to agree voluntarily to suspend publication for a short time—until both sides could properly prepare and present their arguments and he could render a judgment. *The Times* refused, and an angry Judge Gurfein, noting that "there's never been a case like this," granted the government its temporary order barring publication. "The ques-

Attorney General John N. Mitchell

tions raised by this action are serious and fundamental," he said. "I believe that the matter is so important . . . that a more thorough briefing than the parties have had an opportunity to do is required."

Three days later, on June 18, before hearing the government's case, Judge Gurfein remained in an anti-*Times* mood, observing that "a free and independent press ought to be willing to sit down with the Department of Justice and as a matter of simple patriotism determine whether publication . . . is or is not dangerous to the national security." As the hearing progressed, however, the judge betrayed a growing impatience with the government. Again and again, he asked the Justice Department attorneys to identify the "specific documents" that would compromise national security and in effect received no response. Again and again, he gave the government "one more chance" to demonstrate how publication of the Pentagon Papers would put the country in jeopardy, and every chance was declined. (In point of fact, at this time no one in the Justice Department had read even a substantial portion of the Pentagon Papers, let alone all of the massive dossier.) It soon became evident that the military case against publication was so feeble that it was virtually nonexistent. Since the most recent documents in the archive were more than three years old, it was just about impossible to prove that any of the contents would imperil the ongoing war effort. The best that the government's chief military witness could offer was the vague argument that "there is an awful lot of stuff in [the Pentagon study] that I would just prefer to see sleep a while longer."

Although it went unmentioned in the attorney general's first telex message to *The Times*, the functional heart of the federal case for prior restraint had a diplomatic beat: the potential harm publication could cause to our relations with foreign countries. The two installments that had already appeared had brought embarrassment to the governments of such allies as Australia and Canada. As the deputy under secretary of state testified, "I just don't see how we can conduct diplomacy with this kind of business going on."

Here was an argument at least worthy of consideration, but to Judge Gurfein it was too weak to support the government's challenge to the First Amendment. If the only question was one of embarrassment, he was to write, "we must learn to live with it." This comment was part of the ruling he delivered the day after the hearing, on Saturday, June 19, as he found for *The New York Times* in a decision that defines the role of the press in words that have the ring of history.

> From the time of Blackstone* it was a tenet of the founding fathers that precensorship was the primary evil to be dealt with in the First Amendment. . . . The security of the Nation is not at the ramparts alone. Security also lies in the value of our free

---

*Sir William Blackstone (1723–1780), eminent English jurist whose *Commentaries* are one of the fundamental documents of English law.

institutions. A cantankerous press, an obstinate press, an ubiquitous press must be suffered by those in authority in order to preserve the even greater values of freedom of expression and the right of the people to know. . . .

In the last analysis it is not merely the opinion of the editorial writer or of the columnist which is protected by the First Amendment. It is the free flow of information so that the public will be informed about the Government and its actions.

These are troubled times. There is no greater safety valve for discontent and cynicism about the affairs of Government than freedom of expression in any form. This has been the genius of our institutions throughout our history. It has been the credo of all our Presidents. It is one of the marked traits of our national life that distinguish us from other nations under different forms of government.

While his decision in itself would have permitted *The Times* to resume publication of the Pentagon Papers, Judge Gurfein, knowing that the government would appeal, did not discontinue the restraining order. And in response to his ruling, Justice Department attorneys simply rode an elevator up to another federal courtroom and soon emerged with an order, from the court of appeals, that kept *The Times* securely locked in its straitjacket.

The stay so readily issued by the court of appeals, which prevented Judge Gurfein's ruling from going into effect, was a hint of the difficulties that lay in store for *The Times* when a few days later the case was argued before that eight-member body. Changing their tactics, the U.S. attorneys focused not on the contents of the Pentagon Papers but on how they had originally come into *The Times*'s possession. At the court of appeals hearing, the documents were variously referred to as "stolen," "embezzled," and "purloined," and all these synonyms were like a prelude to a verdict that, though not an outright victory for the government, was certainly a blow to *The Times*. By a vote of five to three, the court of appeals ordered the case back to Judge Gurfein for additional hearings on the evidence and continued the restraining order. Those who eagerly awaited the next installment of the Pentagon Papers would, it seemed, have to wait quite a while longer.

Actually, the presses started rolling in no more than a week. Rather than return to Judge Gurfein's courtroom, *The Times* filed for an immediate review of the case by the United States Supreme Court. Meanwhile, *The Washington Post*, which, following *The Times*'s lead, had begun publishing excerpts from the Pentagon Papers (their copy, too, made available by Daniel Ellsberg), was also engaged in a legal battle with the Justice Department, before first the district court and then the court of appeals in Washington, D.C. That court, a few days after *The Times* had lost in New York, ruled seven to two in favor of *The Post*, a decision the federal government appealed at once. Thus were the two cases joined, and on Friday morning, June 25, the Supreme Court agreed to hear them both the very next day.

Four of the justices would have upheld the decisions of Judge Gurfein and the Washington court of appeals and allowed publication of the complete papers to resume immediately; the Court as a whole, however, approved immediate resumption of publication only with the proviso that passages the government might deem too sensitive to appear in print be excluded. Neither *The Times* nor *The Post* was inclined to publish under such restrictions. They would leave it to the Court to hear the arguments and decide the legitimacy of any sort of prior restraint.

Saturday morning, June 26. In a courtroom bristling with tension, all present were aware of the historic nature of the case about to be heard by the nine justices. But if the crucial issue was conflict between our security as a nation and the rights of a free press, that was not apparent from the government's opening arguments. Once again the Justice Department, represented by the U.S. solicitor general, chose to dwell on how the newspapers had come into possession of documents that were not rightfully theirs. The justices showed their impatience with this line of attack by fidgeting in their huge leather chairs; finally, Justice Potter Stewart interrupted with a question that forced everyone's attention on the larger picture: What was the proper judgment if publication of the Pentagon Papers might result in the loss of a hundred young lives?

To this question *The Times*'s lawyers were quite ready to concede that in the face of "grave and immediate danger" the First Amendment would have to yield, a position that did not sit well with the Court's free press absolutists, Justices Black and Douglas. And they seemed to be joined by Justice Thurgood Marshall when, commenting on the implications inherent in the government's view, he asked, "Wouldn't we then—the federal courts—be a censorship board?" To this the solicitor general admitted that he knew of no alternative, prompting Black to remark, "The First Amendment might be."

The government's response here, though it began by claiming to defend the First Amendment, soon took a weird turn that brought it frighteningly close to George Orwell's *1984*, where key words mean exactly the opposite of what they appear to mean. Said the solicitor general, in a statement that provides a capsule summary of the Nixon administration's position, "You say that 'no law' means 'no law' and that should be obvious. [The reference is, of course, to the First Amendment: "Congress shall make no law abridging freedom of the press."] I can only say, Mr. Justice, that to me it is equally obvious that 'no law' does not mean 'no law' and I would seek to persuade the court that that is true."

But he could not and did not. He was arguing that "no law" meant that the government could inflict upon newspapers restrictions of its own choosing, but he failed to persuade a majority of the justices that the suppression of "leaks" was sanctioned by the Constitution. And that, in reality, was what he was attempting to do. There was nothing contained in the Pentagon Papers that would have endangered the lives of our military forces in Vietnam. Nor did they hold any secrets that, once divulged, would have seriously hampered the conduct of our diplomacy. No, there was only the troublesome fact that these official documents had been given to the press in a surreptitious manner. And this the administration could not tolerate. In its fight against publication of the Pentagon Papers it strove to protect not the nation's security but its own. Indeed, since the Vietnam Archive dealt entirely with acts of previous administrations, it was trying to uphold the concept of constitutionally approved government secrecy as a guard against *future* "leaks" that might prove equally embarrassing or even more destructive.

While the solicitor general was in the midst of challenging the absolutist position on the First Amendment, Justice Stewart again interrupted to point out that the newspapers had already agreed (though certain justices did not) that freedom of the press had its limits. And so, after a little more than two hours, the hearing of the Pentagon Papers case came to a close and the court adjourned. Four days later, at 2:34 P.M. on Wednesday, June 30, it announced its decision. By a vote of six to three it held:

> Any system of prior restraints of expression comes to this court bearing a heavy presumption against its constitutional validity. The Government thus carries a heavy burden of showing justification for the imposition of such a restraint. The Dis-

trict Court for the Southern District of New York . . . and the District Court for the District of Columbia and the Court of Appeals for the District of Columbia . . . held that the Government had not met that burden. We agree.

The decision came embroidered with nine separate opinions, ranging from the absolutist concurrences of Justices Black and Douglas to the angry dissent of Justice Harry Blackmun, who saw in the court's ruling a warrant for "the death of soldiers, the destruction of alliances, the greatly increased difficulty of negotiation with our enemies"—in other words, for prolongation of the war. It is, of course, true that publication of the Pentagon Papers resumed the day after the Court rendered its judgment, while our military involvement in Vietnam trudged along for four more

Daniel Ellsberg

years. Today, however, few would suggest a cause-and-effect relationship here. To the contrary, most informed observers believe that the Papers had very little bearing on the duration of the war; if anything, by unquestionably strengthening public and congressional opposition to it, their publication probably helped to "bring the boys home" a bit sooner.

In any event, the primary significance of the Pentagon Papers case lay elsewhere. At the time, the Court decision seemed a triumph for the press and was immediately hailed as such by the journalistic community. Seeing the judgment in a larger context, *The Times* praised it not so much as "a victory for the press as a striking confirmation of vitality of the American democratic form of government." But after the first flush of exhilaration had faded, in certain quarters reaction to the ruling took on a darker and more negative cast. For implicit in the majority opinion is the idea that *under special circumstances the government can justifiably exercise prior restraint* against the press. The Supreme Court had never articulated this view before, and some First Amendment defenders were deeply troubled by it. Moreover, they criticized *The Times*'s attorneys for accepting such a premise in arguing their case before the Court. To these critics, freedom of the press is like a bulwark and, no matter how extraordinary the circumstances, *any* governmental attempt to pierce it must be vigilantly and vigorously opposed.

The circumstances surrounding the next attempt were extraordinary indeed. They took place almost eight years later—and more eventful years would be hard to imagine. Having failed to prevent publication of the Pentagon Papers, the Nixon administration was determined to prosecute the man who had appropriated them, Daniel Ellsberg. And in trying to gather evidence against him, it indulged in certain illegal tactics that, when eventually revealed, not only forced the government to drop its case but became part of the web of scandal that was known as Watergate. As previously noted, the press played a pivotal role in uncovering the conspiracy and misdeeds that finally led to the resignation of Richard Nixon. But as the seventies rolled on—with Gerald Ford succeeding to the presidency, bringing the last troops home from Vietnam, and then losing the next election to Jimmy Carter—the power of the press, symbolized at the beginning of the decade by the Pentagon Papers and Watergate, was gradually, subtly, but perceptibly being chipped away. We had entered the era of the *Stanford Daily* and *Gannett,* the time of Earl Caldwell and Colonel Herbert and Myron Farber, and the press seemed to be in the loser's corner in every Supreme Court confrontation it faced. Early in 1979, it looked as if another case was headed that way, probably to a similar conclusion.

It was spawned by the antinuclear movement, which, in one form or another, has been with us ever since the Atomic Age began, back in August 1945, with the bombing of Hiroshima and Nagasaki. The movement has, however, grown stronger and more vocal as the weapons we and the Soviets produce have become ever more lethal and numerous and as effective arms control seems ever more elusive. Increasingly, demonstrations, peaceful and otherwise, have been massed outside of munitions factories, nuclear power plants, and military installations, and, increasingly, demonstrators have been literally dragged off to jail for acts of civil disobedience. The end of the Vietnam War spurred the movement on; one cause replaced the other for the dissidents among us who see as the essence of American foreign policy only the reality or the threat of military force.

Howard Morland was one of those. Fascinated with flying, he

had enlisted in the air force in 1965, expecting that the Vietnam military action would be over by the time he finished flight training. It wasn't, but before he could be sent into combat he managed to get a medical discharge—in his words, "on the grounds that [he] had acquired a mental disability while in the service—namely, an objection to the war in Vietnam." As he was to write later, in a book called *The Secret That Exploded*, "I saw no call for Americans to be shooting or bombing Vietnamese of any political persuasion." It was quite a while before our government reached the same conclusion, and by then Morland had become interested in resource depletion. From there a very short step led to his involvement in the Clamshell Alliance, a New England environmentalist organization that was fighting the construction of a nuclear power plant at Seabrook, New Hampshire. Two thousand people turned out for the alliance's first huge demonstration at Seabrook, on April 30, 1977 ("It was reminiscent of the civil rights and antiwar movements," wrote Morland), and for refusing to leave, many of them were arrested the following day. Morland, like the others who declined to raise bail, remained in jail for twelve days; by the time he was released he had come upon the path that he still follows today.

It is a path that could bring our country to unilateral nuclear disarmament, and it was a longtime ban-the-bomb activist who, there in the Portsmouth (New Hampshire) Armory, guided Howard Morland to it. This man made him realize "that protests against nuclear power were protests against nuclear weapons in disguise," and he identified what became for Morland the real enemy, the military-industrial complex. Before long, Morland had decided, he writes, "that for the next few years I would try and see how big a dent I could make in the Department of Defense and its system of military contractors. . . ."

Morland began to travel all over New England and then beyond, lecturing and presenting a slide show on the danger of nuclear power and the horror of nuclear war. His audiences were composed of community and college groups that, at the very least, felt concerned about such matters as the arms race, the levels of radiation in the atmosphere, and the effects of nuclear fallout. And if they gave a sympathetic hearing to his "ban the bomb" message, it was partly because his past gave him credibility: He "had once bored holes in the sky with needle-nosed Air Force jets, and . . . had color slides to prove it."

Knowledge, he realized, served as a key that opened people's minds. Most Americans were not inclined to question the government's nuclear weapons policy largely because "in a general sense . . . they were not qualified to discuss matters about which nothing was known, or could be known. . . ." The secrecy that had surrounded the creation of the atomic bomb had, in the postwar world, continued to shroud our nuclear posture, to be lifted only for a select few. To enlighten the public so that they might judge that posture for themselves became for Morland the immediate challenge. He set about to learn the secrets with the intention of divulging them—and putting an end to ignorance.

Now, in his own words, "an amateur atom spy," Morland abandoned his antinuclear slide show and embarked on a new strategy. To combat secrecy, he started on a journey that would take him from laboratories to libraries, from scientists and engineers to journalists and peace activists, from those who had helped develop nuclear weapons to those whose only goal was to destroy them. Along the way Morland made contact with *The Progressive,* a magazine published in Madison, Wisconsin, that, since its founding in 1909, has been a crusading force against monopolies, imperialism, racial discrimination, and all forms of warmongering. It was agreed that *The Progressive* would provide Morland with press credentials and would eventually publish the articles that resulted from his research.

And, as time went on, Morland's efforts were gaining both momentum and results. Later he wrote: "As I questioned more and more people I learned that information was like money: it was easier to get more if you already had a lot to start with." Putting together facts gleaned from many different sources, he came to realize that there was essentially just one secret that explained the working of the hydrogen bomb. That secret eluded him for a long time—but not forever. To quote now from the article he wrote, "I discovered it simply by reading and asking questions, without the benefit of security clearance or access to classified materials." His search ended, Morland was ready to reveal all that he had learned.

Early on, he had become aware that an article on making an H-bomb might seem to put him in violation of the Atomic Energy Act of 1954. This sweeping law allows the attorney general to try to restrain publication of all data—lawfully obtained or not—relating to the design, manufacture, or use of nuclear weapons and certain nuclear materials. When he read the Act, Morland thought, "It must be a joke. Everything in the entire area of atomic science and technology had been declared classified until it was declassified. Any new idea, no matter who had it, was automatically classified, just as the oldest ones were. . . . The only way anyone could be sure he was not disseminating classified information was never to discuss the subject at all, or else to first reveal everything in front of a classification officer."

Morland was not inclined to accept either of these options, but when his article was ready for publication by *The Progressive*, one of the magazine's editors suggested "sending a copy to the government to get their reaction." Morland resisted this idea at first, suspecting that Washington would either ignore the article or, more likely, try to prevent its publication. But the latter probability soon took on an appeal of its own. The purpose of the article, after all, was certainly not to teach people how to make a hydrogen bomb. Rather, it was to strengthen "a popular movement against nuclear weapons," and with that aim in-mind, Morland thought, "how much more impact on the public consciousness the whole thing would have if it turned into a kind of Pentagon Papers case." Thus, he and the editors of *The Progressive* were not merely prepared for the consequences, they were actively courting them when, in mid-February 1979, the Department of Energy was sent a copy of "How a Hydrogen Bomb Works,"* by Howard Morland.

It was not ignored. On March 1, *The Progressive* received a call from the chief legal officer of the Department of Energy, formally advising them "that in the judgment of the DOE the article . . . contained restricted data" and warning that its publication would risk the civil and criminal penalties provided by the Atomic Energy Act. The editor's reaction was to tell Morland on the phone, "Congratulations. They took the bait." Writes Morland, "The fish arrived in Madison the next day . . . four from the DOE and two from Justice." One of these government lawyers confirmed the accuracy of the article, except for a few details that "were not substantial," news that Morland later "received . . . with . . . glee." Otherwise, the official visit had little effect. In the face of government threats of prior restraint, *The Progressive* re-scheduled the article for May (for a short time the editors had planned to run it in the April issue) but, as the magazine's attorney notified the DOE five days later, it would definitely appear "as it

---

*This was the title the government was to use in referring to the article. It was, in fact, no more than the heading over a series of diagrams that illustrated the article, which was itself untitled at that time.

Howard Morland, right, with an editor of The Progressive. *On Morland's T-shirt is a schematic diagram of an H-bomb.*

stood." The following day the government announced that it was going to court to stop publication, on the ground that it represented a clear and present danger to the security of the United States.

On March 9, Judge Robert Warren of Wisconsin's Eastern District Court, in Milwaukee, granted the Justice Department a temporary restraining order pending another hearing to be held a week later. He decided, he said, on "common sense grounds," that "hydrogen bombs could do a lot more damage" than could the mildest form of prior restraint. The lawyer for *The Progressive* argued that Morland's article contained no classified information and was protected by the First Amendment, but in the context of the hearing he was like a lonely figure protesting that a burning house violated the zoning laws while everyone else was busy fighting the blaze. Judge Warren, their leader, unquestionably reflected popular opinion when he commented that he would have to think "a long hard time before I gave the hydrogen bomb to Idi Amin."*

He was, of course, not only reflecting popular opinion but molding it. Not having read the Morland article (he had had the opportunity to do so, but had chosen not to, at least at that point), the judge had nevertheless referred to it in open court as "the recipe for a do-it-yourself hydrogen bomb," and this characterization was immediately embraced by the media. An NBC News anchorman called the article a "how-to" for anyone "who might like to build a hydrogen bomb in his garage." Could the public, then, be blamed for thinking of Howard Morland as some mad subversive who should have been writing not for a political magazine but for *Popular Mechanics*?

Even among those who might have been expected to side with Morland, opinion was generally against him. Opposed to publication of his article were, for example, the Milwaukee law firm he approached in search of personal legal representation; Daniel Ellsberg, "the Great Leaker himself" (as Morland tags him), who thought the article "would abet the proliferation of nuclear weapons"; and *The New York Times*, *The Washington Post*, and many other prominent newspapers, all of whose editorials tended to sound a common theme: *The Progressive* should print a government-edited version of the article rather than risk losing so emotional and controversial a case and thereby endanger the press's protections against prior restraint.

But *The Progressive* would not be moved. Said its editor, "As

---

*At the time Idi Amin was the despotic and, many thought, deranged ruler of the African nation of Uganda.

for this notion that we should voluntarily surrender our freedom so that theirs won't be imperiled, the answer is very clear. Rights exist only when they can be exercised. If there is no First Amendment for *The Progressive*, there is no First Amendment for anyone."

And Morland and *The Progressive* did not stand entirely alone. Their most important support came from two very different sectors and, in themselves, they suggest the "split personality" the magazine's defense had almost instantly developed. On the one hand, Morland sought and found nuclear physicists who confirmed that the information in his article was common knowledge among many scientists, including those without access to classified data. (Said Dr. Edward Teller, "Father of the H-Bomb," and not a Morland ally, "What is known to a million people is not a secret.") On the other hand, the American Civil Liberties Union sided with *The Progressive* on constitutional grounds, attacking the Atomic Energy Act, the basis for the government's action, as being vague and excessively broad.

Because collecting affidavits and briefs from all these varied and interested parties took a good deal of time—and a judicial reading of them would require even more—*The Progressive* requested and received a ten-day postponement of the second hearing. Meanwhile, the government was amassing its own mountain of material. Upon inspection, these documents, too, revealed a split— indeed, not merely a split but also an inconsistency. Their primary charge was that the Morland article contained information, not to be found in the public domain, that could be used to harm the United States. But one government affidavit alleged that the article was so full of mistakes that it could not possibly have been derived from the respected sources that Morland claimed. Clearly, whatever its sources, if the article was riddled with inaccuracies and glaringly incomplete, as stated in this affidavit, its usefulness as a guide to H-bomb building had to be seriously deficient—in which case, what harm could it do, to the United States or anyone else?

But at the next hearing, on March 26, the government's lawyer, Morland recalls, "did not mention any mistakes, and anyone listening in the courtroom, including reporters, would have supposed that my account of the H-bomb was both complete and accurate." Since at that time Morland thought so himself, he was not at all displeased to hear this "accusation." But in stressing the soundness of Morland's designs and data, the government had in mind purposes other than commending the quality of his research. First, it argued that under the Atomic Energy Act, Congress had tried to protect the secrecy of the kind of information the article contained; if on occasion leaks occurred, the material itself was still covered by the Act and thus those who disseminated such material were breaking the law. The government's second line of attack sprang from the Pentagon Papers decision, thereby confirming the fears of those who saw that ruling as considerably less than a First Amendment triumph. For in their signed opinion two Supreme Court justices had found prior restraint justified if and when publication would cause "direct, immediate, and irreparable harm to the nation and its people." At the hearing, the government attorney referred to this as the "*New York Times* test" and, applying it to *The Progressive* case, he found the Morland article eminently censorable. Indeed, he considered its publication a threat not only to the nation but to "the world, if not the entire universe."

Brandishing as his weapon a volume of the *World Book*, *The Progressive*'s lawyer began his counterattack. He turned to an entry in the encyclopedia entitled "How the Hydrogen Bomb Works" and contended that there was no significant distinction to be made between the information available there for his nine-year-old daughter to read and the supposedly "secret restricted data" in the Morland article. "It was secret according to the government . . . but not *really* secret. That," writes Morland, "was the important point." The lawyer proceeded to cite the many scientists whose affidavits supported the defense in its position that the article was merely a "summary of published information," and to point out the obvious and "un-American" absurdities of the Atomic Energy Act. In conclusion, he said that by trying to suppress the article, the government had "given it the stamp of authority" and had so heavily publicized it that, should *The Progressive* not be permitted to publish it, the underground press certainly would.

The Progressive's lawyer proved to be better at prophecy than persuasion. Having heard both sides in the case, Judge Warren declared a five-minute recess and then returned to the court with a fifteen-page "Memorandum and Order" that gave slight consolation to Morland and at least an interim victory to the government. Between hearings Warren had read the article and now he at least partially retreated from his Idi Amin comment by asking, "Does the article provide a 'do-it-yourself' guide for the hydrogen bomb?" and answering, "Probably not. . . . One does not build a hydrogen bomb in the basement." He recognized that highly sophisticated technology, a large industrial capacity, and "resourceful scientists" were essential to the creation of the bomb, and therefore the worst the article could do would be to expedite the entry of a medium-sized nation into "the thermonuclear club." The judge went on to note that any move toward prior restraint runs headlong into constitutional protection of the press and that "many wise, intelligent, patriotic individuals can hold diametrically opposite opinions on the issues before us." But on one issue Judge Warren seemed adamant: "The court can find no plausible reason why the public needs to know the technical details about hydrogen bomb construction to carry on an informed debate on the issue."

Torn, then, between a concern for the First Amendment and a conviction that the article had only serious mischief as its purpose, Judge Warren proposed that he choose a five-member panel to mediate the case out of court. The defense, like the government, would have nominated eight experts, from among whom the judge would have made the final selection; nevertheless, *The Progressive* lost little time in rejecting this compromise. If mediation resulted in even one word being cut from the article, "it would be a censored document," writes Morland, "and the First Amendment would be diminished. Self-censorship was even worse than imposed censorship." So, convinced that it would win the case on its merits, the magazine preferred to take its chances in higher courts.

Although the government may have felt just as confident that it would ultimately prevail, it accepted, somewhat grudgingly, the mediation proposal. Thus, it was the defense alone that caused Judge Warren severe disappointment, forcing him to the wall— and giving him, in his mind, no choice but to issue an injunction that barred publication of Morland's article until a full trial could be held.

As they left the courthouse, Morland and the defense team had all sorts of prepared statements ready to deliver to the press: "Today marks the beginning of the end of the use of secrecy to promote the production and deployment of nuclear weapons." "When the Founders framed the First Amendment they did not put it out for mediation." Accepting the judge's offer "would have been a frightening and tragic precedent to set for all Americans." But these pronouncements did not carry much beyond the courthouse steps, for on that day, March 26, 1979, the Carter Administration won another major victory. Egypt and Israel signed the

Camp David peace accords, the first formal agreement between Jews and Arabs in modern history, and news of that momentous event all but swamped the developments in Milwaukee. Two of the television networks mentioned the H-bomb case briefly and the third ignored it altogether. As a result, many Americans went unaware of the day's other historic "first"—the government's success in legally barring for an extended period publication of a significant piece of journalism.

The "extended period" turned out to be six months. The urgency with which the courts viewed the Pentagon Papers case, involving as it did daily newspapers of commanding prestige and influence, did not seem applicable to a small-circulation monthly magazine. Defense efforts to expedite the schedule of hearings, though they went as far as the Supreme Court, proved unsuccessful. But Morland used the time to good advantage—lecturing, helping to research and write legal briefs, and revising his article in the light of new information and understanding. The defense team was busy, too, of course, planning strategy and mounting a two-pronged attack on the government's case: *The Progressive's* attorneys emphasized that since everything in the article was in the public domain and therefore not secret, the Atomic Energy Act did not apply, while the ACLU, representing Morland, chose the more ambitious approach of challenging the very constitutionality of the Atomic Energy Act itself. Perhaps busiest of all during this waiting period were various writers and reporters for the underground press who were more than eager to pick up the ball Morland had been forced to drop. Denied access to his article by the courts, they were gaining vital yardage by doing research on their own, and, as the date of the next hearing neared, one of them was about to score.

The Seventh Circuit Court of Appeals, in Chicago, heard the

case on September 13. This time the defense was armed not only with affidavits from scientists but also with supporting articles, editorials, and briefs from magazines, major newspapers like *The New York Times* and *The Boston Globe*, and such highly respected press organizations as the American Society of Newspaper Editors, the National Association of Broadcasters, and the Association of American Publishers. Clearly, in the past six months, the climate of opinion had quite markedly changed. With a congressional committee now looking into charges that the government's policy on atomic secrecy was being manipulated for political purposes, the basis of the defense case had taken on both respectability and credence. Laid to rest were worries about Idi Amin and backyard H-bombs, and after the burial the government's case seemed far more feeble than before. At the hearing, the appeals

A cartoon comment on the Morland case.

OLIPHANT—WASHINGTON STAR

'MISS CLAGTHORPE, PLEASE DIRECT THIS GROUP OF STUDENTS TO WEAPONS, NUCLEAR (HYDROGEN), TRIGGER MECHANISMS, TOP SECRET, DECLASSIFIED.'

court judges themselves appeared to be confused by what was classified as secret and what was not. And the government, as if aware that its case was slowly sinking, grasped at straws, arguing, for example, that the kind of information contained in the Morland article was comparable to obscenity—and therefore not protected by the First Amendment.

The court of appeals hearing lasted one day, a Thursday, and over that weekend, the case, like a terminally ill patient, suddenly but not unexpectedly, died. On Monday, September 17, the government dropped its suit. Writes Morland: "The months of absurdities came to an end with a short, emotionless statement. The government 'respectfully moves this court for an order vacating the preliminary injunction, dismissing the consolidated appeals as moot . . .'—that is, meaningless, superfluous, unnecessary, inconsequent."

What had prompted this governmental turnabout? Ostensibly, publication that Sunday of a letter in the Madison (Wisconsin) *Press-Connection*, an underground newspaper, that divulged much of the contents (not entirely accurately) of Morland's article. The writer of the letter, one Chuck Hansen, a longtime antinuclear activist, had gathered his information the same way Morland had, had transmitted his "letter to the editor" to seven publications in various parts of the country, and had sent a copy to the Department of Energy, which had immediately classified it as "secret" and taken legal steps to prohibit its publication. But we live in an age when technology has brought us not just nuclear weapons but also photocopying machines, and soon "copies of the letter were multiplying like rabbits" and newspapers not among the original seven had received them—without the government's knowledge and therefore under no restraints against publication. One of these papers was the Madison *Press-Connection*, which ran the letter as a 12,000-copy special edition on September 16. That, said the government, was the ball game.

But many observers were not persuaded. They believed—and still believe—that the government used the Hansen letter as an excuse to drop the suit. They point out that between March and September other articles had appeared covering much the same material. Why hadn't they rendered *The Progressive* case moot? No, Morland and his supporters are certain that the government "had merely seized upon the pretext of the Hansen letter . . . before the appeals court had a chance to overturn Judge Warren's injunction."

By not permitting the higher courts to rule on that injunction, the government managed to leave the conflict between press freedom and national security in the clouded corner of the Pentagon Papers decision where publication may be restrained in order to prevent "irreparable harm to the nation and its people." But what kind of information poses such a threat? In *Near v. Minnesota,** the 1931 decision frequently cited in various Pentagon Papers opinions, Chief Justice Charles Evans Hughes wrote that in time of war a government could without question prevent "the publication of the sailing dates of transports or the number and location of troops." In the *Progressive* case, the government claimed that wartime restrictions upon the press also applied to the nuclear arms race and that "telling the H-bomb secret was like warning the Germans in advance about the Allied plans for D-day." To this Howard Morland replies: "Military secrecy of that sort, however, is obsolete. Deterrence makes it not only unnecessary, but undesirable. Each side must know exactly what the other side is

---

*A landmark case in the fight against prior restraint, in which the Supreme Court, voting five to four, declared unconstitutional a Minnesota law that allowed a single judge to shut down a scandalmongering "public nuisance" of a newspaper.

doing. Secrets can breed misunderstanding; misunderstanding, fear; fear, war." Morland cites as his authority no less an eminence than Albert Einstein, among the first to recognize the vast potential of nuclear energy. To Morland the following passage deserves immortality: "There is no secret, there is no defense, and there is no possibility of control except through the aroused understanding and insistence of the peoples of the world."

All too often, then, the issue of national security versus a free press can be reduced to a simple, if sweeping, disagreement over a political policy. Publication of the Pentagon Papers was viewed as harmful by those who supported the Vietnam War, useful by those who opposed it. Publication of the H-bomb article was an outrage to those who favor a nuclear arms buildup, an act of courage (however futile) by those who would have us disarm unilaterally. But the First Amendment should tower above such political disputes and not be challenged by them. In all our history we have yet to encounter a time when the press would have endangered our security had it not been restrained by government action.

Nor are we likely to—but that is not to say that the press has never been prevented from reporting developments of national concern. In October 1983, the Reagan administration succeeded where earlier administrations had failed. It struck at the very root of the journalistic process by effectively suppressing the gathering of news. When United States Marines invaded the tiny Caribbean island of Grenada, to protect American citizens there and to prevent a Communist takeover of the government, the press was given no advance notice of the action and, for two days, no opportunity to cover the landing and occupation. The reasons for this unprecedented act of omission were variously put forth as a need to maintain absolute secrecy in order to ensure the success of the mission and an inability to provide for the physical safety of the journalists who would have accompanied the invading forces. Apparently forgotten were all the battles in all our earlier modern wars that newsmen observed at close range, never divulging vital information, never seeking special protection, and, on occasion, dying in the line of duty just as gallantly as the most honored combatant.

What happened in Grenada, supposedly in the interest of national security, added a new dimension to the concept of prior restraint. As the invasion proceeded, NBC News commentator John Chancellor observed, "The American government is doing whatever it wants to, without any representative of the American public watching what it is doing." But, aside from the press itself, did anyone care? The Reagan administration seemed willing—indeed, eager—to risk the wrath of public opinion, for it knew that times had changed, drastically, since Vietnam and Watergate. Said a high White House aide, "Kicking the press is a surefire applause line with almost any audience."

PART FIVE

Conclusion

10.
"A Sort of Wild Animal"

In the wake of the Grenada news blackout came the angry sputter in editorial pages and television commentaries. But then, in response to those inevitable cries of "unfair," "unreasonable," and "un-American," the voice of the people could be heard and, in letters to the editor, it sounded like this:

So the press was not allowed to go to Grenada and do its usual liberal, biased reporting. Whoopee!

The press long ago abdicated its role as impartial observer. It no longer reports. It editorializes.

Who besides the press views its exclusion from Grenada as "a bad mistake"? Newspeople have become so smug, arrogant, and manipulative that they overreact to any attempt to get balance into their reporting.

... you say, "The press has a ... function as a representative of the public." This statement is essentially correct. However, the function is self-assigned. The public, on the other hand, has not complained that the press was denied for a time its sensational headlines and pictures of Grenada.

And indeed, the public had generally not complained. Of course, some people agreed with the California woman who asked, "How can I form an opinion of what happened in Grenada when the only viewpoint I have of the first three days is Government-censored film? I feel cheated, angry, and sad." But surveys showed such objectors to be vastly outnumbered by those whose sentiments were fairly accurately reflected by the quotations cited above.*

Public reaction to the media freeze-out became perhaps the biggest story to emerge from the invasion. Certainly it was the only one, aside from the military action itself, that contained an element of great surprise. Sophisticated observers found the Reagan administration running true to form in imposing the press ban and, while they could not have anticipated it, they regarded it as simply the latest dramatic evidence of the deep distrust in which the government held the media. And for their part, the indignation and rage of the shut-out newsmen were about as unexpected as the roar of a trapped lion.

Scarcely more than a decade earlier those same newsmen had seemed to be basking in the warmth of public favor. The Pentagon Papers decision had led former *New York Times* editor Harrison Salisbury to write, "It was, as far as anyone could see, a famous victory. Right and Justice had triumphed. Opinion polls showed

---

*Letters and calls to NBC supported the press ban 5 to 1; to ABC, "99 percent" (said its news anchorman); to *Time*, 8 to 1; to a dozen daily newspapers informally polled, 3 to 1.

that the country strongly supported the press." And two years later, journalists achieved even greater acclaim when the relentless efforts of a team of *Washington Post* reporters broke the story of the Watergate scandals. While the Nixon administration was sent reeling, eventually to stagger and fall, the reporters' own account of their investigative exploits, a book called *All the President's Men*, rose to the top of the best-seller lists and was made into a popular, award-winning motion picture. What had happened in the ten years that followed to cause much of the public to turn against the press and look upon it not as an honored ally but as a rather sinister adversary? "Why do they hate us?" asked Robert MacNeil, the executive director of the PBS "MacNeil/Lehrer News Hour."*

To a considerable extent, the press had become the victim of its own success. Every victory means a defeat for someone, and the triumphs that journalists enjoyed in the seventies generally spelled failure to those on the far right of the political spectrum. Although most Americans viewed our disengagement from Vietnam as a too-long-delayed assertion of reason and humanity, a highly vocal minority, as we have noted, saw it as an ignominious rout brought on largely by biased reporting on the part of the media. They denied they were blaming the messenger for the bad news; they charged that the messenger had, by distortion, *created* the bad news. Whatever the truth of the matter, members of this faction have never forgiven the press and continue to regard it on the whole as a dangerous force, blind to the worldwide Communist menace and trying unflaggingly to swing our foreign policy to the left. To the chairman of Accuracy in Media, an organization that

---

*In an address delivered at Columbia University and reprinted in the June 1985 issue of *Columbia, The Magazine of Columbia University.*

trumpets this point of view, the Grenada news blackout "deprived [the press] of the opportunity to publish the facts in advance" and in that way prevent the military operation from proceeding. However much newsmen might deride this attack as baseless and absurd, there was no denying that in the political climate of the early eighties, it struck a responsive chord. Said the editorial-page editor of *The New York Times*, "The most astounding thing about the Grenada situation was the quick, facile assumption by some of the public that the press wanted to get in, not to witness the invasion on behalf of the people, but to sabotage it."

Thus, while accusations of slanted reporting were not new, the belief that journalists tilted heavily to the left had gained wider currency as the country itself seemed to have turned more conservative. In truth, surveys have shown that on social and political issues, reporters and editors—but not publishers and newspaper owners*—do tend to have personal views that are distinctly liberal. The popular television interviewer Barbara Walters has said, "The news media in general are liberal. If you want to be a reporter, you are going to see poverty and misery, and you have to be involved in the human condition." But she and other journalists are quick to deny that their own values are reflected in the way they handle their news-gathering function.

It is, however, doubtful that journalists can achieve total objectivity in reporting, no matter how sincere their intentions to do so may be. But it is also doubtful that media bias is primarily responsible for the negative attitude that so many people feel toward the press. At least as important—and probably more important—in shaping that attitude is a quality perceived as arrogance. Critics

---

*In 1984 a national survey of newspapers reported that 58 percent endorsed President Reagan; 9 percent, Walter Mondale. The remaining 33 percent backed neither.

of the press find and condemn arrogance at least as frequently as editorialists bewail the "chilling effect," with both groups tracing the source of their concerns to the same root—the First Amendment. While media people are keenly alert to any attempt to limit or reduce their constitutional rights, their detractors charge that they use those rights in ways that were never intended: as a barrier from behind which they can shoot at whatever targets they choose, without regard for accuracy, decency, or compassion, or as a cloak of immunity in which to wrap themselves as protection against demands of accountability for their offenses.

When the charge is arrogance, the supposed offense is most likely to fall within the category of libel or invasion of privacy. The huge wave of sympathy that swept Carol Burnett to her record-setting jury award exemplified an all-too-common sense of outrage—a feeling that the press has "gone too far" and must not be allowed "to get away with it." As we have seen, this reaction has led in recent years to a sharp increase in the number of libel actions instituted, the number lost by journalist defendants, and the size of the damages juries have awarded. Observed one newspaper editor, "Juries are the American people. They want to punish us."

That's probably something of an overstatement. If jurors tend to find for plaintiffs in libel suits, the reason is usually not that they are angry at the media but that most people are quicker to identify with a victim—to feel the pain of an injured reputation or the embarrassment of a revealed secret—than to recognize the value of an abstract concept like freedom of the press. But to the extent that the remark is true, it implicitly acknowledges that in performing their job, vital though they are, journalists seem more and more to have blithely overstepped certain boundaries of human consideration and ordinary courtesy. Displays of arrogance and rudeness are common, if varied: from reporting as fact a wild rumor about a television star, to camping outside the home of the widow of a president, to shoving a microphone under the nose of a bereaved parent. And while such practices as these may be acceptable under the Constitution, no Bill of Rights can compel the public to approve of them.

Nor can anyone approve of a reporter's deliberate failure to distinguish between fact and fiction. This may well be the ultimate act of journalistic arrogance—to pass off as truth what one knows to be false. Unless a real person is somehow victimized by the fake story, the offender will probably not be hauled into court. But the consequences of such a hoax—if and when it is exposed—can be damaging indeed. In the early eighties a rash of fiction-as-fact incidents infected three major newspapers, the New York *Daily News* and *The New York Times* among them. The most highly publicized involved a reporter for *The Washington Post*, Janet Cooke, who in 1981 won a Pulitzer Prize for her series "Jimmy's World," about an eight-year-old heroin addict. An affecting, insightful account of a doomed childhood, it seemed richly deserving of the honor it received. But, sadly, it was a fraud, made up of bits and pieces of reality and the author's imagination, artfully intermingled. And later, when its authenticity was questioned and Janet Cooke had to confess that there was no Jimmy, for her there was no longer a Pulitzer Prize or a job.

But the loss suffered by responsible journalists everywhere was perhaps even more serious, for the Janet Cooke episode, a front-page story throughout the country, diminished the press's most valuable asset, its credibility. When the public has good reason to question the truth of news reports, the old adage "Don't believe everything you read" becomes not cynicism but common wisdom. And between 1976 and 1983, one survey showed, the number of people who had a great deal of confidence in the news media declined by over 50 percent, to barely more than one person in ten. Such a statistic suggests that the press, one of the pillars of our democratic society, has been seriously undermined in its function as reporter, interpreter, and critic of the events and policies that form our present and will determine our future.

Since popular sentiment toward such large institutions as the press, the law, and the government tends to swing like a pendulum, chances are that the precipitous drop in public trust will prove temporary: The press will recover at least some of its esteem and, indeed, may go on to new heights of approbation. To help make this happen—and in response to the recent waves of criticism and lawsuits—many newspapers and television stations have taken various steps that should ensure greater accuracy, fairness, and balance in their news coverage. They require increased documentation or verification for stories of uncertain origin. They publish corrections of errors more quickly and more prominently—the retraction of a false charge that appeared on page one is less often found buried on page eighty-four. They have opened their columns and their airtime to expressions of opinion that are at odds with their own. And more and more frequently they have made the press itself—their own performance and that of their affiliates and competitors—the subject of extended discussion and analysis.

The conspicuous adoption of such measures should enhance both the image and the reality of the press as a responsible institution. But the changes that time brings are certain to have just as much of an effect. And within the halls of the Supreme Court, which is uniquely influential in molding public opinion, a shift in outlook is inevitable, too. As new justices ascend to the High Bench, taking the place of those retired or deceased, the current trend toward antipress rulings may even intensify, but someday the tide is sure to flow in the reverse direction.

So, while the media may seem beleaguered and out of favor during any one period, the situation will not last. What *is* timeless is the power of printed words. It was recognized as long ago as the end of the fifteenth century, when the English Crown imposed its licensing laws and the valiant few who circulated unauthorized books and pamphlets risked their very lives. It is recognized today in the controversies of the recent American past that we have considered in these pages and that, in many cases, still fester. And it will be recognized in the future, for as long as we remain a free people, whenever someone may be moved to rise in wrath against the press or an arm of government feels compelled to lay its heavy hand upon it.

The power of printed words is equaled—or perhaps even surpassed—only by the power of the ideas they express. Herbert Agar, a distinguished American editor and historian, wrote in 1942, shortly after the United States had entered the Second World War, "There is nothing worth fighting for except an idea, for it alone can last, can provide a basis for the developing future." It is hard to imagine an idea that could not live on in the minds of men and women forever, or until it ceased to have meaning or usefulness. But in *1984* George Orwell suggested that ideas could indeed be killed. He envisioned a world in which despotic governments could so distort the meaning of words and could impose such deep and sweeping thought control that a blanket of conformity would smother entire populations. It is to guard against this danger that our press, which keeps ideas alive, must be afforded the highest possible degree of freedom.

The First Amendment absolutists believe that under the Constitution the press has total freedom—that it cannot be subject to any kind of outside restraint. Few of us share that view. Someone once described the press as "a sort of wild animal in our midst—restless, gigantic, always seeking new ways to use its strength . . . acknowledg[ing] accountability to no one except its owners and publishers." And we have seen that, at times, the wild animal demands to be tamed, as it tramples over reputations, privacy, justice, and even truth. Yes, freedom of the press is lodged in the First Amendment, but it is not the only freedom that resides there, nor is the First the only amendment to our Constitution. Nevertheless, whenever the press is penalized or restricted, however justifiably in the public mind, there is a risk that the people will also lose. The chance of a libel suit causes a magazine to be excessively cautious in what it publishes, the threat of a jail term forces a reporter to reveal his confidential sources—these are scenarios in which, whether we recognize it or not, we all become victims. It may well be that we are prepared, even happy, to suffer this role. The greater good may not be on the side of the press.

But, in this writer's opinion, that is rarely the case. For all its sins—and they are not to be minimized—the wild animal that is the press is also a watchdog, alerting us to abuses of power by the forces, institutions, and individuals that in so many ways dominate our lives and determine our future. The importance of this function is overriding, for it works to protect and preserve the entire range of our freedoms. Those who fear the power of the press have good reason to do so because, in reality, what they fear is the power of an informed people.

Bibliography

An asterisk (*) indicates a book published in paperback.

Barth, Alan. *Prophets with Honor: Great Dissents and Great Dissenters in the Supreme Court.* New York: Alfred A. Knopf, Inc., 1974.

Black, Hugo. *One Man's Stand for Freedom*, ed. Irving Dilliard. New York: Alfred A. Knopf, Inc., 1973.

*Bonsignore, John J., et al, eds. *Before the Law: An Introduction to the Legal Process*, 2nd ed. Boston: Houghton Mifflin Company, 1979.

*Chafee, Zechariah. *Free Speech in the United States.* New York: Atheneum, Publishers, 1969.

*Emerson, Thomas I. *The System of Freedom of Expression.* New York: Random House, Inc., 1970.

Farber, Myron E. *Somebody Is Lying: The Story of Dr. X.* New York: Doubleday & Company, Inc., 1982.

*Friendly, Fred W. *The Good Guys, the Bad Guys and the First Amendment: Free Speech Vs. Fairness in Broadcasting.* New York: Random House, Inc., 1976.

*———. *Minnesota Rag: The Dramatic Story of the Landmark Supreme Court Case That Gave New Meaning to Freedom of the Press.* New York: Random House, Inc., 1981.

*————, and Elliott, Martha H. *The Constitution: That Delicate Balance.* New York: Random House, Inc., 1984.

*Hentoff, Nat. *The First Freedom: The Tumultuous History of Free Speech in America.* New York: Delacorte Press, 1980.

Morland, Howard. *The Secret That Exploded.* New York: Random House, Inc., 1981.

*Morris, Richard. *Fair Trial: Fourteen Who Stood Accused, from Anne Hutchinson to Alger Hiss*, rev. ed. New York: Harper & Row, Publishers, 1967.

*Obst, Lynda Rosen, ed. *The Sixties: The Decade Remembered Now, by the People Who Lived It Then.* New York: Random House, Inc., 1977.

*Rembar, Charles. *The Law of the Land: The Evolution of Our Legal System.* New York: Simon & Schuster, 1980.

*Salisbury, Harrison E. *Without Fear or Favor: An Uncompromising Look at The New York Times.* New York: Times Books, 1980.

*Schimmel David, and Fischer, Louis. *The Civil Rights of Students.* New York: Harper & Row, Publishers, 1975.

Seale, Bobby. *A Lonely Rage: The Autobiography of Bobby Seale.* New York: Times Books, 1978.

*Sheehan, Neil, and Kenworthy, E. W. *The Pentagon Papers.* New York: Times Books, 1971.

Court Decisions

Branzburg v. Hayes, United States v. Caldwell, 408 U.S. 332 (1972)*

Gannet Co. v. DePasquale, 443 U.S. 368 (1979)

Herbert v. Lando, 441 U.S. 153 (1979)

New York Times Company v. Sullivan, 376 U.S. 254 (1964)

New York Times Company v. United States, 403 U.S. 713 (1971)

Quarterman v. Byrd, 453 F. 2d 54 (4th Cir. 1971)**

Richmond Newspapers, Inc. v. Virginia, 448 U.S. 554 (1980)

Time, Inc. v. Hill, 385 U.S. 374 (1967)

Zurcher v. Stanford Daily, 436 U.S. 547 (1978)

---

*To explain methods of legal citation: This means that *Branzburg v. Hayes* and *United States v. Caldwell* were decided by the United States Supreme Court in 1972, and that the opinion begins on page 332 of volume 408 of the United States Reports, the official volumes of the Court's decisions.

** This means that *Quarterman v. Byrd* was decided by the United States Court of Appeals, Fourth Circuit, in 1971, and that the opinion begins on page 54 of volume 453 of the Federal Reporter, Second Series.

Index

Numbers in *italics* refer to illustrations.